.87

D0935110

Readings
from the new book
on nature

The
University of
Massachusetts
Press

Amherst,
1981

READINGS
FROM
THE NEW book
ON NATURE

Physics and metaphysics in
the modern novel

ROBERT NADEAU

Copyright © 1981 by
The University of Massachusetts Press
All rights reserved
Printed in the United States of America
Library of Congress Cataloging in Publication Data
Nadeau, Robert L., 1944–
Readings from the new book on nature.
Bibliography: p.
Includes index.
1. American fiction—20th century—History and
criticism. 2. Physics in literature. 3. Literature
and science. I. Title.
PS374.P45N3   813'.54'09356   81–2625
ISBN 0–87023–331–9   AACR2

To my parents,
Richard E. and Mary Virginia Nadeau,
and to my daughter Langdon.

CONTENTS

Acknowledgments   I wish to express my special thanks to Professor Molly B. Tinsley for her encouragement and helpful suggestions during the preparation of this manuscript. I am also extremely grateful to Professor Stephen G. Brush for his invaluable assistance in researching and writing the portion of this book dealing with the origins and history of scientific concepts. To the National Endowment for the Humanities, which provided the opportunity to study with Professor Brush, let me also indicate my indebtedness.

preface

Not so many years ago a rocket plunged through the sweet milk of the earth's cloud cover into the whisperless dark of outer space. The on-board camera panned through the glittering immensity beyond to focus on the only object on that alien horizon that seemed designed for warm and secure habitation. And what an impossibly beautiful sight it was! Against the backdrop of the interstellar night hung the great ball of the earth, with the intense blue of its oceans and the delicate ochres of its land masses shimmering beneath the vibrant and translucent layer of its atmosphere. The distances between us seemed suddenly contracted, the ecosystem more fragile, but the impression that sent the adrenalin flowing through my system was the overwhelming sense that the thing was alive! The teeming billions of organisms writhing about under the protective blanket of atmosphere ceased in the shock of that visual moment to be separate—they were interdependent, fluid, blending presences in the one organic dance of the planet's life.

Although everything in the above paragraph may seem true in emotional terms, or at least fit the preconceived, a cursory examination of implicit assumptions would probably lead to the conclusion that it is anything but an objective analysis of the content of the visual image. What we have here is an attempt by a humanist to communicate my own value-laden, subjectively based conception of existence in a world presumably represented by a visual image. In addition to the anthropomorphizing of various details of the image, we also detect here a metaphysical assumption, i.e., all life forms are interdependent and may even participate in some fundamental unity.

The fact that I readily made that assumption and that many readers of the passage might have little difficulty assenting to it may imply a good deal about our present intellectual climate, but there is nothing in the image itself that makes the assumption either actual or necessary. If the impulse were to free us of cultural bias in order to seek a more objective view of the elements in this visual field, we would probably turn to the work of scientists, like those of NASA.

The presumption that scientific analysis has greater epistemological validity than any other mode of analysis can also be ascribed to cultural bias, but most members of this culture would probably resist the characterization. As Gerald Holton puts it, we tend to suppose that the "main difference between scientists and humanists" is that the "former . . . do not preempt fundamental decisions on aesthetic grounds; they do not make a priori commitments; and only let themselves be guided by the facts and the careful process of induction." This account of scientific procedure is not wrong, explains Holton, in that it has its uses in "broadly characterizing certain features of science as a public institution," but it is clearly deficient. If we "try to understand the actions and decisions of an actual contributor to science," Holton continues, we discover that the "process of building an actual scientific theory requires explicit or implicit decisions, such as the adoption of certain hypotheses and criteria of preselection that are not at all scientifically 'valid' in the sense previously given and usually accepted."[1]

Not only are metaphysical assumptions—as Holton and others have convincingly demonstrated—just as important and primary in the creative work of scientists as we have long known them to be in humanistic endeavors, the implications of new scientific theories (as we shall see later in this discussion) have often had unexpected impact upon those assumptions. It is also conceivable, although there is no precedent for it, that a radically new scientific paradigm, like that of the new physics, could prove so inconsistent with received metaphysical assumptions as to occasion a massive revolution in thought, out of which an alternate metaphysic would emerge. This is, I am convinced, our present situation. Not long after the publication of Einstein's special theory of relativity in 1905, many of the architects of what was fast becoming a revolution in scientific thought began to realize that they were not simply in the process of redefining concepts in a discipline, but were raising some formidable questions about the character of reality itself. They perceived, in short, that the revolution in physics seemed to be leading inexorably to a revolution in metaphysics, that a full acceptance of this new scientific view of the nature of things necessitated some profound changes in the conceptual machinery upon which an entire cosmos had been constructed.

As a self-confessed humanist writing for other humanists who have a similarly high tolerance for the excesses of our kind, allow me to return for the moment to my earlier ruminations about life on planet earth. The decision to do so is not entirely wanton, in that the discussion should serve as a useful introduction to epistemological and ontological dilemmas posed by concepts from the new physics. My impression that the earth is alive would not disturb anyone in the scientific community—organic life bubbles away even in the most remote deserts of this planet in enormous variety and extent—but we also know from fairly recent scientific research that this was not always so. About 4.5 billion years ago, after the swirling gases had constricted under the force of gravity to hard, material substances, the atmosphere was noxious and the temperatures blazing. Over billions of years, through a countless series of accidents, enough molecules in the right combinations began hanging around together to form the primordial soup out of which organic life came. When some wandering lightning bolt banged together the complex organic acid forming genetic materials, the first cell made its appearance. If we can be said to have a first parent, that tiny organism is it—the diversity of life forms found everywhere around us probably derived from that single cell. The resemblance of enzymes in whales, pigeons, people, and the crab grass that grows on our lawns is very difficult to account for in the absence of that assumption.

Although the progress has in ways been pretty sloppy—evolution in terms of the life of individual organisms is a wasteful business—that first cell definitely took the highroad toward more complex configurations of life forms. My candidate for most complex configurations of cells would certainly win no beauty contest, but its internal dynamics, inasmuch as we can understand them, are a wonder to behold. Although it is only about the size of two clenched fists, weighs roughly three pounds, and is not even capable of supporting itself outside its container, the 30 billion cells of the human brain converse with one another in such intricate ways that it will be a long time before we fully understand what the conversation is all about.

4

Everything the brain does deserves a little respect, but it is the activities of the frontal and prefrontal lobes that are the most astonishingly complex. It is in these areas that microstructures and biochemistry come together in those processes called *language* and *intellect*. And if there is any place in the body that we can correlate with the existence of that little deity and sometime despot called personality, this is it.

The rapid increase in the size of the forebrain that made symbolic language and conscious manipulation of the environment possible was, from our point of view, another happy evolutionary accident. The enlargement in brain size was due principally, we now speculate, to survival through natural selection of those human or prehuman organisms capable of elaborate hand movements. The brain cells and brain connections in early man and ourselves are, incidentally, no different from those of the apes; both brains are composed of the same kind of material and are constructed on essentially the same plan. The difference is simply that man's is larger. The additional cells in the brain of our prehistoric forebears made it possible to discover—and it could well have been the discovery of a single tribe—that the range of sounds made by air from the lungs vibrated through the larynx and nasal passages, and, refined by tongue and lip movements, could function as symbols put together in crude syntactical patterns. During this stage in evolutionary history the creature that can now properly be called man began to have something more at his disposal in the terrible struggle to survive than instinctual responses to bodily need and physical danger. The ability to conjure up in that enlarged forebrain a symbolic world, a world in which the harsh realities of existence could be represented and manipulated on the level of abstractions, made it possible to construct a future time based on experience in the remembered past, and to anticipate and plan for contingencies that would not otherwise have been known. Imagine growing up without any exposure whatsoever to language systems, and the debt owed that tribe of early men is immediately apparent. We might exhibit an interesting range of instinctual responses, but there would be nothing beyond our physical appearance that would be distinctly human.

It is impossible to know what thoughts early man had, but there is no question that a visit to his mental landscape would be more than a little disconcerting. I suspect it would not be dull there—surely his visual field would be more arrestingly bizarre than any painting in the Guggenheim or Hirshhorn—but it would probably be so different from our own that a psychotic break could well be a consequence of remaining there too long. Our own mental landscape has been in the process of cultivation for some time, seeded and tended courtesy of the collective efforts of countless human beings whose own ideas about the way things are happened to survive into the learned experience of successive generations. But no two landscapes are the same, as any effort to fully communicate with even the most like-minded person will demonstrate, and the overlap with those of people from other cultures that have had little converse with our own can seem almost nonexistent.

When symbolic language became an activity in nature, however, the relationship between the human organism capable of that activity and the world of its being was fundamentally altered. Events in nature, which prior to this development must have seemed no more mysterious or alien than rain to an orangutan, were apprehended quite differently as features of the symbolic landscape. Subsumed under a complex field of categories, constructs, and ideas, the heretofore overlapping and blending presences in the seamless stream of consciousness were now somehow separate from one another—the world, in short, had become in the experience of man that which is *other*. The processes in the cells of the forebrain that made it possible to posit the existence of self and world as disparate categories were now obliged to establish an acceptable ground for believing that the distinction was not absolute. As the symbol-making animal fragmented his world into discrete identities, he needed mythological thinking to pull the jumble of particulars into some meaningful pattern. Myths made connections, bespoke causes and origins, and, in general, imparted to the world of his creation the sense that it was his world indeed. That which made the myth-making both possible and necessary was symbolic language, and the fruits of the enterprise can be witnessed in the elaborate mytho-religious heritage of any people.

Language, as linguists have been defining it for some time, is an arbitrary system of sound symbols that has meaning to a given cultural community. More recently linguists have come to view language not simply as a device for reporting experience, but also as a way of defining it. This understanding of the function of language, generally referred to as the Sapir-Whorf hypothesis, assumes that the form of language not only directs our perceptions, but also contains habitual modes of analyzing experience into categories. It is, says Sapir, a "self-contained, creative symbolic organization" which "defines experience for us by reason of its formal completeness and because of our own unconscious projections of its implicit organization upon the field of experience." Or, as Whorf puts it in a slightly different way, the "linguistic system (in other words, grammar) of each language is not merely a reproducing instrument for voicing ideas but rather is the shaper of ideas, the program and guide for the individual's mental activity, for his analysis of impressions, for his synthesis of his mental stock in trade."[2]

As the symbol-making animal set about the business of bridging the gap between the categories of *self* and *world*, he was obviously making use of the large mass of cells floating in his cranium. Although there is no question that the cells evolved from and exist in nature, the activities of those cells that allowed for the development of language systems were capable of generating ideas about nature that bore little correspondence to physical events as we now scientifically view them. And more important for the purposes of this discussion, the perception of the character and meaning of those events was a function of the internal organization of the system itself. Does this mean that people with very different linguistic and cultural heritages often have disparate conceptions of their relationship to the natural, or that their perceptions and feelings in response to nature could be very unlike one another? Obviously it does.

Examples of the manner in which language systems condition approaches to and definitions of human reality are numerous and growing all the time, but let us choose one close to home. The color vocabulary of the Navaho includes five terms that are used to categorize certain color impressions. One is roughly equivalent to English *white* and another bears close correspondence with English *red*, but there are two terms in Navaho for our term *black* and one that includes both *blue and green*. This does not mean that English speakers cannot perceive the two blacks of the Navaho, or that the Navaho speaker is unable to differentiate between blue and green. But it is likely that the sensitivity to these colors and their configurations differs between the two groups as a result of the difference in color categories.

Move in the other direction, from ideas about nature to the form of the language containing the ideas, and the role of language in the creation of human reality is even more apparent. The Navaho developed, apparently quite early in his religious history, the idea of the self living in a universe of eternal and unchanging forces within which he attempts to maintain an equilibrium. The activity of the self is viewed as intimately involved with the balance of powers in nature, and a failure, intentional or not, to observe a set rule of behavior or perform certain rituals can disturb that balance. Illness, unexplained death, or any other personal or communal misfortune or disaster, signals a disturbance in the relationship to nature. Through a re-enactment of one or more of a series of religious dramas that represent the events through which early, mythical figures in Navaho culture first established the harmony between man and nature, it is hoped that the symptoms of the disturbed relationship are eliminated.

If a traditional Navaho is sickened by the spectre of a four-lane highway running smooth across the land his people once inhabited, there is nothing in our own mytho-religious heritage that would allow us to finally comprehend the source of that revulsion. He is not, for example, responding like some latter-day American transcendentalist or Eastern mystic living in sympathetic communion with the eternal One, nor is he simply troubled by the thought that some earthly paradise created by a providential deity is being defaced. It is more that in his symbolic universe this kind of trouncing upon natural forces represents a direct threat to his survival and that of his community because it appears to disturb the delicate balance of forces within which he takes his being.

The idea of relatedness to nature reverberates throughout the language system of the Navaho. Consider the following relatively simple example. When the Navaho speaks of *actors* or *goals*, which he could never do in the usual sense of these words, he is not describing performers of actions or one to whom actions are performed. In his language system entities are associated with actions that are already defined in part as pertaining to a particular class of beings. "You have lain down" in Navaho is better represented in English as "you now belong to, or equal, one of a class of animate beings moved to rest." Similarly, "you have lain me down" in English would mean in Navaho something like "you have set a class of beings to which I belong to motion to arrive at this point."[3] Imagine a Sartre or Camus growing up as a Navaho Indian, and we can begin to appreciate how different this language system is from our own. Their philosophical positions, presuming that they could have been developed in this cultural context at all, would sound like perfect jibberish. The notion of self as wholly disparate from the world of its activity discovering its identity through willful confrontation with that which is completely *other* simply does not make sense in the symbolic universe of the Navaho.

The suggestion that so-called "primitive" people have developed ideas about nature arising out of the structure of their individual language systems that are not, in our view, scientifically valid, does not, at first, seem too problematic. It is our cultural bias that explanations for natural events not arrived at through scientific method cannot begin to describe that which is pristinely true in nature. Since the method requires scientists to draw conclusions through a careful and direct investigation of what *is*, any assumptions not derived from empirical data are presumed invalid. Although this understanding of the character of scientific knowledge has proven enormously useful in the progress of science, and remains something of a credo in the practice of what Thomas Kuhn calls "normal science," it is now viewed, at least by those physicists sensitive to the metaphysical implications of the new physics, as lacking in ontological validity.

As Holton describes it, the "ontological status of scientific knowledge itself has been turned completely upside down since the beginning of the twentieth century. The experimental detail is now not simply the token of a real world; on the contrary, it is all that we can be more or less sure about at the moment."[4] Or, as the situation is described by another formidable historian of science, Karl Popper: "I think we shall have to get accustomed to the idea that we must not look upon science as a 'body of knowledge,' but rather as a system of hypotheses; that is to say, as a system of guesses or anticipations which in principle cannot be justified, but which work as long as they stand up to tests, and of which we are never justified in saying that we know that they are 'true' or 'more or less certain' or even 'probable.' "[5] This does not mean, of course, that investigators in the new physics do not rely heavily upon the empirical method, but it does imply that the knowledge gained through carefully controlled experiments should not be presumed objective in the strict sense, or as a direct consequence of induction alone. Something more is involved here, and that something is the world-constructing mind of the individual.

The physicists then have been forced increasingly to recognize, for reasons other than those of the cultural anthropologists and linguists, that it is the organization of their own symbolic universe that conditions the selection of problems that can be presumed to have a solution. The ways of looking at and evaluating nature that make the experiment and to some extent determine the meaningful results are not, in the view of many quantum theorists, givens in nature. One such theorist is Martin Deutsch, a nuclear physicist at the Massachusetts Institute of Technology. "In my own work," says Deutsch, "I have been puzzled by the striking degree to which the experimenter's preconceived image of the process which he is investigating determines the outcome of the observations. The image which I refer to is symbolic, anthropomorphic representation of the basically inconceivable atomic process."[6] Henry Stapp, a physicist who is perhaps best known outside the scientific community for his lucid commentary on the Copenhagen interpretation of quantum theory, resolves the quandary perceived by Deutsch by choosing to view science as "an invention of the human mind that man constructs for the purpose of incorporating into the world of human ideas abstract structural forms that capture aspects of the empirical structure of man's experience."[7]

We should not conclude from these comments that physicists have given up all hope of learning about subatomic processes —which is anything but the case—or that what they do know is simply fictive. But there is the growing suspicion in the scientific community that knowledge in the sense of an absolute transcription of physical reality may be a kind of necessary illusion for the symbol-making animal. It could also mean, if the present scientific revolution continues to have an impact upon the subjective experience of members of this culture, that absolute knowledge in other aspects of our lives might come to be regarded in the same way. Science, as Holton notes, "has always had a mythopoeic function" in that "it generates an important part of our symbolic vocabulary and provides some of the metaphysical bases and philosophical orientations of our ideology,"[8] and there is little or no prospect, as I see it, that this particular function of science could cease to operate in this abundantly scientific age.

The notion that the analytical mind is capable of discovering the unalloyed essence of physical reality dates from the time of classical Greek civilization. During that period a number of individuals started relying upon the activities in the cells of their forebrains to raise questions that came to be called *philosophical*, and some ideas about the "nature of things" entered the mainstream of Western thought. What is truly remarkable about this particular set of ideas is their staying power—they are still basic features of the mental landscape most of us inhabit. The notions about substance and identity, form and number, which were invented or formalized by Greek philosophers, proved so remarkably durable because they were derived from what turned out to be one of the most basic features of the symbolic universe of Western man—a belief in the duality of Being. If that same belief had not been a feature of Judeo-Christian cosmology as well, there is good reason to suspect (as I will attempt to illustrate in the first chapter) that thinkers like Copernicus, Galileo, Kepler, and Newton—all of whom had a consuming passion for cosmic unity—would not have conceived of a model of the physical universe in which these ideas are presumed to have absolute ontological validity.

If this is as obvious as I am apparently suggesting it is, why did Newton and his followers presume that all the major assumptions in classical physics were necessitated by the experimental data, or that all the basic concepts and laws of this physics were "scientifically valid" in the strictest sense of that phrase? Or more important, why did anyone believe them in the first place? The most obvious reason is that classical physics is highly predictive of the results of physical interactions at speeds considerably less than the speed of light. In terms of what anyone in the eighteenth and most of the nineteenth centuries knew how to measure or predict, Newtonian science worked. It was only in the early decades of the twentieth century that physicists began to realize that the closed and wonderfully precise mathematical scheme that is classical physics is not the complete and final picture of physical reality the Newtonians thought it was. If that had been the case, it would never have required any modification. From the perspective of the new physics it is apparent that classical physics embraced common-sense assumptions which had long been the bedrock of the symbolic universe of Western man with a mathematical formalism that represented those assumptions as a priori truths. But they do not now appear true in that sense at all. They originated in an open-ended debate over metaphysical reality in which scientific method—not yet invented—played no role whatsoever. The makers of these assumptions were simply trying to create in their own minds, as myth makers have always done, some abstract model that establishes a relationship between self and world which could be assimilated into the structure of their symbolic universe. Like the Navaho, they perceived the world as the internal organizations of their thought would allow them to perceive it. And the same limitation was at work in the world constructing minds of classical physicists, and, as many students of quantum theory are quick to point out, is at work in our own minds as well.

That concepts from the new physics appear to undermine common-sense assumptions in classical physics that also happen to be basic features of our symbolic universe should unnerve any of us, but that is not all of it. If the implications of the Copenhagen interpretation of quantum theory are taken seriously, there is also the possibility that the most pervasive organizing principle within that symbolic universe is also suspect. The system of logic that we use on the conscious or preconscious levels at least, to weave threads of connection between that boisterous crowd of neurological events labeled thoughts, feelings, impressions, and impulses is premised upon the efficacy of a structuring principle that may not be commensurate with the life of nature on its most basic level of functioning. I refer here to the habit of mind reified into a necessary precept for intelligent, rational discourse by another ancient Greek—the principle of the either-or, or the "law of the excluded middle." Since every major controlling symbolic or belief system in the West is also premised upon the efficacy of the either-or, as Aristotle conceived it, the prospect that it too is not a given in nature obviously has enormous implications. As we shall see in some detail in chapter two, quantum theoretical physicists, who are perhaps the supreme embodiment of the analytical tradition in Western thought, do not as a group easily accept this prospect, and a number of rather bizarre theoretical models have been advanced which are indicative of their resistance to it.

The first phase of this discussion will consist of an effort to examine the development in Hellenic culture of those ideas incorporated into the understanding of the organization of material reality that is Newtonian science. Once we perceive that the common-sense assumptions in that science are not a priori truths, but rather a consequence of the experience of man in this particular culture, we should be better prepared to digest the concepts from the new physics that appear to undermine them. We should then be in a position to explore the mythopoeic function of this new science as it is now manifesting itself in the contemporary novel. Although most of the concepts from physics that have had an impact upon the novelists studied here can be traced to theoretical advances in physics made in the 1920s and '30s, we will also briefly review more recent controversies in quantum physics. Some of the novelists, like Pynchon and DeLillo, appear to have followed these developments rather closely, but the principal benefit of reviewing them is, I think, that they reveal a good deal about the fundamental organizing principles in the symbolic universe of Western man. Nothing in this discussion will be terribly hard to grasp intellectually. Any number of practicing physicists and historians of science have translated concepts from the new physics into perfectly intelligible, and often quite beautiful, prose, and I will draw very heavily upon them here. The greatest obstacle to acceptance of the implications of these concepts in lived experience is not our inability to understand them, but rather our emotional resistance to them.

The comment by William James that the greatest obstacle to new truths is old truths very definitely applies here. In this discussion we will be tinkering around with the very foundations of Western metaphysical reality, or with the scaffolding upon which our entire symbolic universe rests. If a psychic surgeon could immediately extract from our consciousness all the assumptions about self and world that do not appear commensurate with our most advanced scientific knowledge, there would be little in our experience that would not be altered beyond all recognition. The world "out there" that seems safe and certain as an enduring presence that sustains our psychological well-being would simply dissolve. We would not be merely confused; we would go perfectly mad. And this is not hyperbole. Concepts from the new physics constitute a direct, frontal assault on virtually everything we have thought and felt about ourselves from at least the time of classical Greek civilization. The death of the ideas about substance and relation that could come about as a result of the assimilation into our symbolic universe of these concepts is necessarily a kind of death of ourselves, and we are likely to resist it with something like the bone-chilling terror felt by prisoners standing blind-folded before a firing squad.

If this is the case, why should we, or the novelists studied here, bother with the metaphysical implications of the new physics, and even if we do bother, surely our powers of rationalization should be sufficient to diffuse those implications of any lasting significance. Perhaps; but I don't think so. We can no more successfully resist over time a transformation of ourselves in the face of these latest pronouncements than our cultural ancestors could resist the transformation of themselves when confronted with the assertions of a Copernicus or a Darwin. Although it is true that the assimilation of the ideas of these scientists was within existing frameworks, as opposed to major adjustments in the framing process itself, there is still no prospect, as I see it, that we could avoid being radically changed by ideas from the new physics.

The likelihood that the assimilation of these new truths will be prolonged and difficult does not mean, however, if we can trust the judgment of the artists discussed here, that the new truths will not prove beneficial to mankind. It does not require much sensitivity to conclude that there is entirely too much human misery and conflict in the global village, or much intelligence to know that the village itself runs the risk of being destroyed in nuclear holocaust with ever-increasing certainty. The once-prevalent faith in this culture that science and its handmaiden technology could wrest from the forces of nature all that was needed to sustain and nurture the entire human population dims, and yet the mushroom-shaped cloud hovers perpetually in the recesses of our minds as sign and symbol of our dreadful mastery over these forces. But science is not just technology; it is idea as well. The change in the manner in which we use our minds that may follow upon the integration into the fabric of our intellectual and emotional lives of ideas from the new physics could not only prove beneficial in terms of our individual sense of well-being; there is even the delicious prospect, as several novelists whom we will study see it, that it might prolong the existence of the symbol-making animal in the organic dance of the planet's life.

When Western man has been obliged to confront scientific discoveries that were not commensurate with his sense of relation to the whole, it is the artist who has generally been most responsible for the full assimilation of those discoveries into his subjective life. Philosophers and theologians may provide us with the clearest description of the intellectual dilemmas posed by a Copernicus or a Darwin, but it is the artist who insinuates these threatening ideas into the emotional fabric of our lives. Outfitted with their usual hypersensitivity to the intellectual currents that eventually transform us, artists in the modern period appear to have sensed far earlier than any other group outside the scientific community the implications of ideas from the new physics. All of the novelists studied here attempt to envision the alternate metaphysic that could well evolve out of these concepts, fashioning in the process the intellectual and emotional landscape that may well emerge as we rebuild our conceptions of self and world upon this quite new foundation.

It should be noted at this point that I have not attempted in the chapters on the novelists to arrive at a definitive analysis of the work of any one individual. The novels that I have chosen to discuss here are, in my view, documents of culture providing insights into the manner in which dramatic implications of ideas from the new physics might be assimilated into subjective experience. In the chapter on Fowles, for example, several of his major works are simply not dealt with because he does not appear in those novels to be struggling overtly with the implications of these ideas. Although Barth and Pynchon do confront the implications in virtually everything they have written, I elected to devote most of the discussions to *Giles Goat-Boy* and *Gravity's Rainbow* because these novels contain the most imposing investigation of the metaphysics implied in the new physics provided by either novelist to date. Updike is a somewhat special case in that he derives from physics a notion of duality that looms large in his moral and theological debates with the reader, and an encompassing discussion of most of his fiction proved the most useful way of illustrating that influence. In the chapter on Vonnegut, the effort to ferret out his speculations on this topic resulted, given the relative simplicity of his narrative structures, in a discussion of virtually all his work as well. The novels of the two relative newcomers on the literary scene, Tom Robbins and Don DeLillo, are, finally, examined in some detail because ideas from modern physics are pervasive concerns in each canon. For those who would object that Robbins and DeLillo do not belong in the select society of Barth or Pynchon, I would argue that the novels of Robbins and DeLillo

are just as important as documents of culture as those of their somewhat older contemporaries.

Although some formal elements of structure and narrative technique are examined in each of the chapters on individual novelists,
the critical approach in those chapters, given the original impulse
behind this study, tends to be thematic. A more focused examination
of those formal elements will take place in an additional chapter
dealing with the impact of metaphysically based assumptions about
the character of physical reality upon the evolution of the form of the
novel. That concluding section will also discuss the problems faced
by the contemporary novelist in circumventing received narrative
conventions while creating a fictional landscape in which the metaphysic implied in the new physics is a feature of both narrative structure and technique.

These particular novelists are not, of course, the only modern
artists to discover metaphysical implications in concepts from physics. Cubist painters, as many experts in art history have noted, were,
for example, quite taken with the implications of relativity theory.
Although we have not yet even begun to develop a significant body of
criticism tracing the influence of ideas from the new physics upon art
in the modern period, there is, I think, little doubt that they provided
metaphysical, or epistemological, justification for a host of artistic
experiments. The writers dealt with here seemed the obvious choice
for a first effort of this kind, primarily because all of them seem conscious of the extent to which their acquaintance with these concepts
has conditioned their conception of reality, and because most make
specific reference to them within the art itself. The more difficult task
is, of course, to delineate the less explicit force of this radically new
view of the nature of things in the art of individuals who do not so
openly recognize the influence.

There are, I think, two reasonable objections that are likely to be
raised in response to this particular study. The first is that since
change in nature on its most basic level of functioning does not appear to proceed—as we will see in the section on quantum theory—in
terms of neat, linear, causal connections and every event involves,
and in some sense *is*, every other event, the suggestion that the novelists are causally influenced by ideas from physics appears specious.
A second objection might be that many of the themes, structures, and

narrative techniques that are associated here with the mythopoeic function of the new physics could just as easily be explained in terms of other, more pervasive tendencies in culture, like those articulated by Tony Tanner in *City of Words*.[9]

My general response to both objections is that I am inclined to view change as it is conceived in quantum physics as analogous to that form of change on the macro level called civilization. From this perspective civilization, like all processes in nature, is a complex interplay of forces within which it is impossible to isolate a particular idea and determine its fixed and final relationship to any other idea. *Intellectual climate* is that vague but useful term we normally use to denote these forces, the effects of which we witness in diverse products of a given culture that closely resemble one another in form and meaning in spite of the fact that they might be produced by individuals who had no direct contact with one another's art or ideas. One can easily make the case, for example, that the novelists would not have been receptive to the ideas from the new physics if other non-scientific developments, like the romantic movement in philosophy and literature, had not been a force in culture, and also that the course of science itself would have taken different directions without such influences. The ideas generated by truly creative scientists, like those generated by truly creative people in any endeavor, do not evolve strictly within the confines of closed universes of meaning called *disciplines*, but are happenings in the vastly more complex field of forces called *culture*. Although the concepts from physics featured in this discussion constitute one such force among the many overlapping and blending currents of our time, and cannot be said to have caused the mind and sensibility of the artists whose work is studied here to evolve in a particular way, they are catalysts for some rather large reactions, and the results, as we shall see, are similar.

1 • COMMON SENSE AND THE NATURE OF THINGS

If you learned in high school or college physics, as I did, that the atom, also cutely described as nature's little building block, was composed of small, indestructible particles, you did not study the new physics. That view of *things* was among the ideas invented by early Greek philosophers that found their way into Newtonian science. Reality, as classical physics conceived it, consisted, says John Dewey, of "those fixed immutable things philosophy called Substances. Changes could be known only if they could be reduced to recombinations of original, unchanging things."[1] This conception of *substance* is not only pervasive in all our dealings with things, it also governs, to some great extent, our sense of relatedness to everything, including other individuals, in our environment. The empirical evidence from the new physics suggesting that substance, as we have understood it for 2,500 years, is without scientific foundation is not an innocuous scientific oddity—it is the stuff out of which major revolutions in thought are made.

On the macro level, where we seem to derive our expectations of "the way things are," high-speed collisions between masses, like that of cars on the freeway, normally results in their breaking apart into smaller pieces. The force of these collisions can be predicted in terms of classical mechanics, and the fragmentation of the masses involved also seems consistent with Newton's presumption that change is recombinations of original, unchanging things. But if there is anything the new physics will almost inevitably violate, it is common-sense expectations. Bubble chambers are used in particle accelerators, some of which are seven miles in circumference, to study the results of collisions between subatomic particles. Subatomic particles, accelerated to velocities close to the speed of light, collide with other particles sitting in the chamber. The behavior of the individual particles becomes detectable as bubbles, which are many orders of magnitude larger than the particles themselves, form around the lines of movement. In examining the thickness and curvature of the lines in photographs taken at the time of collision, physicists are able to identify the various types of particles present in the interactions. Although most of the particles created in these collisions live an extremely short period of time (less than a millionth of a second), this is a technological peep show well worth the price of admission.

When two particles collide in the chamber they do not break up, but are transformed through the interaction into new particles that are often considerably greater in number, and in collective size and weight, than the original particles. The graceful, spiraling lines in the photographs show matter, the stuff out of which we all are made, becoming, simply as a result of banging together at terrific speeds, not only some *thing* they were not originally, but additional *things* with aggregate mass greater than themselves. If cars on the freeway were somehow to collide at those speeds, the results of the interaction of subatomic particles in those respective masses could be the same. Some obvious questions come to mind here: Where does the new matter come from, and where does it go when the particles disintegrate? Is this something coming out of nothing, as we might first be inclined to believe, or is there another presence here that is not a *thing* at all?

The explanation is the relationship between matter and energy represented in the best known and least understood equation outside the scientific community—$E=MC^2$. That relationship, as the physicist Werner Heisenberg describes it, is not terribly hard to grasp: "Since mass and energy are, according to the theory of relativity, essentially the same concepts, we may say that all elementary particles consist of energy."[2] In the bubble chamber we witness the complete mutability of matter in the interplay with the other aspect of its being —energy. Make the calculations that allow the results of these interactions to become intelligible in scientific terms, and we are obliged, along with the physicists, to view mass as bundles of energy. That which is conserved, or remains constant, is not the total mass, but the total energy, i.e., kinetic energy (energy of motion), and the energy contained in all the masses.

Since we do not go around bumping into other masses at velocities close to the speed of light, the matter that composes our bodies seems fairly predictable on a day-to-day basis. This bag of skin called *self* may undergo dramatic changes over time through processes like growth and aging, but the suggestion that our particular collection of atoms is not a definite *something*, separate and distinct from all other things, is another proposition entirely. Although the particles in the mass of atoms that is me, traveling at considerably slower velocities, may not behave like the particles in the chamber, I cannot escape the conclusion that they bear the same relationship to the energy of life. This mass, like all matter, is a manifestation of energy, and that energy exists, quite literally, everywhere in the cosmos.

If common sense were ever likely to score a clear victory over so-called scientific fact, this would seem to be the instance. Assuming that the relationship between matter and energy is as the new physics describes it, the matter that is my body cannot be separate from the energy from which it takes its being. If I am one with the cosmos, a mere pulse of energy wed like a wave in a river to the vast space-time continuum, then I, as a discrete and definable something, would not appear to exist at all. I can not be liquid fire bubbling from some unseen cosmic soup called energy. Could the new physics be so preposterous to suggest otherwise? The answer is "yes," or, more accurately, "yes and no." And yet this new sense of relation to the cosmos poses, as I see it, no foreseeable threat to the concept of human freedom.

What the new physics finally implies about human identity and its relation to the whole is taken up in the next chapter. Our concern here is with the metaphysical foundations of Newtonian physics which the new physics appears to undermine. The idea of the nature of physical reality subsumed by Newton with mathematical formalism, which most of us continue to unwittingly endorse, is premised upon conceptions of substance and identity, form and number, that were early products of the dualistic Western metaphysical tradition. The Greek philosophers largely responsible for developing these conceptions were simply using their own mythopoeic imaginations to posit an understanding of physical reality consistent with preexistent assumptions about the character of spiritual reality.

The texts used in introductory courses in the history of Western philosophy often create the impression that the early Greek philosophers were supremely rational beings whose love of *Truth* made them somehow immune to the usual preoccupations of other members of their culture. It is as if they had sprung whole out of the head of Minerva without any substantive contact with the social and intellectual climate that contains the deep structure of any idea in civilization. Anyone who has stood on the remains of the Temple at Delphi, with even the vaguest conception of the role which that remote religious center played in Hellenic culture for over 2,000 years, would have to feel different. This was a culture in which sacred forces were presumed to be active agencies in the affairs of men, and the spot chosen for the oracle, like all centers of its kind, appears to advertise that possibility in every visual detail. The rugged, undulating hills, strewn with poplar trees that seem planted by some celestial gardener with a penchant for geometric design, are passable by foot. And yet the clouds hover about these hills as if earth had wedded sky with the ease and passion of human lovers. Here one feels close to beginnings, to essences and sources of luminous power, and the mind is easily seduced into the conviction that the ineffable can be deciphered, decoded, and known after all. No matter that modern geologists do not believe that the fissure in the earth—from which the sacred vapor came that presumably allowed the illiterate priestesses to babble forth divine truth—could have existed in this locality. And no matter that the literate priests who interpreted the babblings may have been the greatest con artists in the history of the West. There is magic in this place no matter how elaborate the attempt to demystify it.

The same Greek mind that sensed the presence in nature of sacred forces, with a certitude that is difficult for modern man to even imagine, was also remarkably confident in its own force. The remains of the architectural masterpieces that sit atop the Acropolis in modern Athens signal a new relationship between mind and nature that is not apparent in the architectural achievements of any previous civilization. Against the background of the hills beyond these buildings assert a studied unwillingness to blend with the natural.

There is a sense of geometrical order and precision in the confluence of line that asserts itself as prior to, or beyond, the visible world. The pyramids may also testify to mathematical precision in the builder's art, but those structures, painted white after stones were set in place, suggest, against the background of mountains of shifting sand, that which was from nature, not something beyond it.

Without some appreciation of this idea of the sacred and the sense of relation to the natural that is a function of that idea, the contributions of the early Greek philosophers cannot really be put in proper perspective. The Greeks may be credited with such scientific sounding accomplishments as the discovery of mathematics and deductive reasoning, but their method of developing these conceptual tools was not the scientific. The Greeks reasoned deductively from what appeared self-evident, and not inductively from what had been observed. In fact the impulse which fueled the act of imagination that led to these formulations is comparable to that of mystics in any culture—it was the quest to uncover the essence of metaphysical reality. What distinguishes this quest from that of mystics in other traditions, particularly from the East, is that the unifying principle out of which all things evolve and into which they transform themselves again could be represented, as the Greeks saw it, in linguistic signs or symbols. These thinkers tended to talk about unifying principles as if they were substances.

The stage is set for the debate over the nature of metaphysical reality that would culminate in a picture of material reality that has proved such a sturdy feature of our symbolic universe with the appearance of Heraclitus. This obstreperous Greek was not only in the habit of viciously attacking every position taken by his eminent predecessors, he also thought of war as "the father of all and the king of all." And yet he alone among the early Western philosophers arrived at a conception of change in the cosmos that is almost entirely consistent with the view of change in modern physics. What appeared self-evident to Heraclitus was that the fundamental life principle is perpetual transformation and eternal becoming. "All things," he said, "come out of the one, and the one out of all things," and what keeps the whole from simply passing away is the tension between opposites. The unity of the One, which is the strife of all opposites, was called by him the *logos*, and his symbol for the perpetual transformation was fire. If we substitute, as Werner Heisenberg says we might, *energy*, as the new physics uses that term, for Heraclitus' term *fire*, virtually everything he says about change is acceptable from the modern scientific view.[3]

The fundamental life principle, as Parmenides conceived it, was unique, invariable Being rather than Becoming. He supported that position, significantly from our point of view, with an argument based upon an analysis of the character of language. Thinking or naming involves, he reasoned, the presence of *something*, and this makes both thought and language dependent upon the existence of objects outside themselves. Since it is possible to think or speak of something at various times, that which can be thought or spoken must exist at all times. This led to the conclusion that *nothing* changes for change requires things coming into existence or ceasing to be. Since the infinite and indivisible One cannot change, all that we perceive as change is illusory. The One of Parmenides is not, we should note, the One of Hinduism, Taoism, or Buddhism—it appears to be a material and extended universal substance.

The impossibility of all change is obviously not the feature of this philosophy that became a taken-for-granted assumption in a science investigating laws governing motion of material bodies. What survived, due to one of those curious turnings that are not unusual in the resolution of metaphysical debates, was the idea of substance as indestructible. That resolution occurred as the atomists, Leucippus and Democritus, attempted to make compatible the notions of Heraclitus' Becoming and Parmenides' unchanging Being. They asserted that Being is manifest in invariable substance (*atoms*) which through blending and separation make up the things in the changing world. Although these thinkers were conspicuously vague about the causes of this motion, they were in general agreement that the forces behind it were of spiritual origin, and, therefore, different in kind from the material atoms. It is also significant that both Leucippus and Democritus were strict determinists. "Naught happens for nothing, but everything from a ground of necessity," said Leucippus.

The picture of reality derived from metaphysics that carries over into Newtonian physics is made complete with the addition of wildly speculative assertions by one of the most eccentric of the Greek philosophers. Pythagoras was first and foremost a mystic who, like Heraclitus and Parmenides, apparently had few doubts about his ability to uncover the essence of spiritual reality. Convinced that his

own being was at least semidivine, he founded a religion in which
devotees, presumably taken with his occult powers, engaged in a
variety of interesting practices. To enter the Pythagorean order, followers were required to believe in the transmigration of the soul, and
to refrain from such sinful activities as eating beans, breaking bread,
plucking garlands, and walking on highways. Although the perceived world, taught Pythagoras, was illusory, he also urged upon his
following the notion that truth of a very precise nature could be discovered through reason and contemplation, and, more important,
that this truth was mathematical in form. His use of mathematics for
demonstrative deductive argument, his recognition of the importance of mathematical relationships in musical forms, and his
famous dictum that "all things are numbers" were simply out-
growths of this revelation. If these ideas seem consistent with our
own conception of the scientific, that is not surprising. The impact of
Pythagoras upon the formation of that conceptual paradigm is
enormous.

The distance between these acts of the imagination in early
Greek philosophy and the rise of modern science in the seventeenth
century is traveled through a metaphysical tradition that reinforced
the picture of the real already formulated in every particular. The
most formidable architect in that tradition, Plato, wholeheartedly
accepted Pythagoras' conception of the nature of both truth and
knowledge, and also concluded that the foundations of physical reality rested upon immaterial mathematical or geometrical forms. Platonic idealism, which posits the existence of a realm of being and
value higher than and distinct from the realm of phenomena, would,
I suspect, have seemed considerably less feasible to Plato without the
influence of Pythagoras, and might not have developed at all in the
absence of it. If geometrical forms can be presumed to exist immate-
rially on some other plane of being, then the prospect that other mental constructs (*ideas*) could reside there as well does not seem terribly
farfetched. (When Plato describes regular solids, for example, he
imagines them to be constructed of two basic triangles, the equi-
lateral and the isosceles. The triangles have no extension in space,
and are, therefore, immaterial.)

The shift in emphasis from mathematical idea to other disembodied essences in the work of Plato was not, however, conducive to
the progress of science for this reason—it was accompanied by the

assumption that the material world experienced by the senses is inferior to the immaterial experienced by the mind. Since matter in the metaphysics of Plato represents a falling away from the *Good*, Western man, who remained committed to the same dualistic model of the nature of Being, tended to view substance as defective, incomplete, and undeserving of the closest scrutiny. This curious Platonic bias, that mutability is a barrier to intelligibility, remained a large conceptual stumbling block in physics right up through the time of Galileo.

Aristotle's more down-to-earth, common-sensical approach to the understanding of nature would seem to make him a better scientist than Plato. But on closer examination we discover in Aristotle the same division between the immutable and transcendent found in Plato. The conception of matter as immaterial potentia capable of actual existence by passing into form is not unlike Plato's notion that the immaterial form or idea is reflected in its material image. Aristotle's matter is, in other words, a nonmaterial essence comparable to those essences in the heaven of ideas. This dualism also appears in Aristotle as part of his explanation of the mechanics of motion. In the region of the cosmos above the moon, said Aristotle, things are ungenerated and indestructible because they remain in continuous and infinite circular motion. It was possible for Aristotle to conceive of this higher realm of being in circular motion without undergoing change, in the sense of transformation, because he believed, as Plato and Pythagoras did, that perfect geometrical forms have actual existence in that higher realm.

The cause of this motion, the Unmoved Mover or First Cause, not only clearly exists outside the realm of things, it closely resembles the Judeo-Christian conception of deity. Aristotle became the supreme authority in physics shortly after his works appeared in Latin in the twelfth century, not only because his system seemed more credible than any other, but also because the metaphysics in his physics reinforced the controlling symbolic of the age. It is no accident that when the defenders of that symbolic felt threatened by Copernicus' argument for the heliocentric universe in the sixteenth century and Galileo's description of the mechanics of motion in the seventeenth, they turned to the physics of Aristotle. The cosmology of this enlightened pagan definitely seemed on the side of the angels.

The dualism prevalent in Greek philosophy, that habit of mind that posits the existence of a world of abstract, disembodied forms or ideas more essential or more important than the world of sensible objects and movements, did not suffer from neglect and die. It became the most characteristic feature of Western philosophical and theological thought. Purge the historical record of every document in these disciplines that implicitly relies upon it, and there would probably not be enough material left to justify a sophomore-level survey course in either area. Although this habit of mind undoubtedly served to retard, if not actually undermine, scientific knowledge, there is one important respect in which it made the first phase of the scientific revolution possible.

In contrast to the great religious systems of the East (Hinduism, Buddhism, Taoism), Western metaphysics enhanced the true believer's sense that he could know in an analytical sense the nature of the physical world. Believing that his soul partook of the essence which is God, that he possessed, however feebly, the divine faculty of reason, Western man did not fundamentally doubt the reliability of his sense perceptions, or his ability to interpret them correctly. Nature seemed immediately present and fully intelligible to his mind, and the mental categories he developed to classify natural events (substance, essence, matter, form, and quantity) were not regarded as metaphors for that which language could not finally describe or contain, but as actual transcriptions of what *is*. It was this confidence in the ability of mind to derive the essence of material reality that accounts as much as anything else for the first great theoretical advances in physics in the sixteenth and seventeenth centuries.

Copernicus did not, for example, arrive at a conception of the structure of the cosmos that occasioned so much fright and dismay among his contemporaries by pondering over carefully developed scientific data with some primitive slide rule in hand. His claim that a system with thirty-four epicycles with the earth in motion was superior to the Ptolemaic system with eighty epicycles and the earth at rest was not the inevitable consequence of scientifically based inductive reasoning. It was based most fundamentally upon his conviction that his model represented a simpler and more harmonious mathematical order of the sort that the supremely rational creator of the universe would obviously prefer. Although it was the geocentric model of Claudius Ptolemy of Alexandria (second century A.D.) that Copernicus set out to modify, he did so under the influence of another ancient Greek, Aristarchus of Samos (ca. 310 to 230 B.C.).

Aristarchus had also advocated a heliocentric system, but was unable to prove that the motion of celestial bodies as then known could be represented by a combination of uniform circular motion in the system.

The work of the scientist—which after all is a word that did not enter the English language until about 1840—was more avocation than vocation until fairly recently in our history, and science was not a full-time commitment for Copernicus, Kepler, Galileo, or Newton. Copernicus was, for example, not merely an able astronomer and mathematician, but also an administrator, diplomat, physician, avid student of the classics and economics, and, most important for our purposes, a highly placed and honored church dignitary. The placement of the sun at the center of the universe was not in the mind of this terribly devout and essentially conservative man an act of irreverence, but rather another concrete demonstration, within the context of his own mythopoeic imagination, that the intelligent and intelligible God of the West was making his divine purpose manifest in the experience of man. As he puts it in the *Revolution of Heavenly Orbs*: "In the midst of all the sun reposes, unmoving. Who, indeed, in this most beautiful temple would place the light-giver in any other part than that whence it can illumine all other parts?"[4] Although the heliocentric model constructed by Copernicus did provide somewhat greater mathematical simplicity than the geocentric model of Ptolemy, it was not, in Copernicus's time, any more useful in making astronomical calculations than the accepted model, and, in operational terms, was even more complicated to implement. It seems clear in retrospect that Copernicus's attachment to his model, or his conviction that it was right and necessary, was primarily a consequence of his aesthetic sense that sun as the symbol for the Divine Architect should radiate its presence from the absolute center of all existing things. It was not, as it is often represented, another instance of the analytical mind moving in lockstep toward complete scientific logos.

The role of Johannes Kepler in the development of classical physics has been strangely neglected and misunderstood. Perhaps the explanation is that since physics and metaphysics, astronomy and astrology, geometry and theology, commingle in Kepler's work in a manner that is unsavory to the more austere sensibilities of the scientifically minded individual in our own age, it has been difficult to take him seriously. And yet it is Kepler, says Holton, who was the "first to look for a universal physical law based on terrestrial mechanics to comprehend the whole universe in its quantitative details," and Kepler who succeeded in "throwing a bridge from the old view of the world as unchangeable cosmos to the new view of the world as playground of dynamic and mathematical laws."[5] While working on the *Astronomia Nova* in 1605, Kepler offered the following account of what he hoped to accomplish:

I am much occupied with the investigation of the physical causes. My aim in this is to show that the celestial machine is likened not to a divine organism but rather to a clockwork. . . , insofar as nearly all the manifold movements are carried out by means of a single, quite simple magnetic force, as in the case of a clockwork all motions are caused by a simple weight. Moreover I show how this physical conception is to be presented through calculation and geometry.[6]

Although this work is now known for containing Kepler's First and Second Laws of planetary motion, and not the "one unifying principle," later revealed in Newton's *Principia*, Kepler's ambition to do so signals a dramatic change in Western man's conception of physical reality.

Kepler's impulse is to unify the classical picture of the world in which there is a split between celestial and terrestrial regions by subsuming the whole under the influence of a universal physical force. In his own words, he wished to "provide a philosophy or physics of celestial phenomena in place of the theology or metaphysics of Aristotle."[7] For Aristotle, Ptolemy, and Copernicus, the forces between bodies were presumed to be a function of their relative positions or geometrical arrangements, and not of the mechanical interactions between objects themselves. In shifting the focus to those interactions, Kepler introduces a conception of the universe in which Pythagoras, who conceived of himself as semidivine in any case, becomes very godlike indeed. "For next to the Lutheran God revealed to him [Kepler] directly in the words of the Bible," says Holton, "there stands the Pythagorean God, embodied in the immediacy of observable nature and in the mathematical harmonies of the solar system whose design Kepler himself had traced."[8] The creator of the "celestial machine," whose beneficent presence is symbolized in this universe—as it was in that of Copernicus—by the sun, is, says

Kepler, also the maker of "laws" that "lie within the power of under-standing of the human mind; God wanted us to perceive them when he created us in His image in order that we may take part in His own thoughts. . . . Our knowledge of numbers and quantity is the same kind as God's, at least insofar as we can understand something of it in this mortal life."[9] The god who imbued man with the mathemat-ical idea and who expresses himself through mathematical laws was no less real or vital in Kepler's mythopoeic imagination for having made the orbits of planets around the sun elliptical. Quite the con-trary. The mathematical laws evincing communion with the mind of God not only accounted for the shape of those orbits, but also sug-gested that the sun, emblem of his active agency, was located in the center of a mathematical harmony that was more consistent with the observed motions of the planets than the Copernican system allowed.

Galileo, apparently out of his own aesthetic need to preserve the godlike circle, did not use, or even refer to, the planetary laws of Kepler when those laws would have made his ardent defense of the heliocentric universe more credible. But it was Galileo's science, nevertheless, that laid the groundwork for the acceptance of those laws. In spite of their differing views on the shape of the planetary orbits, Galileo, like Kepler, was also an avid devotee of the Pythago-rean mathematical idea. In his *Dialogue Concerning the Two Great Systems of the World*, Galileo makes the following response to Simplicio's remark that he is probably sympathetic to the position of the Pythagoreans: "I know perfectly well that the Pythagoreans had the highest esteem for the science of number and that Plato himself admired the human intellect and believed that it participates in divin-ity solely because it is able to understand the nature of numbers. And I myself am inclined to make the same judgment."[10] As Alexander Koyré has nicely demonstrated, the reliance upon the Platonic dia-logue as the mode of discoursing upon the fundamental laws of na-ture is itself significant in the progress of science. In allowing these laws to be deduced by Sagredo and Simplicio, or by the reader him-self, Galileo believes, says Koyré, that "he has demonstrated the truth of Platonism 'by fact.' " The new science represented for Galileo a proof of Platonism, or of the Platonic notion that the es-sences of nature consist of mathematical or geometrical forms also contained in the mind, in that it assumes, according to Koyré, that the "formulation of postulates and the deduction of their implications precedes and guides the recourse to observation."[11]

The first of the mathematical laws established by Galileo, a constant describing the acceleration of bodies in free fall, is a dramatic example of the application of the new scientific idealism. It was a bold analytical leap on Galileo's part, not only because it violated the received view of motion contained in Aristotelian physics, but also because there was simply no way in the seventeenth century to subject it to experimental proof. In the physics of Aristotle objects have by their nature a proper place within the harmonious and ordered whole, and movement out of that place connotes inequilibrium. From this perspective a state of rest requires no explanation, for it simply means that a body is where it should be and will seek by its own nature to return to that place in the speediest manner. Since the fastest and most direct path in movement back to the natural place is a straight line, Aristotle reasoned that the body would return there at infinite speed if there were not some medium to resist its movement. Since instantaneous movement seemed, reasonably enough, entirely impossible to Aristotle, he concluded that no natural movement could take place in a void.[12] This conception of natural place also led Aristotle to suppose, in contrast with Plato, that since the space of geometry is an empty space, or an abstract representation of form without actual content, terrestrial movement can never be exactly represented in geometrical or mathematical forms. As Simplicio, the dogged Aristotelian in the *Dialogues*, puts it, "All these mathematical subtleties are true in abstracto. But applied to sensible and physical matter, they do not work."[13]

The notion that bodies accelerate at a constant speed in free fall not only presupposes the existence of a vacuum, but also subjects movement to the law of number. Classical physics, as Koyré sees it, can be said to have its beginning with the formulation of Galileo's first law governing motion in that it "asserts that the real is, in its essence, geometrical and, consequently, subject of rigorous determination and measurement."[14] But what is most remarkable is Galileo's extraordinary confidence in the absolute validity of this law when it could not be proven experimentally. Pneumatic pumps capable of creating vacuums had not yet been invented, and the experiments which Galileo thought would yield proof—designed to show that the movement of pendulums is isochronous—only succeeded in showing that pendulum movements are not isochronous after all. Galileo is obviously asserting here that there is something more primary and credible than that which is actually revealed in nature, and that that something is the godlike capacity of mind to discover the immaterial mathematical and geometrical forms.

Since Galileo's conception of scientific method was premised on the assumption that mind was capable of discovering truth in mathematical and geometrical forms, Pythagoras' notion of a realm of being beyond the material containing those truths soon became something more than mere philosophical speculation. With the emergence of classical physics it did appear that change in the physical world could be entirely explained in terms of disembodied, immutable essences called *natural laws* that were mathematical in form. Rigorous application of those laws did seem to allow the investigator to trace precise, causal connections between phenomena that produced results predictable to the nth degree. The fact that the new science lent credence to an idea of an ancient cult figure seems little more than an intellectual curiosity until we also realize that it provided grounds for a divorce between man and nature in the West that has yet to culminate in a reconciliation.

Throughout most of his recorded history Western man had been able to maintain the sense that he could accurately perceive and fully participate in his world because he believed in the imminent presence of a Being that bridged the gap between his atomized identity and all things *other*. In presenting us with a conception of nature in which God is not immediately present, Galileo lit the fuse resulting in the explosion that destroyed that ontological bridge. In fact the only role that the God of the Judeo-Christian tradition could play in this cosmos was First Efficient Cause or Creator of original substance—the immutable natural law neither needed, nor permitted, any other kind of assistance. This is not, incidentally, a dilemma that Galileo failed to recognize: "Nature," he said, "doth not that by many things, which can be done by a few,"[15] acts only "through immutable laws which she never transgresses," and cares "nothing whether her reasons and methods of operation be or not be understandable by men." [16] We are confronted here with a conception of the universe as a vast machine within which man is buffeted about by forces that have no regard whatsoever for his central place and importance. The

long-range impact upon the mytho-religious heritage of Western
man is as obvious as it was inevitable—a profound sense of alienation from the processes of nature.

The philosopher who was probably most responsible for instill-
ing this bone-chilling perspective into the emotional fabric of the life
of Western man was René Descartes. Galileo may have firmly believed that God made the world as an immutable mathematical system, but he did not believe, as Descartes did, that he had arrived at
that conclusion through divine revelation. On the evening of No-
vember 10, 1619, Descartes claimed to have been visited by the
Angel of Truth who provided him with the supernatural insight necessary to perceive that mathematics was the conceptual key that un-
locked the secrets of the universe.[17] Firmly grounded in mathematics
as a result of his studies at the Jesuit College of La Fleche, he invented, shortly thereafter, analytical geometry. What is significant
about this particular sequence of events is that analytical geometry is
a conceptual scheme that presupposes exact correspondence between number as abstraction (arithmetic and algebra) and the form
of concrete physical reality (space). The insight imparted by the celestial visitor can also be linked to another important event in
Descartes's intellectual life—the formulation of his famous metaphysical dualism. This terribly influential idea was primarily a consequence of his desire to provide logical proof for that which he already
knew on the best of authority to be valid—that immaterial mathematical forms were eternally true.

Taken with the Platonic bias that mutability is somehow a
barrier to intelligibility, Descartes would not accept Galileo's empirical method of proving the validity of the mathematical idea because
the senses are capable of deceiving us: "In things regarding which
there is no revelation, it is by no means consistent with the character
of a philosopher . . . to trust more to the senses, in other words to the
incomprehensible judgments of childhood, than to the dictates of
mature reason."[18] We discover the "certain principles of physical
reality," he concluded, "not by the prejudices of the senses, but by
the light of reason, and which thus possess so great evidence that we
cannot doubt of their truth."[19] Since revelation had shown that essential or primary truth in nature was mathematical form, how did
Descartes explain other qualities perceived as belonging to objects

that cannot be explained in terms of the mathematical idea? If they are not part of the identity of the objects themselves, those qualities must be due, he asserted, to the deceitfulness of the senses.

It was the need to establish a firm division between what actually exists outside ourselves, spatial magnitude and geometrical form, and all other aspects of nature that are present in our perceptions of this world, that led to the establishment of the domains of existence for immaterial cognitive functions—the res extensa and the res cogitans. Simply put, the primary, mathematical qualities reside outside subjective reality in the res extensa, and the secondary qualities are manifestations of that reality in the res cogitans. The problem then became to find a way out of the disturbing conclusion that subjectively based activities (perception, willing, feeling, imagining) are mere phantasm unrelated to anything outside themselves. His resolution of that particular dilemma was even more radical—reify the thinking substance: direct one's attention inward, and sense the existence of that substance in the absence of all extended things, and one will know with complete certainty, said Descartes, that one actually exists. This is the context in which the famous *cogito ergo sum* is properly understood.

If the division between the two domains is, however, as absolute as Descartes claimed it to be, how can we presume that our mathematical knowledge of the essence of material objects is reliable when our perceptions of external things are necessarily distorted and approximate? Why is it that we are not locked away in the abyss of subjectivity with no prospect of arriving at any certain judgments of the outside world? At this point the rigor of philosophic discourse gives way to an article of faith—God constructed the world, said Descartes, in accordance with the mathematical concepts intuited by our minds. When scientifically minded people after Descartes began to view such theological arguments not only as unlikely but also as inappropriate to the practice of genuine science, the sense that mind is a discrete, atomized function in the world became even more inevitable. Cartesian dualism was not, of course, a notion that the scientific community chose to resist. The scheme legitimated the assumption that mind, separate from world, could use the mathematical idea to arrive at a wholly objective description of the behavior of material objects, and served—ironically to be sure—to dispel the bias that provided impetus for the formulation of the scheme in the first place: that mutability is a barrier to intelligibility in the study of nature.

When Newton set to work fashioning his own idea of nature, the metaphysical assumptions about the character of physical reality originating in Greek philosophy were so basic to the construction of the symbolic universe in the West that no sane person would even dream of openly questioning them. With the emergence of classical physics as the single most pervasive paradigm for scientific thought, however, the connection between atomism and the Pythagorean mathematical ideal became more vital and necessary than ever before. Newton, like Galileo, easily accepted the notion that matter is composed of absolutely hard, indestructible particles because it allowed the form of matter to be reduced to mass points corresponding exactly with numerical integers. The wedding of the two constructs made it possible, in other words, to conceive of physical reality as being entirely contained within the mathematical idea. Change as Newton saw it was, therefore, separations, associations, and motions of permanent atoms in varying compliance with natural law.[20] Newton felt that if the scientist could represent all of those laws in mathematical form, he could arrive at the irrevocable and final truth about the material world. Since the body of laws devised by Newton, as we noted earlier, was highly predictive of the results of interactions on the macro level at speeds considerably less than that of light, the mathematical idea now appeared to be precisely what Descartes said it was—the conceptual key that unlocks the secrets of the universe.

Although the great dream of the Newtonians that mind is capable not only of understanding, but also of controlling, events in nature, was enormously useful in the progress of science, the impact upon the emotional life of Western man was not so positive. Within the context of the new scientific paradigm, there is, first of all, nothing that would indicate that the behavior of man, like the behavior of any other collection of matter, is not completely predetermined. Another, equally disturbing implication is that the qualities we perceive in objects (collections of atoms) cannot reside in the objects themselves. If the physical world is composed of minute, indestructible particles moving in mathematical harmony, all other aspects of that world are simply psychic additions of the perceiving mind. And that is precisely the conclusion that Newton came to. God alone, he said, can directly perceive external objects. If the thinking or feeling self has no immediate contact with the outside world, where, then, does that self reside? It is locked away, said Newton, in a remote corner of the brain called the *sensorium*.[21]

At this point in our intellectual history, Cartesian dualism —which we are obliged to accept from Descartes only if we endorse his initial assumptions—takes on the aura of scientific truth it has maintained ever since. The world outside ourselves becomes a vast machine containing within itself only those qualities that can be reduced to mathematical forms. All the other qualities we thought to be manifestations of the life of nature (beauty, color, fragrance, sound) must now be considered as only happenings in a remote corner of our brains. Any conceptions of design, purpose, and meaning in natural process are valid only to the extent that we are willing to believe, as Newton did, that they mirror the machinations in the mind of God.

"Newton the man" is, interestingly, a subject that was relatively unexplored until the last two decades of this century. It now appears likely that the British caretakers of the documents that have provided some startling insights into this complex personality chose to suppress them for chauvinistic reasons. After the first sale at Sotheby's in 1936 of a portion of what turned out to be a considerable number of private papers and theological and alchemical treatises that had been held by the Portsmouth family, a picture of the great man began to emerge that is still considerably at variance with the popular conception. The most consuming passion in the long life of Isaac Newton, who died in 1727 at the age of eighty-five, was not the laws of physics, but metaphysical or religious concerns represented, in the extant documents alone, by more than a million words of prose in his own handwriting.

Frank Manuel in three very fine books on Newton, *Isaac Newton, Historian*, *The Religion of Isaac Newton*, and *A Portrait of Isaac Newton*, has provided through careful study of these documents a view of Newton that has yet to be represented in most textbooks in physics. Newton as historical scholar sought to develop "an interpretation of mythology, a theory of Egyptian hieroglyphs, a radical revision of ancient chronology founded on astronomical proof, an independent reading of the sense of the Bible, and circumstantial demonstrations of the fulfillment of prophecy in the external world.''[22] Newton's interpretation of Old Testament prophecies and the Revelation of Saint John, for example, indicates that the earth will still be inhabited after the day of judgment, and he even speculated on the dimensions and cubic footage of a New Jerusalem large enough to accommodate both the quick and the dead—"the cube root of 12,000 furlongs."

The documents also indicate that Newton, who apparently had a psychological breakdown in 1693, suffered from extreme anxiety, loneliness, and repressed sexual desires. His notes contain fantasies about killing his stepfather, his mother, and himself, and reveal a terrible dread of punishment for entertaining such morally reprehensible impulses. According to Manuel, Newton discovered two refuges from the terrors of his psychological reality: "One was the bible literally interpreted as historical fact, de-allegorized, de-mythologized of everything vague and poetic, reduced to the concrete; the other was mathematical proof. . . . The discovery of his mathematical genius was his salvation; that the world obeyed mathematical law his security." Newton, in the words of Wallace Stevens in "Idea of Order at Key West," was perhaps more than any other architect of this scientific revolution, possessed by the "maker's rage for order." In "whatever direction he turned," says Manuel, "he was searching for a unifying structure. He tried to force everything in the heavens and on earth into a grandiose but tight frame from which the most miniscule detail could not escape."[23]

Not only does Newton, perhaps out of fear of being derided if not persecuted by the orthodox thinkers of his day, elect to suppress these concerns in his scientific work, he creates the impression that he is entirely committed to divesting the scientific endeavor of all metaphysical constructs. "Our business," he tells other natural philosophers, "is with the causes of sensible effects,"[24] and experimental verification is mandatory at each stage in the development of hypotheses. Principles like mass, gravity, and cohesion are not to be considered as "occult qualities, supposed to result from the specific form of things," but as "general laws of nature, by which the things themselves are formed."[25] The task of the investigator is to uncover general laws that govern behavior of all corporal things and not to concern himself with the ultimate causes of those laws. In spite of Newton's concerted effort to keep his theological imagination a subdued presence in his scientific work, however, there are two very important concepts in his physics in which his need to sustain a fundamental feature of his symbolic universe seems to prevail.

"Absolute, true and mathematical time, of itself, and from its own nature, flows," said Newton, "equably without regard to anything external," and "Absolute space, in its own nature, without regard to anything external, remains always similar and immovable." Since Newton recognized, as Galileo did, that the motions detectable to the senses are "relative motions" that are probably somewhat accelerated or retarded in relation to absolute time, how did this supposedly avowed experimentalist who disdained mere hypotheses uncover the experimental evidence that proved the existence of absolute space and time? Although he did speculate that "in the remote regions of the fixed stars, or perhaps beyond them, there may be some body absolutely at rest"[26] which would prove the existence of absolute space and time, there was clearly no opportunity to validate that hypothesis. If we accept Newton's criteria for scientific investigation, which he insists we must before accepting scientific knowledge, then his assertions about space and time constitute massive errors in the main body of his most classic work. The willingness of Newton to allow these fundamental concepts to remain in his physics was, I suspect, a product of his need to ensure the continued participation of the God of the Judeo-Christian tradition in a cosmos that could operate perfectly well without it.

God, says Newton in the *General Scholium*, "is not eternity or infinity, but eternal and infinite; he is not duration or space, but he endures and is present. He endures forever, and is everywhere present; and by existing always and everywhere, he constitutes duration and space."[27] The man who came to be known as largely responsible for disseminating the idea of the clockwork universe could not bear, as his violent reaction to Leibniz's proselytizing of this notion testifies, to view his God merely as clockmaker. In insinuating God's presence within the conceptual framework of his physics, Newton as metaphysician was able to circumvent the profound sense of alienation from the natural that would soon become a feature of Western cosmology. This subtle, and, for the most part, unnoticed stratagem allowed Newton to continue to conceive of God as the Divine Will that sustains creation, rather than as some coldly disinterested cosmic craftsman. And it also explains why he could so easily accept the observed deviations from natural law in the motions of planetary bodies. God, said Newton, was present to correct all such irregularities.

Although Newton may not have been troubled by the prospect that the providential deity of the Judeo-Christian tradition might not be an active presence in the cosmos, his paradigm for the organization of physical reality made that leap of faith several furlongs longer than it had ever been before. It was not only that the Newtonian universe did not appear to require the presence of any transcendent power other than the natural law to remain operational, but also that this mathematically precise, closed universe would simply not permit intervention of any external agency. (The well-known connection between the attempt to assimilate the new scientific knowledge and the dispiritualization of nature in eighteenth-century literature speaks for itself.) After God had been locked out of His creation, Western man would never quite recover, even in the romantic period, his earlier confidence that he could commune with aspects of his environment not transcribable in number.

If the impact of Newtonian science upon our symbolic universe had such adverse consequences, why is it that the metaphysical foundations of that science have not been investigated earlier? The most obvious reasons are that Newton's laws were representations of common-sense views of physical interactions, and that they appeared to allow precise predictions of the results of those interactions. But apparent scientific validity, as we are discovering in our own time, has rarely been sufficient justification for widespread acceptance in culture of insights that threaten basic features of controlling symbolics. Where in the age of Newton is the intellectual and emotional furor that arose in response to the discoveries of Copernicus and Darwin in their times? The almost total absence of adverse reactions makes sense when we realize that Newton's physics was itself a manifestation of, and, therefore, highly congruent with, the same metaphysical assumptions found in the controlling symbolic. The conception of natural law as transcendent absolute is, for example, not only a corollary of the Western conception of moral law, it is also commensurate on a more basic level with the dualistic conception of Being assimilated from the Greeks. The view of change as recombinations of original, unchanging things, which coincides with the emergence of ontological dualism in Greek philosophy, is also retained and reinforced in Newtonian physics. Since the Western conception of identity as atomized substance, which also applies, by extension, to human beings as well, was a feature of the new science, classical physics posed no threat to the idea of self as essentially a fixed and static identity. The understanding of death as either the cessation of all being in the self-entity, or the point at which the primary self-entity (the soul) is elevated to a higher, distinct level of being was likewise reinforced. Newtonian paradigm and controlling symbolic mirror one another to this extent because both are built upon the same foundation—the Western metaphysical tradition.

All of which explains why the various defenders of the faith, the high priests of culture who maintain and disseminate knowledge of the symbolic universe, did not perceive the potential of the new science to damage the belief systems they were pledged to protect. Assuming that the threat had been perceived, and that Newton, consequently, had been targeted, like Galileo or Darwin, as the purveyor of heretical doctrine, it is doubtful he would have survived the onslaught as well as they did. The man who considered his scientific work as fundamentally an act of worship and thought his greatest achievement a lengthy and largely forgotten commentary on the Revelations of Saint John, could not have dismissed such charges, as the modern scientist might, with the assertion that the truths of science are prior to, or more fundamental than, the truths of philosophy or religion. And yet Newton laid upon the altar of scientific truth a set of ideas that, perhaps more than any other, served to banish God from the subjective experience of Western man.

2 · METAPHYSICS AND THE NEW PHYSICS

The Greek conception of the atom as discrete, indestructible substance that served in the Western metaphysical tradition to reinforce the notion of self as a separate, essentially immutable entity first became suspect in the nineteenth century with the discovery of the phenomenon of radioactivity. Not long after Pierre and Marie Curie discovered radium and polonium in 1898, it became apparent to the New Zealander Ernest Rutherford that not only are atoms composite structures, but also that they transform themselves into different substances as a result of radioactivity. Rutherford speculated that by firing a certain kind of particle given off by radioactive substances at atoms and studying the manner in which they are deflected, he could arrive at a more realistic picture of the internal structure of the atom. Like so many breakthroughs in modern physics, the experiments suggested something that gave the heretofore rocklike face of external reality a startling new appearance. Atoms were apparently composed primarily of vast regions of space in which extremely small particles (electrons) moved around a tiny nucleus.

In order to appreciate how puzzling this new picture of the internal structure of the atom was to the scientists, imagine the mass that is your body so greatly reduced in size that you could walk into the space of the atom. Assume that this space is the size of the Houston Astrodome, stroll inside, and locate the pitcher's mound. Place a grain of salt on top of the mound, and then strain to see a speck of dust moving furiously around the outside of the enormous dome

—the analogy provides a rough approximation of the relative distance between nucleus and electrons in atomic structures. Now travel in the same fashion into the things that surround you, or better yet, journey down through tissue, bones, organs, cells, molecules, and atoms that make up the organic structure that is a human body. If the mind's eye can even begin to entertain this vision of the rock of material reality dissolving into seemingly vast reaches of nothingness inhabited by tiny activities of somethingness called subatomic particle, then you can begin to appreciate the bewilderment of Rutherford and his colleagues.

This new view of the life of substance was difficult to accept, not only because of its strangeness, but also because it could not finally be explained in terms of classical physics. How was it that atoms composed of so little matter could collide billions of times a second with other such structures and yet return to their original form after each collision? Newtonian physics could explain with some minor deviations the stability of the orbits of planets in our solar system, but the stability of the atom could not be accounted for with the same conceptual tools. These tools also proved inadequate in the effort to demonstrate why large collections of matter made up of atoms that were almost entirely empty could not simply pass through one another.

Scientific progress rarely proceeds in the manner in which it is represented in most traditional textbooks on the history of science —as neat linear progression from problem to solution. Scores of recent books and articles now exist detailing the subtle, nonlinear progress of modern scientific thought in which we witness the unsuspected and often surprising influences of earlier and virtually forgotten scientists upon major figures in the present scientific revolution, and even the impact of literary and philosophical developments upon the evolution of scientific concepts. We will not, of course, be able to fairly represent that considerable body of scholarship in one chapter, but we can at least arrive at some understanding of the major developments in the new physics, and begin to perceive their startling implications in metaphysical terms. The most expedient manner of going about this is, I suspect, to begin with an examination of the implications of Einstein's special and general theories of relativity, and then confront the more enigmatic, mind-bending issues in quantum physics that are still being hotly debated.

In order to better appreciate the situation confronted by Einstein in 1905 it might prove helpful to introduce some terms from Thomas Kuhn's *Structure of Scientific Revolutions*. Physicists from Newton to Einstein practiced, says Kuhn, "normal science"—a mode of scientific investigation "predicated on the assumption that the scientific community knows what the world is and looks like." In normal science widely accepted scientific paradigms determine the criteria for the selection of problems that can be presumed to have a solution. Radically new insights into the life of nature commence, says Kuhn, "with awareness of anomaly, i.e., with the recognition that nature has somehow violated the paradigm-induced expectations that govern normal science."[1] We see, in other words, even in scientific endeavors, only that which the distorting lenses of our conception of the real will allow us to see. When scientists confront such an anomaly and arrive at a new explanation based upon an entirely different paradigm, they are not simply finding the right words for the same crossword puzzle. They are seeing a world that had no prior existence because the basis for its conception was not known, a world that so violates our normal expectations of the real that it seems, initially at least, unreal. "It was," said Einstein, "as if the ground has been pulled from under one, with no firm foundation to be seen anywhere, upon which one could have built."[2]

The anomaly presented itself to Einstein in the results of investigations into the area which came to be known as electrodynamics by the nineteenth-century physicists Michael Faraday and Clerk Maxwell. Their study of the effects of electric and magnetic forces provided the first concrete demonstration that there were processes in nature that lay outside the province of classical physics. When Faraday managed to produce an electric current in a coil of copper by moving a magnet near it, he demonstrated that the mechanical work of moving the magnet could be converted into electrical energy. Nothing dramatic would have been learned from the experiment if the phenomenon had been interpreted in Newtonian fashion as the interaction of a positive and negative charge that results in attraction, like that between two masses. The scientists speculated, however, that each charge creates a disturbance, or a condition, in the field around it which causes the other charge, when it is present, to feel a force. In Newtonian physics force had to be viewed in terms of bodies interacting. In choosing to view force not simply as the result of the interaction of particles, but as a property of a field created by a single charge and existing even if another charge is not present to feel its effects, Faraday and Maxwell went beyond classical physics.

The anomaly confronted by Einstein consisted, then, of two disparate views of the nature of force which he sought boldly to resolve with the publication of two papers in a single year (1905) that thoroughly revolutionized the study of physics. The first paper, entitled "On the Electrodynamics of Moving Bodies," contained what would later be called the special theory of relativity, and the second, an understanding of electrodynamic radiation that would become the basis for quantum theory. The reverberations of the speculations of the obscure German thinker rattled not only the foundations of the old science with amazing alacrity, but also appeared to strip away much of the theoretical ground upon which it rested. Since the features of Newtonian physics displaced by the new physics mirror common-sense assumptions about the real grounded in a metaphysic implicitly accepted and endorsed in the Western world for about 2,500 years, the architects of the new physics made their discoveries with an anguish and confusion not at all commensurate with the popular image of the coldly analytical man of science. As notions fundamental to Newtonian science, like absolute space and time, the elementary solid particle, simple causality in natural process, and the possibility at least of a wholly objective description of natural events, began to dissolve like so many desert mirages, scientists had every right to feel that the "ground had been pulled from under one." In metaphysical terms that was precisely the case.

Albert Einstein generated, unwittingly to be sure, more public curiosity about his private life than any scientist in our history, and we need not dwell upon the well-known, exhaustively researched aspects of that life. But some understanding of Einstein as metaphysician is essential if we wish to comprehend the special character of his scientific work and his own emotional confusion over the results. In contrast with Newton, who believed in the literal truth of biblical events all his life, Einstein, in "Autobiographical Notes," describes himself as being disillusioned with that belief at the age of twelve after reading a number of popular scientific books. This loss of faith in the conservative, orthodox view of religious verities was accompanied, as the following passage from the "Notes" suggests, by the emergence of an alternate, although in some sense parallel, religious belief:

Thus I came—despite the fact that I was the son of entirely irreligious [Jewish] parents—to a deep religiosity, which, however, found an abrupt end at the age of 12. Through the reading of popular scientific books I soon reached the conviction that much in the stories of the Bible could not be true. The consequence was a positively fanatic [orgy] of freethinking coupled with the impression that youth is intentionally being deceived by the state through lies; it was a crushing impression. Suspicion against every kind of authority grew out of this experience. . . . It is quite clear to me that the religious paradise of youth, which was thus lost, was a first attempt to free myself from the chains of the "merely personal." . . . The mental grasp of this extra-personal world within the frame of the given possibilities swam as highest aim half consciously and half unconsciously before my mind's eye.[3]

What is most interesting in this passage is Einstein's feeling that belief in transcendent, immutable biblical truth allowed him to dwell in a "religious paradise of youth," or in a psychological state in which he felt distanced, or disassociated from the harsh realities of state or social environment. Although this "deep religiosity" ceased—after exposure to the scientific—to be associated with biblical truth, Einstein describes himself as seeking to recover that psychological state by developing an intellectual understanding of the "extra-personal world within the frame of the given possibilities," or, as I think we can safely infer, within the context of the transcendent, immutable laws of physics. That Einstein, along with Kepler, Galileo, and Newton, also reified the Pythagorean mathematical ideal into a godlike agency is apparent in the following commentary on the uses of mathematics in the study of nature:

Nature is the realization of the simplest conceivable mathematical ideas. I am convinced that we can discover, by means of purely mathematical constructions, those concepts and those lawful connections between them which furnish the key to the understanding of natural phenomena. Experience remains, of course, the sole criterion of physical utility of a mathematical construction. But the creative principle resides in mathematics. In a certain sense, therefore, I hold it true that pure thought can grasp reality, as the ancients dreamed.[4]

The depth of Einstein's commitment to this metaphysical assumption, comparable in many respects to that of Galileo, is also revealed in his response to the news that the Eddington eclipse expedition (1919) had apparently provided experimental proof for an aspect of the general theory. As Ilse Rosenthal-Schneider, who visited Einstein shortly after he had received a telegram describing the results, writes, "When I was giving expression to my joy that the results coincided with his calculations, he said quite unmoved, 'But I knew the theory is correct,' and when I asked, what if there had been no confirmation of his prediction, he countered: 'Then I would have been sorry for the dear Lord—the theory is correct.' "[5] Since Einstein was not known to make flip, irreverent comments on matters of religion, and apparently had little patience with those who did, we can take seriously the suggestion that his belief in the ontology of number provided a sense of communion with some higher realm of being containing immaterial mathematical forms. Without some appreciation of this deeply felt need to fashion a vision of cosmic forces that bespoke the coherence and harmony of aesthetically pleasing mathematical paradigms it is difficult to comprehend the resolution of the anomaly which Einstein perceived in Maxwell's study of electrodynamics.

In 1905, physics was still premised upon the idea that physical events could be explained in terms of things and the forces that existed between them sitting in, or traveling through, a medium called the ether. Since the Michelson-Morley experiment failed to detect the velocity of earth with respect to the hypothetical ether, and suggested through this failure that the ether may not exist, it is described in most histories of modern science as providing the experimental evidence that led Einstein to the conclusion that light traveled in free space at a constant speed unaided and unretarded by anything else. As Gerald Holton has beautifully and quite convincingly demonstrated, however, this was simply not the case. Not only was Einstein apparently unfamiliar with the results of this experiment in 1905, he appears to have arrived at the conclusion that the ether is nonexistent in the effort to eliminate what he perceived as "assymmetries" in Maxwell's theory. The fact that there was one equation in this theory for finding the electromagnetic force generated in a moving conductor when it goes past a stationary magnet, and another equation when the conductor is stationary and the magnet is moving was simply not consistent with Einstein's expectation that nature is the "realization of the simplest conceivable mathematical ideas." In order, says Holton, "to extend the principle of relativity from mechanics (where it worked) to all of physics, and at the same time to explain the null results of all optical and electrical ether-drift experiments, one needed 'only' to abandon the notion of the absolute frame of reference, and with it, the ether."[6] As Einstein put it in the paper on electrodynamics, "The electrodynamic fields are not states of the medium (the ether) and are not bound to any bearer, but they are independent realities which are not reducible to anything else."[7] Surmising that the empirical evidence for the existence of ether would never be found, he proclaims that the ether does not exist and proceeds to establish the principle upon which the special theory is constructed—the constancy of the speed of light. His problem then becomes to explain why every observer regardless of his state of motion could possibly perceive the speed of light as constant.

In order to appreciate how preposterous the principle seemed at the time to classically trained physicists, let us imagine ourselves aboard a spaceship moving at 86,000 miles per second away from a beam of light that has just begun to emanate from a distant point in space, and calculate when the light will become visible. Using classical transformation equations, we would be obliged to compute the speed of the massless photons (light) approaching at 100,000 miles per second and determine how much time is required to travel the distance between the two points. If we reverse the situation and move toward the light source at 100,000 miles per second, the same method of calculation indicates that spaceship and light are approaching one another at the rate of 286,000 miles per second. Incredible though it seems, our calculations would be wrong in both instances—the photons travel, regardless of our state of motion, at a constant 186,000 miles per second. Even if we give chase to the beam of light at a velocity approaching the speed of light itself, it would still be leaving us at its own constant speed.

Einstein, with his great talent of dealing with what seemed actual in scientific terms regardless of the violence done to common sense, surmised that if the speed of light measured by an observer at rest relative to a light source is the same as the speed of light measured by an observer in motion relative to the source, then the measuring instruments must change from one frame of reference to the other such that the speed of light always appears to be the same. Because classical mechanics since Galileo had recognized that the laws of motion valid in one frame of reference are only valid in other frames of reference which move uniformly in relation to it, Einstein did not invent the principle of relativity per se. What he sought to do was expand the Galilean relativity principle to include all the laws of physics, which in his own time included the laws governing electrodynamic radiation. The mathematical scheme devised by Einstein which, for reasons we will examine later, stressed a mechanistic world view, inferred that light speed is constant from one frame of reference to another regardless of motion relative to the source because the tools of measurement—rods and clocks—vary in accordance with the motion itself. If moving measuring rods become shorter and moving clocks run more slowly, then the moving observer with his shorter measuring rods and slower clocks could conceivably calculate more distance and more time for light to travel than the observer at rest. Although light speed would appear constant to both observers, each in his particular frame of reference would notice no change in length of rods or speed of clocks. Theoretically this would remain the case right up until the moment when the velocity increases to that of the speed of light, at which point objects would become so contracted in the direction of motion that they would disappear altogether and clocks would cease to run entirely.

Since human beings, like mechanical clocks, also consist of atomic structures, we can safely presume that the biological clock would be affected in the same manner. Let us put ourselves back aboard our imaginary spaceship traveling on this occasion at speeds approaching the speed of light while our twin brother or sister awaits our return on earth. If our spaceship maintains this velocity for several years (our frame of reference), we would probably return to discover that our twin was not only dead, but had been so for centuries (relative time in earth's frame of reference). The Twin Paradox, which has intrigued physicists for decades, is not without experimental justification. Experiments in high energy particle physics have shown, for example, that an object with a certain length in a frame of reference at rest does become shorter with increasing velocity relative to an observer. Similarly, particles approaching the speed of light in such experiments have been observed to live many times longer, on the average, than identical or "twin" particles traveling at lower velocities.

Although these experiments clearly show that space and time are not absolute and separate dimensions but part of what Einstein called the space-time continuum, we find no indication that this is the case in the course of normal, everyday experience. We can, of course, control our location in space, but there appears to be no prospect at all of having any effect upon the flow of time. Since this three-dimensional reality we occupy in space does appear, as Newton said, to move forward in one-dimensional time, any talk about time as the fourth dimension seems a bit fantastical. The impression that events can be arranged in a unique time sequence (past, present, and future) is due to the fact, explained Einstein, that the velocity of light is so high in comparison with other velocities in our experience that we have the illusion we see an event in the instant in which it occurs. If we get back aboard our spacecraft and imagine ourselves observing some events on Mars, for example, it is apparent that we would order events differently in time than our twin studying the same events in his frame of reference on earth. If there is no absolute time existing independently of an observer, it follows that space cannot be understood to contain a definite configuration of matter every instant in time as the concept of absolute space clearly implies.

In the space-time coordinate system physicists use to account for such differences in the observational process, time is a coordinate added to the three space coordinates forming the four-dimensional continuum space-time. In relativistic physics, transformations between different frames of reference express each coordinate of one frame as a combination of the coordinates of the other frame, and a space coordinate in one frame usually appears as a combination, or mixture, of space and time coordinates in another frame. The space-time coordinate system represents this situation in the language of mathematics, and allows the mixture of space and time to be transcribed in a well-defined manner in the four-dimensional continuum space-time. Time as the fourth dimension in the mental landscape of mathematics does not, of course, translate well into the mental landscape associated with ordinary language, and can perhaps best be described as "a label given to a relationship." We could review the various diagrams and illustrations that have been developed to communicate this four-dimensional reality in ordinary language, but it would not be useful in helping us to finally visualize it. The mathematical idealization of this reality that yields precise results in relativistic physics may serve to describe the condition of our being, but our world-constructing minds are not yet equipped to fully construct it in nonmathematical terms. But, as Herman Minkowski proclaimed in a now famous lecture in 1908, "Henceforth space by itself, and time by itself, are doomed to fade away into mere shadows, and only a kind of union of the two will preserve an independent reality."[8]

The concept from the special theory with the most potential to transform us is the new relationship between matter and energy discussed earlier. $E=MC^2$ reveals mass as a form of energy and energy as having mass, or, as Einstein himself put it: "Energy has mass and mass represents energy."[9] The thought that the energy contained in any piece of matter is equal to the mass of the matter multiplied by the extraordinarily large number that is the speed of light squared is certainly imposing, but the recognition that the Western idea of substance, thing, or identity may be without scientific foundation has exceedingly profound implications. As the situation is aptly described by James B. Conant: "To some, the real disappearance of matter seems as disturbing as the loss of life and ruin of the city, for associated with the word 'matter' in most people's minds is the word 'reality.' "[10]

The special theory did not take into account the force of interaction between massive bodies (gravity), and in 1915 Einstein sought to extend its framework in the general theory to include that phenomenon as well. The effect of gravity, said Einstein, is to curve the space-time continuum. The terrain of space-time, if we had eyes to see it, is mountainous in the region of large or massive bodies, like our sun, and evens out into something like a flat plain in those remote areas of space where matter does not exist in any great concentrations. For our purposes, however, what is most interesting in general relativity is that it is impossible to distinguish between the gravitational field, existing everywhere in the cosmos, and the structure or geometry of space. Since both are represented in Einstein's field equations by the same mathematical quantity, we are obliged to view matter and space as interdependent aspects of one seamless whole. "We may therefore regard matter," said Einstein, "as being constituted by the regions in space in which the field is extremely intense. . . . There is no place in this new kind of physics both for the field and matter, for the field is the only reality."[11] Concentrations of matter, such as our bodies, do not from this perspective move as separate and discrete entities through an ether or a void, but exist as manifestations of a field that is quite literally everywhere in the cosmos.

The essential unity of natural process that Einstein perceived on the macro level was later discovered to be a feature of nature on the level of the very small—the world of subatomic activity. Rutherford's experiments suggested that the internal structure of the atom, consisting of very little mass with enormous distances separating electrons and nucleus, could not be reasonably explained in terms of Newtonian mechanics. Max Planck's hypothesis that energy from heat, a form of electromagnetic radiation, is not emitted continuously, but rather in discrete energy packets, provided the first significant breakthrough to an acceptable theory. When Einstein, in a paper on the photoelectric effect, demonstrated that light energy is also emitted in discrete units, which he called quanta, he initiated a line of investigation that grew into quantum physics. The fact that Thomas Young had shown 102 years earlier that light travels in waves may not, at first, seem terribly significant, but the suggestion from Einstein that it also behaves as particles laid the groundwork for a controversy among physicists over the fundamental character of material reality, and our ability to know it, that rages to this day. Before beginning our own struggle with the metaphysical implications of the dual wave-particle aspects of matter, let us briefly review the major theoretical breakthroughs in quantum physics that kept the controversy alive.

In 1913 Niels Bohr, whom we will hear a good deal more about later, speculated, based on the spectroscopic data gathered from the study of hydrogen atoms, that electrons revolve around the nucleus in orbits, or shells, which occupy specific distances from the nucleus. Each of the shells, which are theoretically infinite in number, contains, says Bohr, a specific number of electrons. The one electron of the hydrogen atom occupies the first shell in the lowest energy level, or ground state, and jumps outward to another shell, suggested Bohr, with the introduction of energy—which it will re-emit in the form of light in the exact amount—in returning to the ground state. Bohr's calculations show that the energy differences between states of the electrons are proportional to the frequencies in the hydrogen spectrum. The next major development occurred when Louis de Broglie in his doctoral dissertation in 1924 suggested that the point-like electrons swarming around the nucleus in Bohr's model propagate as waves. It was de Broglie's hypothesis that just as massless photons (light) behave like waves as well as particles, electrons should behave in the same manner also. The reason, speculated de Broglie, that the energy levels in the atom are quantized is the same reason that the frequencies of overtones in vibrating strings are quantized. If the standing wavelike patterns in the movement of electrons assumed, like vibrating strings, a limited number of well-defined shapes, then electrons might be confined to a specific set of orbits with definite diameters. When it was later discovered that all so-called material particles (protons, neutrons, heavy nuclei) share this wavelike behavior, de Broglie's insight proved to be a great theoretical advance for quantum physics.

It was de Broglie's theory on matter waves that stimulated the Viennese physicist Erwin Schrödinger, a year later, to develop his own theory. Schrödinger in his wave mechanics seeks to eliminate what he perceived as certain ambiguities in Bohr's planetary model featuring hard, spherical electrons revolving around the nucleus at specific levels. The model, as Schrödinger saw it, did not provide a mechanistic explanation for why it is that each shell can contain only a certain number of electrons, or how it is that the electrons do their jumping from one orbit to another. Choosing to view electrons as quantized standing waves existing in three dimensions—length, width, and depth in lay terms—Schrödinger analyzed the standing wave patterns of hydrogen, with its one electron, and calculated with the use of his wave equation a multitude of possible shapes. With the addition of a postulate formulated by another Austrian physicist, Wolfgang Pauli, that no two of the standing wave patterns in the atom can be the same, and therefore, the formation of one particular pattern excludes all others—Pauli's exclusion principle—an explanation for the numbers assigned to electrons at various energy levels in Bohr's model was provided. The Schrödinger equation, with the addition of Pauli's exclusion principle, reveals only two possible wave patterns for the ground state of the hydrogen atom, eight for the second level, and so on to the theoretical limit.

The feature of the Schrödinger wave mechanics that is most important for the purposes of this discussion is that it is mechanistic in the Newtonian sense and presumes direct, causal relationships between events that predetermine results. If we can assume that the wave equation is accurate for a system propagating in isolation, or evolving into different wave patterns undisturbed by an observer, the order of those patterns strictly coincides with the order given in Schrödinger's wave equation. Since one pattern will presumably follow another in an unvarying sequence, the suggestion is that the subatomic event might follow deterministic laws of motion just as macroscopic events follow the laws of Newtonian mechanics. There are, however, other developments in quantum physics that appear to contradict this interpretation, and most respected theorists in quantum physics seem to openly reject it. Although Schrödinger's famous equation remains an integral part of quantum theory, there are some limits to its application, which we will soon discuss, that suggest that the microcosm of the atom is not simply a much smaller version of the cosmic machine.

The alternate theory to Schrödinger's wave mechanics, developed by Werner Heisenberg, is matrix mechanics, and the two theories, in spite of a dramatic difference in the assumptions about the actual character of subatomic processes, are mathematically equivalent and are still considered alternative formulations of the single theory—quantum mechanics. The difficulty with Schrödinger's theory, like that of de Broglie, is that it does not explain precisely what it is that is vibrating or waving in the wave pattern. Strictly interpreted the theory suggests that the electron is spread out over the entire orbit in Bohr's atom displaying a wide range of different speeds. Although waves, like those of sound, do propagate in this fashion in a continuous medium, this proved not to be an accurate picture of the behavior of electrons. Working independently of de Broglie and Schrödinger, the twenty-five-year-old Heisenberg made the theoretical leap to matrix mechanics in 1925 by taking the positivist, or empiricist, position that physics can deal only with observables, or, in this instance, only that which can be known at the beginning of an experiment and the end. As he would put it much later in his life, we should "abandon all attempts to construct perceptual models of atomic processes."[12] After developing a method for organizing data into mathematical tables called matrices, Heisenberg created tables that could be used to calculate probabilities associated with initial conditions that could be applied in the analysis of observables in subatomic processes.

As Max Jammer, who has extensively analyzed developments in

quantum theory, notes: "It is hard to find in the history of physics two theories (wave and matrix mechanics) designed to cover the same range of experience which differ more radically than these two."[13] Whereas Schrödinger's theory emphasizes continuity of physical processes and the wavelike behavior of the electron, Heisenberg's theory features discontinuity of physical processes and regards the electron as particle without assigning it a definite space-time description in the classical sense. These logically irreconcilable but mathematically equivalent theories raise, as we shall soon discover, some formidable epistemological questions about the relationship between mind—or the symbolic universe of Western man—and nature that could, over time, fundamentally alter the terms of construction of the symbolic universe itself.

Before discussing those questions, we must entertain two more theoretical propositions in quantum mechanics that became key issues in this controversy—Max Born's proposal that the electron is really a particle with the wave function representing the probability that it is located at a particular point in space, and Heisenberg's more famous indeterminacy principle. The term *probability* as it had been used earlier in areas like kinetic theory did not imply that the exact properties of molecules in a system could not be determined exactly, but was rather a term of convenience in doing calculations with the available data. Born's use of the term is quite different, in that it assumes that positions and velocities of each subatomic particle do not have definite values, but are random processes with only certain probabilities of displaying particular values. As he put it, the behavior of subatomic particles is "in the nature of the case indeterminate, and therefore the affair of statistics."[14] It is important to stress here that Born is not indicating that the definite values are there and that we only lack the tools to find them, but rather that these processes are by nature random and unpredictable, except within a certain range of probable occurrence. Heisenberg's indeterminacy principle (1927) states that there are certain pairs of physical properties in a particle, like position and momentum, that cannot simultaneously be measured with a high degree of accuracy. Since Heisenberg illustrated the inability to directly observe position and momentum by demonstrating that if we probe the atom with a particle with a wavelength short enough to locate the electron, the energy of the probe would disturb the electron's momentum, or if we use a particle with energy low enough not to disturb momentum, the wavelength would be so long that the particle could not be precisely located, there is the widespread impression that he meant that position and momentum were definite but unobservable values. In actuality Heisenberg meant precisely what Born did—both are indeterminate as random events within a certain range of probability.

The suggestion that so-called material particles in subatomic processes display a dual nature (particle and wave) which has been subsumed by two mathematically equivalent theories that focus upon each aspect seems of no great concern, metaphysically or otherwise, until we take a more studied look at the implications. The quandary is not, incidentally, eliminated by isolating an individual particle, for even that single particle "interferes with itself" in experimental conditions and displays a wavelike characteristic. To provide some indication of the consternation experienced by physicists when faced with this paradox, consider the following two comments. Heisenberg characterized his view of the situation with the analogy that it is as if a box were "full and empty at the same time."[15] Or, as Robert Oppenheimer puts it with the maddening logical inconsistencies that the description demands: "If we ask, for instance, whether the position of the electron remains the same, we must say 'no'; if we ask whether the electron is at rest, we must say 'no'; if we ask whether it is in motion, we must say 'no.' "[16] Physicists, as perhaps the most extreme embodiment in this culture of the Western analytical tradition with all of its metaphysical underpinnings, are (as we will see in some of their more bizarre attempts to evade the paradox) ill-equipped to deal with this view of the fundamental character of physical reality.

Niels Bohr, recognized along with Heisenberg as the founder of the Copenhagen interpretation of quantum theory, is also responsible for positing a mode of cognitively dealing with this situation that lies at the very center of the epistemological dilemma in modern physics. Bohr counseled the physicists to hold wave and particle in their minds as complementary views of one reality recognizing the inherent limitations of each in accordance with the indeterminacy principle. Opposites from this point of view have meaning only in terms of their participation in one another, and can never be finally viewed as categorically different. As Leon Rosenfeld has demonstrated, Bohr did not conceive of his principle of complementarity as having applications in the area of physics alone, and "devoted a considerable amount of hard work to exploring the possibilities of application of complementarity to other domains of knowledge."[17] Although the resistance of physicists to this notion has at times been fierce, it appears likely that it will come to enjoy increasingly larger acceptance in that community. Since more general constructs, like force and matter, motion and rest, and even existence and nonexistence, also appear in the new physics as to be complementary views of one unified process, physicists, struggling with a habit of mind operating almost everywhere else in their experience, are increasingly obliged to recognize the limitations of either-or categorical thinking.

Since the Bohr-Einstein debate, comparable in many respects to the more heated controversy between Newton and Leibniz, was the means through which the epistemological questions raised by quantum physics became widely known, perhaps we should pause, as we did in discussing Einstein, and consider the metaphysical assumptions and philosophical influences at work in Bohr's mythopoeic imagination as well. Most remarkably like Einstein, Bohr (1) was preoccupied in his early life with religious verities; (2) experienced profound disillusionment as he came to recognize the improbable nature of biblical events; (3) developed, as a consequence, a deeply skeptical attitude toward authority; and (4) eventually discovered in the scientific endeavor an alternate approach to metaphysical reality. As Oscar Klein, one of Bohr's earliest collaborators, tells it, Bohr in childhood believed "literally what he learned from the lessons on religion in school. For a long time this made the sensitive boy unhappy on account of his parents' lack of faith. When later, as a young man, he began to doubt, he did so with unusual resolution and thereby developed a deep philosophical bent similar to that which seems to have characterized the early Greek natural philosophers."[18]

Although Bohr may have been as enamored with the Pythagorean mathematical ideal in youth as Einstein appeared to be throughout his life, the influence of at least two major theorists outside the hard sciences—Sören Kierkegaard and William James—apparently led Bohr to develop a different perspective on that ideal. As Gerald Holton, who has carefully researched Bohr's acquaintance with Kierkegaard, evaluates that particular influence: "Kierkegaard's stress on discontinuity between incompatibles, on the 'leap' rather than the gradual transition, on the inclusion of the individual, and on inherent dichotomy was as 'nonclassical' in philosophy as the elements of the Copenhagen doctrine—quantum jumps, probabilistic causality, observer-dependent description, and duality—were to be in physics."[19] According to Henry Stapp, Bohr's exposure to William James's version of pragmatism provided much of the epistemological foundation for the Copenhagen interpretation. The subjectivist character of that interpretation, which we will soon examine, may owe a good deal, suggests Stapp, to James's position that a "relationship between an idea and something else can be comprehended only if that something else is also an idea. Ideas are eternally combined in the realm of ideas. They can 'know' or 'agree' only with other ideas." This assumption about the character of knowledge leads easily enough to the notion, adopted by Bohr, that external realities "could be structurally very different from human ideas. Hence there is no *a priori* reason to expect that the relationships that constitute or characterize the essence of external reality can be mapped in any simple or direct fashion into the world of ideas."[20]

To better appreciate why Bohr was attracted to these positions in the study of physics, and why Einstein vigorously objected to the Copenhagen interpretation, we must consider two thought experiments that were central to the Bohr-Einstein debate—the Einstein-Podolsky-Rosen experiment and Schrödinger's cat. Einstein's famous and often quoted statement that "God does not play dice" has created the impression that his principal objection to the Copenhagen interpretation was its emphasis upon indeterminacy, but it is probably more accurate to say that he was most committed in the debate with Bohr to preserving the realist position that if a quantity can be determined with certainty it actually exists. This concern developed in response to the assumption in the Copenhagen interpretation that the act of observation itself causes all the probabilities in Schrödinger's wave function to collapse to only one possibility—that which has actually been observed.

Presume, for example, that we have calculated the probability of a result occurring in either region A or B prior to making a measurement as a photon, propagating in isolation, realizes deterministically all possibilities given in the wave equation. When the measurement is made, indicating that the observer has now interacted with the observed system, the photon will appear in either region A or B, without our being able to predict which region, and all other possibilities become zero. Einstein, who felt that the particle has an actual existence in nature regardless of whether or not it is measured, assisted in the preparation of a paper in 1935 entitled "Can Quantum Mechanical Description of Reality be Considered Complete?" which contains the EPR-thought experiment. The notion was that two systems, like two electrons, should be allowed to interact and then be assumed to be completely separated from one another so that there is no mutual influence. It was then suggested that if both systems behave, as quantum mechanics says they must, in accordance with the various possible wave functions in Schrödinger's equation, then measurement of a property in the first system, like momentum, should make it possible to single out a particular wave function in the second system. In other words, if we can assume that the systems can be actually separated, a real property of the second system can be determined by measuring the first without the intervention of the observer, and, therefore, that property is real in the absence of the observer.

One of the many ironies in modern physics is that the EPR-thought experiment, designed to discredit the Copenhagen interpretation, became through actual experiment the "EPR effect" that is now used to support the interpretation. When it was discovered that the spin of a subatomic particle can be oriented (up, down, right, left), and that a beam of light could be split into two equal smaller beams, it was possible to attempt to create a spacelike separation in which the two particles (systems) would not presumably interact with one another. The results show that if the spin of a particle in region A is measured, let us say, as *right*, then its twin particle with its spacelike separation in area B will spin left—the spin of the twin particle is invariably equal and opposite in these experiments. In short, what was done, or measured, in region A affects the particle in region B even though the particles themselves, light, are traveling at the maximum velocity that any signal could presumably be carried. The principle of local causes, which says that what happens in one region does not depend upon variables subject to the control of an observer taking a measurement in a distant spacelike separated region, does not appear valid in this situation.

Schrödinger, a realist like Einstein, also could not believe that one aspect of a physical process could collapse, or disappear, as a concrete, identifiable something as a result of a human observer making a measurement. To illustrate what he perceived as the fundamental absurdity of that assumption held by some advocates of the Copenhagen interpretation, Schrödinger conceived of a Rube Goldberg-like thought experiment in which a cat is placed inside a box with a device that could release poisonous gas. The release of the gas would be determined by a random event—the radioactive decay of an atom. Since the box is sealed the experimenter cannot know whether the gas has been released or not, or whether the cat is alive or dead, and the question *is*, "What is happening inside the box in the absence of observation?" If we accept, as Schrödinger does, the proposition that the wave function describes the ensemble of events that is the cat, then the collapse of the wave function, which occurs when a measurement is taken, determines if the cat is dead or alive. The intention is to demonstrate the implausibility of the view of the notion in the Copenhagen interpretation, as Schrödinger derisively represents it, that the cat as wave function is both dead and alive prior to the act of observation as both possibilities remain actual in the isolated system, and that it is the act of observation itself that causes one of these possibilities to actualize or occur.

Before we examine the bizarre recent attempts to resolve the wave-particle paradox in epistemological terms, let us briefly discuss the impact upon the world-constructing minds of contemporary physicists of the theorem that has, most recently, conferred upon the Copenhagen interpretation its enormous authority. Bell's theorem (1964) is a mathematical construct, indecipherable to the nonmathematician, which shows that either the statistical predictions of quantum theory are false or the principle of local causes is false. Both, in other words, cannot be valid in terms of the mathematical formalism of the theorem. (The other alternative, which we will soon explore, is simply to give up realism altogether, and assume that it is the act of observation that confers reality on the observed system.) When hypothetical construct was put to experimental test by Clauser and Freedman in 1972 at the Lawrence Berkeley Laboratory, the results showed that the statistical predictions upon which Bell based his theorem seemed valid, and seven more recent experiments have yielded the same conclusion. Since the experiments on spacelike separated particles, like the one described earlier in connection with the EPR effect, show particles in different regions somehow *communicating*, if one can call it that, at speeds greater than that of light, Jack Sarfatti theorized in 1975 that the spacelike separated particles are not communicating by faster-than-light signals, but are rather interconnected in such a way that they transcend space and time. Since much of modern physics is premised upon the constancy of the speed of light, the suggestion, as Sarfatti put it, that super-luminal communication goes on instantaneously between particles in regions A and B was obviously a radical proposition. It is important to note here that in Sarfatti's theory the wave function on this most basic level is not considered to be a mathematical abstraction, but a something that has actual existence.

What is most imposing about these results is that if the principle of local cause is invalid, then all activities in the cosmos may be viewed as intimately and immediately connected with all other activities in accordance with the wave function. As David Bohm describes the situation: "Parts are seen to be in immediate connection, in which their dynamical relationships depend, in an irreducible way, on the state of the whole system (and, indeed, on that of broader systems in which they are contained, extending ultimately and in principle to the entire universe). Thus, one is led to a new notion of unbroken wholeness which denies the classical idea of analyzability of the world into separately and independently existing parts."[21] Although the idea of the universe as unbroken wholeness, or as fundamentally unified process, has been enthusiastically received of late by Westerners with affection for Eastern religious systems like Buddhism, Taoism, and Hinduism, there are other inferences that have been drawn from Bell's theorem that these holistically minded individuals are either not aware of or have chosen to ignore.

One of the striking features of quantum mechanics, which has been particularly appealing to humanists, is that individual events on the subatomic level are not subject to completely accurate prediction and remain random within a certain range of probability. Bell's theorem implies that what quantum physicists have viewed as a random occurrence, like the decay of a radioactive atom, may not be a random or chance event, but a direct and inevitable consequence of another, spacelike separated event. As Henry Stapp evaluates the implications: "if one accepts the usual ideas about how information propagates through space and time, then Bell's theorem shows that the macroscopic responses cannot be independent of faraway causes. This problem is neither resolved nor alleviated by saying that the response is determined by 'pure chance.' Bell's theorem proves precisely that the determination of the macroscopic response must be 'nonchance,' or at least to the extent of allowing some sort of dependence of this response upon faraway cause."[22] This new determinism, called *superdeterminism*, poses an even greater threat to the concept of human freedom than that posed by classical physics. In the Newtonian paradigm determinism is a feature of isolated systems, and presumes that once the initial situation of the system is established the future of that system will develop in accordance with the inexorable laws of cause and effect. In superdeterminism there is no choice involved in the establishment of the initial situation, for even that is a given. If the universe from its very inception has been developing in accordance with the wave function, all that occurs thereafter could not have been other than what it has been. The experimenter, from this point of view, may be operating under the illusion that he has freely elected to make a measurement in region A which produces a corresponding result in region B, but the correspondence was itself predetermined, and all the speculations upon the effect of the observer in the Copenhagen interpretation are simply a consequence of the attachment of Western man to the notion that choice is, on some level, unencumbered and free of external influence.

All of which brings us to an examination of what most of us will probably perceive as rather zany propositions that serve to preserve the role of the observer as it is conceived by some advocates of the Copenhagen interpretation as well as the prospect that the observations are freely made. Although the Everett-Wheeler-Graham "many-worlds"interpretation was published prior to Bell's theorem in 1957, it is now viewed by some physicists as serving both functions.[23] The basic assumption of this interpretation is that the possibilities represented by the wave function that collapse into one possibility upon observation do not simply disappear, but remain actual in other branches of the universe. As we elect to make the observation and the wave function appears to collapse, the universe splits into two worlds containing both ourselves as observers and the other actually existing wave function. Schrödinger's cat in this fanciful scheme is, astonishingly to be sure, both alive and dead as we open the box and observe it, for the world immediately splits into two branches in which one observer sees the dead cat and the other discovers the cat alive. More recently Wheeler has taken the equally radical position, called the anthropic principle, that the role of the observer in the Copenhagen interpretation should be taken to mean that it is in the act itself of observation by intelligent life that confers reality upon the universe. The early history of the universe, implies Wheeler, came into existence only when the symbol-making animal situated on a planet located at the corner of the galaxy Milky Way in a vast cosmos containing a multitude of other galaxies brought it into existence by perceiving it.[24]

If your tendency at this point in the discussion is either to lapse into deep depression or to presume, defensively perhaps, that the work of scientists has no more relevance in lived experience than the tracts distributed by the most lunatic fringe of cult followers, suspend judgment for just a while longer. The line of investigation in physics that we have been reviewing is, first of all, not the only area in which new insights into the life of nature are being formulated. As Stephen Brush has indicated, there "is no evidence yet for a reversal of the long-term trend toward indeterminism in atomic physics. Stephen Hawkings, a current leader of black-hole theory, has even proposed that 'the quantum emission from a black hole is completely random and uncorrelated' thereby adding a new kind of indeterminism to Heisenberg's principle."[25]

And there is also another alternative response to Bell's theorem which, in my view, is more reasonable, and which will also provide us with an opportunity to examine certain features of the symbolic universe of Western man which may well have led physicists like Sarfatti and Wheeler to adopt conclusions that are not as ontologically grounded in the life of nature as their arguments would suggest.

One of the basic notions in the Copenhagen interpretation that has either, by degrees, been studiously ignored or driven to its less than reasonable epistemological extreme by abandoning realism altogether is that the scientific map is not the actual landscape, or that there is no one-to-one correspondence between subjectively based mathematical ideas about nature and nature itself. It was this feature of the Copenhagen interpretation that provided the basis for Henry Margenau's assertion that the geometric forms which the Greeks assumed to be of divine origin and to exist absolutely in space must now be considered as "a construct of the intellect,"[26] and Mandel

Sach's characterization of the space-time coordinate system as "only the elements of a language that is used by an observer to describe his environment."[27] It might be tempting to infer from this that the idea that originated in the wild imaginings of what must surely be the most influential mystic in Western intellectual history—an idea that determined perhaps more than any other single metaphysical assumption the basic form of the philosophical and scientific paradigms that have governed our investigations of ourselves ever since —is at long last dead. If mathematical language is a system of subjectively based constructs, then truth in mathematical form does not reside, as Pythagoras thought it did, in some supersensible realm of being known to us through reason and contemplation. But as the response to Bell's theorem, which is, after all, a purely mathematical construct, attests, the distinction between map and landscape which is rather easily accepted and endorsed by many contemporary psychologists, linguists, anthropologists, and sociologists, is not recognized, even implicitly, in the work of many contemporary physicists.

Evelyn Fox Keller in an article in the *American Journal of Physics* draws on Piaget's studies of the cognitive development of children to assess the difficulties that many contemporary physicists have in assimilating the new epistemology implicit in quantum physics. According to Piaget an action schema that "cannot be integrated into the system of conscious concepts is eliminated . . . [and] repressed from conscious territory before it has penetrated there in any conceptualized form." Physicists as a group would on some preconscious or unconscious level seek to eliminate or repress awareness of the new epistemology in quantum theory, speculates Keller, because of their exposure to classical physics. "The loneliness which others might find in a world in which subject and object are split apart is," she says, "compensated, for the scientist, by his special access to the transcendent link between the two."[28] Although she does not put it in this manner, it is the implicit belief in the Pythagorean mathematical ideal that provides the physicist with the sense that there is an ontological bridge between the observing intellect and the world observed. The problem in quantum physics, however, is that point-to-point correspondence between mathematical integer and natural event simply does not exist.

The wave function, notes Keller, "does not in general prescribe a definite value for the position, momentum, or, for that matter, any observable of the system, but only a 'probability amplitude.' "[29] The psychological need of some quantum physicists to preserve two basic features of the classical paradigm, objectifiability and knowability of nature, manifests itself, as Keller sees it, in both the statistical interpretation of the collapse of the wave function and in the tendency to attribute to the function an objective, material reality. In the first case the objectifiability of the system is maintained while knowability is sacrificed when the collapse of the wave function is viewed as being no different from the collapse of any probability distribution. In other words, the particle is allowed to retain its reality as discrete, definable substance at the price of abandoning the possibility of mapping that reality directly onto the theoretical constructs. In choosing to attribute reality to the wave function, which leads to the speculations of Sarfatti and Wheeler, the classical independence of subject and object is given up as both are subsumed in the activity of one system, but the attachment to a one-to-one correspondence between theory and reality, or map and landscape, is not.

Keller concludes with the suggestion that the epistemological dilemmas raised by the quantum physicists represent "a continuing belief in omniscience, now translated out of the domain of magic into the domain of science. Based on a vision of transcendent union with nature, it satisfies a primitive need for connection denied in another realm. As such, it mitigates against the acceptance of a more realistic, more mature, and more humble relation to the world in which boundaries between subject and object are acknowledged to be quite rigid, and in which knowledge, of any sort, is never quite total."[30] The many-worlds theory, the anthropic principle and superdeterminism will, I suspect, be viewed in time as curious, and perhaps even comical, attempts to sustain the belief that the mathematical forms contained in the mind have real or actual existence in the realm of transcendence. The great god Pythagoras is not yet dead, and the hubris associated with the Western analytical, logocentric symbolic universe is still very much with us, but one can at least hope that some humbler relation to the world of our being will emerge in the next phase of the scientific revolution.

Bohr's notion of complementarity, which he clearly saw as having applications in various domains of human knowledge outside the narrowly scientific, will, I suspect, prove a useful tool in moving toward that humbler relation. The wave-particle dualism in the behavior of subatomic particles and their associated mathematical formalisms which, taken together, compose quantum theory, will probably serve to reveal more to us in the future about the structuring principles in our world-constructing minds than it has served in the past to coordinate a greater range of our experience in nature. There is, as I see it, the prospect that the law of the excluded middle, which is very much in force in the recent epistemological debates among quantum physicists, will eventually be understood to be incommensurate with the life of nature. Since that principle is a basic feature of all controlling symbolics, and since the defense of the absolute ontological authority of such symbolics in the sphere of political reality threatens to destroy us daily, some fundamental reorganization of the manner in which we use our minds could well be our only hope of survival. If either-or categorical thinking could be perceived as an arbitrarily developed, culturally derived mechanism in the construction of our symbolic universe which is not ontologically grounded in the life of nature, then perhaps we can once again seriously consider, and plan for, the future we hope our children and grandchildren will enjoy.

It is often said by individuals who are intimately acquainted with members of the community of practicing physicists that metaphysical concerns, like those we have raised here, are generally viewed as philosophical issues which these physicists have enormous difficulty taking seriously. As we have seen in our brief examination of the work of truly creative members of this community, however, metaphysical concerns have played an enormously important role in the evolution of the new physics, and, as we saw in the first chapter, metaphysical implications of concepts from physics definitely have an impact upon the subjective experience of members of this culture. In my view it might well be fortunate that the vast majority of practicing physicists do not speculate about the potential impact of the new scientific paradigm upon the construction of our symbolic universe in that the rigorous training necessary to become a physicist often precludes development of the tools of analysis and the broad-based acquaintance with other aspects of culture that are necessary to engage in such speculation. This vitally important business will, I suspect, be left to physicists whose liberal education has also made them humanists, and humanists who are willing to confront and assimilate scientific knowledge. And most important, as I indicated earlier, it will be left to artists versed in the scientific who will employ their own mythopoeic imaginations in fashioning the intellectual and emotional landscape that could emerge as the metaphysic implied in the new physics is assimilated into the subjective experience of Western man.

Some of the novelists studied here who are engaged in this formidable enterprise, like Vonnegut, Pynchon, and DeLillo, have educational backgrounds which exposed them to the language of mathematics, and would probably have little difficulty discussing with the best of the theoretical physicists the intricacies of the new science in purely scientific terms. Although Updike, in a largely ignored collection of poems entitled *Midpoint*, displays an impressive acquaintance with the mathematical formalism of modern physics—equations are actually introduced into the text—his knowledge of the formal aspects of physics may not be as thorough as that of the novelists included in the first group. Fowles, Robbins, and Barth appear to have derived their sense of the metaphysical implications of concepts from the new physics, much in the way that we have here, by extrapolating from the speculations of the physicists themselves. Barth is, however, to be distinguished from the other two novelists in that he also appears to have studied some of the more recent literature on the history of classical physics. What is perhaps most remarkable in this regard is that the presence or absence of extensive training in the field of modern physics makes little difference in terms of these novelists' understanding of the metaphysical implications. Each author adopts a slightly different perspective in speculating upon the shape and contours of the alternate intellectual and emotional landscape, but their sense of what is vitally new and important in our most advanced scientific knowledge is remarkably similar.

3 · john fowles

John Fowles has long enjoyed an enormous following among American students of the novel. There is the comfortable sense in reading his fiction that a connection with the great English novelists of the recent past, like Conrad and Hardy, still exists, and yet we are tantalized by his obvious fascination with contemporary intellectual dilemmas. He is perhaps not as single-minded in his epistemological quests as Barth or Pynchon, but his focus, like theirs, is more upon the force of idea in culture than it is upon the vagaries of human needs and motivations. Since Fowles has been quite open about his indebtedness to the French existentialists, his critics have tended to assume, as William Palmer does, that the "framework" of his "thought in *The Aristos* and the novels is . . . existentialist."[1] Although there is no question that this philosopher-novelist, who did graduate work at Oxford in French literature and remains closely identified with French culture, has been greatly influenced by figures like Sartre and Camus, it is also true that another, quite different set of ideas can be seen at work here. Fowles, in *The Aristos*, and in his most popular work of fiction, *The Magus*, incorporates concepts from the new physics into the general framework of existentialist thought, and manages in the process to escape the more oppressive aspects of that philosophical position.

The form of *The Aristos*, borrowed significantly from Heraclitus, is a series of "pensée" paragraphs on some very broad subjects. In a section entitled "Finity and Infinity," Fowles describes the cosmos as "an infinite proliferation of fire, atoms, mutations, all happening in the space-time continuum."[2] He invites us to look out our windows and realize that everything we see "is frozen fire in transit between fire and fire. Cities, equations, lovers, landscapes: All are hurtling toward the hydrogen crucible" (21). Fully aware of the extent to which the indeterminacy principle lays to waste basic features of traditional Western cosmology, Fowles dares to envision our *place*—if we can call it that—in the scheme of things foisted upon us by the new science:

I live in hazard and infinity. The cosmos stretches around me, meadow on meadow of galaxies, reach on reach of dark space, steppes of stars, oceanic darkness and light. There is no amenable god in it, no particular concern or particular mercy. Yet everywhere I see a living balance, a rippling tension, an enormous yet mysterious simplicity, an endless breathing of light. And I comprehend that being is understanding that I exist in hazard but that the whole is not in hazard. Seeing and knowing this is being conscious; accepting it is being human. (28)

Fowles also understands that nature on its most basic level of functioning is such that all our conceptions of it necessarily remove us from an understanding of the actual situation. Since knowledge requires the use of abstractions that can have only approximate validity in limited contexts and situations, then knowing in any full or absolute sense is an impossibility. "We shall never know," says Fowles, "finally why we are; why anything is, or needs to be. All our science, all our art, the whole vast edifice of matter, has its foundations in this meaninglessness, and the only assumptions that we can make about it are that it is both necessary and sympathetic to the continued existence of matter" (26).

Perhaps the most fascinating of all of Fowles's speculations on the impact of the new physics upon metaphysics concerns the meaning and function of death. Drawing upon Einstein's conception of the integral relationship between matter and energy as well as his principle of the conservation of energy, Fowles suggests that the view of death sanctioned by traditional Western metaphysics is in need of revision:

By death we think characteristically of the disappearance of individuals; it does not console us to know that matter is not disappearing, but is simply being metamorphosed. We mourn the individualizing forms, not the generalized content. But everything we see is a metaphor of death. Every limit, every dimension, every end of the road, is death. Even seeing is a death, for there is a point beyond which we cannot see, and our seeing dies; whereupon our capacity ends, we die. (34)

Death from this point of view is the inevitable limitation of our consciousness of being or our activity as event in natural process. Our characteristic view of death as loss of being, as a complete *is not* where being used to be, is inconsistent, Fowles suggests, with our present understanding of the life process which predicates that no energy, or life, is ever lost through change.

Fowles is terribly aware that a culture's assimilation of a set of ideas which rattles the foundations of the symbolic universe that has governed that culture's perceptions of self and world for two millennia is no easy task. Realizing, however, that we cannot ignore the implications of empirically based scientific insight for any extended period of time any more than we could successfully defuse the Darwinian bombshell in the nineteenth century, he seeks to facilitate our intellectual acceptance of those insights while remaining cognizant of the inevitable emotional trauma of the initial phases of assimilation. "We all live," he says, "in two worlds: the old comfortable man-centered world of absolutes and harsh world of relatives. The latter, the relativity reality, terrifies us; and isolates and dwarfs us all" (39).

The existential philosophers are useful to Fowles in this endeavor; they have sought to resolve many of the difficulties involved in making choices in the face of the proposition that abstractions do not have real existence outside of the intellect of the individual, and, therefore, that reality, as the new physics also proclaims, is subjective. The point at which Fowles radically diverges from the existential position is simply the point at which existential reality no longer seems commensurate with reality as it is perceived in the new physics.

Fowles appears, for example, to be in complete agreement with Sartre's notion that subjectivism means "that an individual chooses and makes himself; and . . . that it is impossible to transcend human subjectivity."[3] The *nemo*, Fowles's term for the emotional or psychological condition occasioned by our present view of natural process, could well have been influenced by Heidegger's concept of *angst*. It is defined in *The Aristos* as "a man's sense of his own futility and ephemerality; of his relativity, his comparativeness; of his virtual nothingness" (49). Similarly Heidegger's "inauthentic Dasein," which connotes "fallenness into the 'they,' " and Sartre's *mauvais fois*, the state in which we mistake the part for the whole or the abstract for the concrete, can both be seen at work in Fowles's definition of the "Aristos" or the enlightened twentieth-century thinker. The Aristos, claims Fowles, is "sometimes of the Many. But he will avoid membership. There can be no organization to which he fully belongs, no country, no class, no church, no political party ... above all he tries to be a free force in a world of tied forces" (212).

Since Fowles, like the atheistic existentialists, views the Judeo-Christian God as another of those abstractions which have no real existence outside our intellects, we might expect him to conclude, as they did, that the individual is locked into his subjective reality without any sense of ontological relation to external reality. This would surely have been the case had he not been familiar with the new physics. Quantum and relativity theories not only suggest that there is a unity and internal integration between all events but also that all phenomena in the cosmos are manifestations of a basic oneness. This empirically verifiable sense of relation becomes for Fowles the foundation of religious belief. We detect in his writings none of that despair so evident in the work of the atheistic existentialists because Fowles, as he frankly admits, is not an atheist.[4] His God, like Whitehead's, is the on-going creative process of life, the never-finished becoming of all being. Since man, as the new physics clearly implies, participates in and in some sense "is" that process, we are, in Fowles's view, anything but alone. This sense of deity, unlike that of the Judeo-Christian tradition, cannot be apprehended in rational or intellectual terms because indeterminacy, or, if you will, creativity, is a condition of its being. "Mystery, or unknowing, is energy. . . . God is the energy of all questions and questing; and so the ultimate source of all action and volition" (28). The Aristos, always conscious of this view of the nature of ultimate being, recognizes that the vast majority of others construct reality in terms of the old, outmoded symbolic, and, consequently, continue to believe in the real existence of absolutes. He "knows the Many are like an audience under the spell of a conjuror, seemingly unable to do anything but serve as material for the conjuror's tricks; and he knows that the true destiny of man is to be a magician himself" (213).

In *The Magus* Fowles gives these disturbingly new ideas thematic expression within the framework of a narrative that would seem easy and familiar to any avid reader of late Victorian novels. Nicholas Urfe, the first-person narrator, describes in a straightforward, albeit highly intellectual fashion, his background and experience before entering a psychodrama (godgame) which serves to externalize internal conflicts. The intent of the godgame, to use Fowles's terms, is to assist Nicholas in the process of curing himself of the condition of "nemo" and preparing to live as a member of the "elect" or the Aristoi. In doing so he learns to assimilate and understand the role of magus or magician.

Nicholas tells us that he became at least superficially acquainted with existential philosophy at Oxford,[5] feels "rejected" by his own age after his arrival on Phaxos, and has, therefore, only the "ability to express his disengagement between his existence and nothingness" (54). Sensing in Sartrean terms that the *pour-soi* cannot become the *en-soi*, or that the *for-itself* (consciousness) cannot fill up and contain the *in-itself* (the realm of raw materiality that perception cannot change), he concludes that he "belonged to nothingness, to the néant" (60).[6] His first and futile attempt to fill the void of nothingness is to become a poet, a role that, as he conceives it, will allow his consciousness to become identical with the world of full being. During this period he is clearly in *mauvais fois* because he is fostering the illusion that the *pour-soi* can become *en-soi* without losing its identity as *pour-soi*—an impossibility as Sartre sees it. Upon discovering that he is not a poet, that he cannot subsume that "other than" with consciousness, he then attempts to make an "authentic choice" (Camus) by confronting death. In confronting the possibility of suicide, however, he finally discovers that he is in bad faith by recognizing as he looks down the barrel of a shotgun that he is "putting on an act for the benefit of someone, that this action could be done only if it was spontaneous, pure, isolated—and moral" (68). It is at this point in the narrative that he begins the godgame.

Conchis, whose name Fowles makes clear on two occasions is pronounced *conscious* (72, 80), will attempt to make Nicholas emotionally and intellectually aware of two important aspects of existentialism—the essential opposition between the *I* and the *they* and the nature of human freedom and responsibility. Most important, however, he will make this representative Western intellectual conscious on the intuitive level of process reality as it is defined in the new physics. The result is that Nicholas is able to assume the position of the existentialists in most important respects without giving way to the solipsism and profound alienation that is usually a consequence of living existential reality.

Take, for example, Conchis's fictive account of his experience in World War I which leads up to the exercise with the die and poison capsules. Conchis intends on the one hand to make Nicholas aware of the absurdity of sacrificing life and freedom in the service of non-existent grand abstractions, but he is also giving him a lesson in the implications of the indeterminacy principle. The combatants in World War I believed, says Conchis, "that we were fulfilling some end, serving some plan—that all would come out well in the end, because there was some great plan over all. Instead of the reality. There is no plan. All is hazard" (129). Similarly, the several acts in the god-game which serve to illustrate the limits of rationality are consistent with the existentialist understanding of the role of reason in a cosmos that is not governed by rational forces. But Conchis also makes it clear that the fact that mystery is a fundamental characteristic of all life processes does not preclude a sense of identification with the whole. Nicholas is not encouraged to label all experience as fundamentally absurd because it evades rational definition, but rather to see that reason, like the new physicist's view of space-time coordinates, is simply a metaphor used in describing a process that precludes definition in static terms.

Conchis assumes that Nicholas, like most of us, operates upon the erroneous assumption that the scientific method reveals the truths of nature in some absolute sense. To convince him otherwise Conchis begins by orchestrating a series of events, like the Robert Foulkes incident, designed, as Nicholas puts it, "to deceive all the senses" (144). Conchis does not wish Nicholas to accept these staged apparitions from other worlds as objectively real, but rather to appreciate the extent to which our perceptions based upon received sensory data are transformed in our subjective constructions of the real by our "conceptions." As Conchis explains: "Verification is the only scientific criterion of reality. That does not mean that there may be realities that are unverifiable" (235).

In the chapter from the fictional autobiography in which Conchis describes the encounter between himself as a young, medically trained idealist familiar with psychoanalytic techniques and the deranged Norwegian Henrik, Nicholas learns more about the nature of unverifiable realities. Conchis notes that he gave up the effort to treat this individual after witnessing one of Henrik's mystical experiences. Posturing as scientific man Conchis claims to have come to the startling realization that Henrik "was not waiting to meet God. He was meeting God; and had been meeting him probably for many years. He was not waiting for some certainty. He lived in it" (308). It was then, says Conchis, that he perceived "in a flash, as of lightning" that "all our classifications and derivations, our aetiologies, suddenly appeared to me like a thin net. That great passive monster, reality, was no longer dead, easy to handle. It was full of a mysterious vigor, new forms, new possibilities" (309).

The suggestion that all human perceptions are equally valid because the real as we now know it is inevitably subjective is reinforced later in the narrative when Nicholas discovers in the *earth*, the underground hideaway for the various players in the godgame, the parable of "The Prince and the Magician." In the parable a young prince who did not believe in princesses, islands, or God, journeys from his father's kingdom and encounters a "man in full evening dress" who shows him both islands and princesses and claims to be God. After the prince is told by his father that the man was a magician, he accuses the man in evening dress of deception during a second meeting. The magician then explains that it is the prince who is deceived because in "your father's kingdom there are many islands and many princesses. But you are under your father's spell, so you cannot see them." After the father confesses that he himself is "only a magician," the prince expresses his desire to "know the real truth, the truth beyond magic." When his father responds that there "is no truth beyond magic," the prince becomes so sad that he resolves to kill himself. The father then causes death to appear and beckon to the prince at which point the young man "remembered the beautiful but unreal islands and the unreal but beautiful princesses" and decides to live after all. His father then concludes by saying that "you too now begin to be a magician" (550–52).

The acceptance of the proposition that the real in human terms can be nothing more than our subjectively based conception of it is, as Fowles makes clear in *The Aristos*, essential if one wishes to become a magus. Our inability to subsume external reality with our private conception of its nature is not, in contrast with the response of the French existentialists, a cause for despair. Since the business of constructing alternate conceptions of the real is, as Conchis sees it, an expression of that creative energy which is the life of the cosmos, any act of the imagination which "breaks the net of science" is anything but an alienating experience—it is communion with the ontological ground of all being. This new metaphysic is best described in the novel by Nicholas in his effort to verbalize his feelings during the drug-induced mystical experience.

In the initial stages of that experience discrete objects, like the stars, begin to dissolve as Nicholas becomes aware that a wind, which later becomes light, is blowing upon him from all directions at one time. Shortly thereafter he ceases to constitute even the wind and light as entities. He feels himself "transforming, as a fountain in a wind is transformed in shape; an eddy in the water," and entering a "state without dimensions or sensations; awareness of pure being" (238). Sensing that he is one with the whole he notes that he "was having feelings that no language based on concrete physical objects, on actual feeling, can describe. . . . I knew words were like chains, they held me back; and like walls with holes in them" (239). The aspect of language—that symbol system through which we constitute knowledge of the world—which makes it an inappropriate vehicle for conveying this sense of communion with the whole is its representation of the world to consciousness in terms of discrete, mutually exclusive categories. Nicholas concludes, therefore, not only that language is ill-equipped to define a universe in which every entity exists in relation to and in some sense is every other entity, but also that all our speculations upon the character of fundamental reality in language can only "taint the description" of its actual nature.

In this state there was, says Nicholas, "no sense of divinity, of communion, of the brotherhood of man, of anything I had expected before I became suggestible. No pantheism, no humanism. But something wider, cooler and more abstruse. That reality was endless interaction." Or, as he puts it more succinctly: "There was no meaning: Only being" (239). That our knowledge of the real, or our constructions of reality, do not correspond to reality itself is not problematic here because consciousness from this point of view is not an isolated event in nature. It is an integral part of the life process. In the last phase of the mystical experience Nicholas, consequently, feels himself related to "millions, trillions of such consciousness of being, countless nuclei of hope suspended in a vast solution of hazard, a pouring out not of photons but nöons, consciousness-of-being particles" (239).

The fact that hazard is endemic to the life process does mean that experience will never entirely conform to any design we attempt to impose upon it, but more important in Fowles's estimation, the indeterminacy principle invalidates the notion that all events in nature are predetermined by abstract and immutable laws. Freedom of choice is, therefore, not only a possibility but also a given in nature. As Mrs. de Seitas puts it quite explicitly in conversation with Nicholas: "The basic principle of life is hazard. Maurice tells me that this is no longer even a matter of debate. If one goes deep enough in atomic physics one ends with a situation of pure change" (628). Nicholas, initially at least, is unwittingly an absolutist and determinist. He is in many respects a smug Western intellectual complacent in the belief that his own set of laws and standards for human behavior is the only possible set, and, as he sees it, choice is a rationally motivated action which produces results commensurate with external expectations and rewards. To break Nicholas out of this delimiting perspective Conchis will force him in the godgame to make choices existentially, that is, without appeal to global abstractions or absolute criteria of judgment, but he will also make him understand that choosing in this fashion affirms the presence in himself of that energy which is all being.

Conchis's extended narrative about his role during the German occupation of the island climaxes at the point at which he refuses to execute the two guerrilla fighters with an unloaded rifle. Since Conchis made it clear during his earlier narrative about his experience in World War I that his primary commitment was to preserve human life, Nicholas assumes that the choice given him by the Germans, to kill the two men or sacrifice the lives of himself and the townspeople by refusing to do so, must surely have undermined his system of belief. As Nicholas puts it: "Those years must have strained your philosophy. The smile." To this Conchis replies: "On the contrary. That experience made me fully realize what humor is. It is a manifestation of freedom. It is because there is freedom that there is the smile. Only a totally predetermined universe could be without it" (437).

What Nicholas cannot appreciate at this point, and will not appreciate until he is forced to make similar choices himself, is that Conchis chose a course of action in the face of a circumstance in which all alternatives are absurd, but affirms his ability to make free choices by choosing nevertheless. Freedom, says Conchis, is the "immalleable, the essence, the beyond reason, beyond logic, beyond civilization, beyond history" (434) because it is a fundamental aspect of the life process which manifests itself through us as the alpha and omega of all existence. In making free choices we affirm our participation in that process, our communion with the source of all being.

Nicholas's absolutism figures large in his inability to fully consummate the relationship with Alison. He explains early in the narrative that "I contrived most of my affairs in the vacations, away from Oxford, since the new term meant I could conveniently leave the scene of the crime" (21). This statement implies not only that he objectifies females by making them conform to his own rationally conceived program for sexual gratification, but also that he sees these encounters as a criminal violation of the terms of such relationships. He further objectifies the female by informing his perception of her with two irreconcilable conceptions of her being. She is either pure, innocent, and virtuous (virgin) or sensual, sexually indiscriminate, and untrustworthy (whore). Alison, initially perceived by Nicholas as "waif-like, yet perversely or immorally so" (23), embodies in his mind both of these conceptions. Since either-or categorical thinking is a feature of the Western mind that is not commensurate with the lesson from the new physics that all particulars exist in relation to and in some sense are every other particular, Nicholas is provided with some rather graphic illustrations of the extent to which this habit of mind distorts and disfigures love relationships.

Lily (virgin) and Rose (whore) function initially in the godgame as externalizations of this false dichotomy. Nicholas predictably falls in love with Lily whom he fully expects in the romantic love tradition (idealism) to redeem him from all personal confusion. Playing off various motifs from ancient myths and legends, Conchis then proceeds to confuse and compound the identities of the twins. This phase of the godgame culminates in the scene in which Lily, known at this point as Julie, allows Nicholas to possess her sexually. Just before Conchis and his helpers break into the room to transport Nicholas to the scene of the trial, Lily-Julie announces that "My name isn't Julie, Nicholas. And I'm sorry we can't supply the customary flames" (488). The comment serves to parody Nicholas's unfortunate association of female sexuality with sin and lends emphasis to the larger point, made explicit by Mrs. de Seitas (601), that the Julie Nicholas claims to love is not an individuated human being but rather a reflection of his conception of the female.

In order that Nicholas can begin to perceive Alison as an individuated human being, it is essential that the old Alison, disfigured in Nicholas's consciousness by the either-or, die. The first suggestion that her suicide was not actual but rather another deception in the godgame occurs during Nicholas's visit to the cemetery where Maurice Conchis is presumably buried. He discovers at the foot of the slab bearing that name "a small green pot in which sat, rising from a cushion of inconspicuous white flowers, a white arum lily and a red rose" (559). Sensing that a pot containing a lily and a rose might convey some other symbolic meaning, Nicholas picks up one of the "humbler background sprigs" and puts it in his pocket. The plant, he later discovers, is called in English "Sweet Alison" and its original name in Greek means "without madness" (566). This is Conchis's way of saying that Nicholas's conception of the female clouded his perception of Alison. She is not Lily and Rose or virgin and whore, but a unique human being who, like all processes in nature, defies final classification and description.

The trial, which is advertised to Nicholas as the climactic event in the godgame in which he is to be ceremoniously accepted into the community of the elect, is simply another effort by Conchis to convince this representative Western intellectual that abstract forms of valuation are only metaphors for a process that cannot ultimately be known or defined. The costumed figures who initially appear in the underground cistern decorated with religious or occult symbols were all perceived historically as representatives of supernatural forces which direct and control the lives of individuals. The group of internationally known psychologists that appears from under these costumes is simply a more recent version of the same. This class of shamans, gurus, high priests, and priestesses claims to have arrived "scientifically" at an understanding of the "laws" governing and determining behavior. Nicholas realizes, however, upon hearing the clinical report on his psychoanalytic history and characterological disorders, that they too are merely providing metaphoric descrip-

tions of a process that remains mysterious because all change is indeterminate in character.

Nicholas's decision to visit John Leverier during his return trip
to London to compare their experiences in the godgame and his compulsion to find and somehow punish Lily for deceiving him suggest
that he has not yet fully assimilated Conchis's view of reality. It is
only after he learns to accept and trust two females, the distraught
Glasgow teenager Jojo and the political activist Kemp, without de-
personalizing them in terms of some abstract schema or design for
personal gratification, that Conchis gives Nicholas the final test.
Nicholas not only refrains from telling the young, naive American selected as the next participant in the godgame about his own experience in that life drama, but experiences envy in contemplating how
rich the young man's experience might be. It is at this point that he is
finally allowed to see Alison once again.

There is nothing in the last interaction between Nicholas and
Alison that suggests that Nicholas views her as a sexual object. His
proposal of marriage is curious in that it is an honest appraisal of the
prospect of living with him in that relationship without any of the
trappings of romantic idealism. At the conclusion of the narrative art
imitates life as Fowles conceives it in that, as Nicholas puts it earlier,
the "maze has no center. An ending is no more than a point in a sequence, a snip of the cutting shears" (645). We leave the couple in the
living present free to decide upon the terms of their relationship because they are one with a process that makes freedom of choice a
possibility. The life of nature, as even Nicholas has now come to see
it, is a lively, mysterious, self-generating process that evinces no intrinsic order, meaning, or design: "All waits, suspended. Suspended
the autumn trees, the autumn sky, anonymous people. A blackbird,
poor fool, sings out of season from the willows by the lake. A flight of
pigeons over the house; fragments of freedom, hazard, an anagram
made flesh. And somewhere the smell of burning leaves" (656).

4 · johN bARtH

Unlike Fowles in *The Aristos*, John Barth has yet to openly declare his indebtedness to ideas from physics, but there is no question that much of his struggle with epistemological questions can be traced to that influence. Although legitimate parallels can be drawn between Barth's philosophical concerns and methods and those of the existentialists, it is an understanding of the character of life consistent with that of the new physics that causes him, as it does Fowles, to part company with existentialism. The first phase of that struggle (*The Floating Opera*, *The End of the Road*, and *The Sot-Weed Factor*) consists primarily of an effort to come to terms with the special character of individuation and valuation in the relative universe of Einstein. In the more experimental fiction (*Lost in the Funhouse* and *Chimera*), Barth plays off the assumption in the new physics that all human constructs are subjectively based events by examining the role and function of the human imagination as maker and transformer of the reality of everyday experience. The habit of mind which quantum theorists have shown to be incommensurate with the life of nature on the subatomic level, that is, either-or categorical thinking, is the focus in Barth's most formidable artistic achievement to date—*Giles Goat-Boy*. Resonances and correspondences with ideas from physics are present throughout this fiction, and there are a number of passages, particularly in *The Sot-Weed Factor*, in which Barth demonstrates his acquaintance not only with the metaphysical implications of discoveries made in the new physics, but also with the metaphysical foundations of Newtonian physics.

The principal source of difficulty for Todd Andrews, the narrator of *A Floating Opera*, is that his belief in a Newtonian universe, which presumes the existence of transcendent absolutes and the ability of mind or reason to know its essences, causes him to run amuck in a world in which experience teaches that life is an indeterminate process. Tending, as he puts it, "to attribute to abstract ideas a life-or-death significance,"[1] Todd concludes in 1937, on the day of his attempted suicide, that his former belief in the ability of reason to direct, control, and define the course of individual experience is no longer justified. "I say this," he explains, "because I know for certain that all major mind changes in my life have been the result not of deliberate, creative thinking on my part, but rather of pure accidents—events outside myself impinging forcibly upon my attention—which I afterwards rationalized into new masks" (21). If life is a series of accidents, and does not, therefore, proceed in accordance with some transcendent purpose or design, meaning or value cannot, as Todd reasons in his Inquiry, be inherent in experience: "I. Nothing has intrinsic value./ II. The reasons for which people attribute value to things are always ultimately irrational./ III. There is, therefore, no ultimate 'reason' to value anything" (218). Unable to provide rational justification for his own continued existence, or of anyone else's for that matter, Todd attempts in the version of the novel preferred by Barth not only to kill himself but also 699 others aboard the Floating Opera. Since the Floating Opera, as Todd explains early in the narrative, is intended to function as a symbol for "life as process," the decision on the part of this categorical thinker to destroy the showboat and everyone aboard it during a performance makes good "logical" sense:

It always seemed a fine idea to me to build a showboat with just one big flat open deck on it, and to keep a play going continuously. The boat wouldn't be moored, but would drift up and down the river on the tide, and the audience would sit along both banks. They could catch whatever part of the plot happened to unfold as the boat floated past, and then they'd have to wait until the tide ran back again to catch another snatch of it, if they still happened to be sitting there. To fill in the gaps they'd have to use their imaginations, or ask more attentive neighbors, or hear the word passed along from upriver to downriver. Most times they wouldn't understand what was going on at all, or they'd think they knew, when actually they didn't. Lots of times they'd be able to see the actors and not hear them. I needn't explain that that's how much of life works. (7)

The handbill advertising the performance on the actual Floating Opera, replicated in the text, and the description of the performance itself provide additional insight into the character of life as Barth conceives it. Both suggest that various acts (events) in the play (life) are not causally related nor do they finally cohere in some rational design, and yet it is a delightful experience for those like Captain Osborn, who are capable of playfulness, openness, and spontaneity. The point is that life is a happening fundamentally indeterminate in its movement or progress. Any design or meaning we believe to be inherent in life, like the order that Todd perceives in his seemingly disordered hotel room, is ultimately a function of subjectively based constructs. When it happens that the explosion aboard the showboat fails to occur for no apparent reason, Todd is suddenly able to entertain the prospect that "in the real absence of absolutes, values less than absolute mightn't be regarded as in no way inferior and even be lived by" (246–47).

If values, like the laws of the physicist, are subjectively based constructs, they are necessarily relative. The problem of undertaking meaningful action in a world in which values are relative is the subject of Barth's next novel, *The End of the Road*. Jake Horner, sitting perfectly immobilized in Pennsylvania Station because there appears to be no rational, absolute criteria for selecting one alternative for action over another, is rescued by an unlicensed Negro "Doctor," taken to a private clinic, and introduced to a mode of therapy devised by this unorthodox physician. Starting with the assumptions that there are no a priori values and that primary motivations cannot be known, "mythotherapy," as the doctor's technique is called, presumes that it is possible to construct an identity for oneself and others out of a series of abstract conceptions of roles in social contexts. Since there is no necessary, rational criteria for the selection of these "masks," Jake is told to make use of mechanical paradigms like *sinistrality* (choosing the alternative on the left) and *antecedence* (the first in a series) as the basis for choice. If mythotherapy is completely successful the patient will learn to keep the masks logically consistent with one another while simultaneously presuming that he has no identity prior to or separate from them. Although mythotherapy is offensive in that it implies that identity is merely an arbitrary system of negotiable conceptions of self, or that there is no essential or primary self manifested in the social self, these are not the grounds upon which it is found unacceptable. The problem is rather, as Jake sees it, that the therapy is premised upon a belief in the ability of abstract categorical definitions to fully define the self. Jake ceases to concern himself with mythotherapy when he realizes that contradictory attitudes toward others is simply a natural and unavoidable consequence of knowing them well.

Joe Morgan, Jake's colleague at Wicomico State Teacher's College, assumes in contrast with the doctor that an essential self in the form of psychological givens generates both values and reasons which become the ground for all action taken in the world. Although the psychological givens cannot be traced to a source and have no inherent value, the fact that they can be known allows the individual in Joe's view to integrate in logical terms all aspects of identity. It is then possible, as Joe sees it, to continuously operate upon conscious, rational motivations; he views failure to do so as a sign of intellectual and emotional weakness. Joe shares with the doctor, however, the assumption that abstract, categorical definitions are capable of defining the essence of what is human. Jake simply and directly refutes both positions when he says: "Existence not only precedes essence; in the case of human beings it rather defies essence."[2]

Unable in the absence of any absolute criteria for judgment to meet Joe's demand that he supply a rational explanation for the sexual involvement with Rennie, Jake realizes, nevertheless, that he does operate upon an absolute or at least upon a principle that serves much the same function: "To turn experience into speech—that is, to classify, to categorize, to conceptualize, to grammarize, to syntactify it—is always a betrayal of experience, a falsification of it; but only so betrayed can it be dealt with at all, and only in so dealing with it did I ever feel like a man, alive and kicking" (119). Although all attempts to impose abstract designs or formulae upon the dynamic flow of life will necessarily result, as the physicists asserted earlier, in distortion and disfiguration, it is this activity which is the basis for our shared conception of the real, and, therefore, all that which is distinctly human. It is Joe's inability to appreciate the approximate nature of the many language systems we use to objectify experience and hence the essential ambiguity of all human behavior that eventually force Rennie into a situation in which she feels compelled to undertake the course of action that eventually kills her.

The confrontation between traditional Western metaphysics, with its ontological dualism, and an alternate metaphysic premised upon the conception of life fostered by the new physics is the central, most pervasive concern in Barth's next novel, *The Sot-Weed Factor*. The decision by Ebenezer Cooke to become a "virgin poet," an identity that he presumes will keep him safe from "Life, from Time, from Death and History,"[3] is obviously a consequence of his belief in a realm of abstract forms and values higher than and distinct from the world of actual experience. Since "Justice, Truth and Beauty," according to Ebenezer, "live not in the world, but as transcendent entities, noumenal and pure" (419), he attempts to make actual people and events conform to his conception of reified essences. Joan Toast, the street-wise prostitute Eben falls in love with in London, is, for example, perceived by him as the very embodiment of innocence, purity, and virtue. Similarly, after encountering a colonial court in Maryland which passes a judgment that blatantly violates all reasonable codes of law, he attempts to restore that corrupt body to a commitment to absolute justice, and unwittingly signs over the title of his father's estate to one William Smith in the process. Upon learning that Smith intends to establish opium dens, whorehouses, and other disreputable businesses on the property, Eben begins to suspect that nature is a good deal more fallen than he originally anticipated.

The spokesman for the alternate metaphysic consistent with discoveries made in the new physics in the narrative is Eben's onetime tutor Henry Burlingame, III. Metamorphosing from one identity into another throughout the novel with no regard whatsoever for the logical coherence of his various selves, Burlingame is himself a metaphor for life as energy perpetually evolving out of itself that which has never been before. As he explains to Eben: "The World's indeed a flux, as Heraclitus declared: the very universe is naught but change and motion" (138). When Eben, committed to the static conception of identity associated with traditional Western metaphysics, expresses concern that Burlingame appears to have no discrete and definable essence, Henry replies: "Your true and constant Burlingame lives only in your fancy, as doth the pointed order of the world" (357). Similarly all assertions made about the nature of self—which are categorical, as our language systems demand—are, says Henry, "acts of faith, impossible to verify" (141). Although we must live with the stark realization that we are "chance's fool, the toy of aimless Nature" (372), it is, Henry suggests, the indeterminacy of nature's processes that allows man the freedom to "make and seize his soul," to declare or assert, "Tis I, and the world stands such-a-way!" (373).

What makes all this particularly interesting from our point of view is that Henry is thoroughly acquainted with classical physics, understands its metaphysical underpinnings, and openly denies its validity. While fending off the passionate advances of his patron Henry More at Cambridge, Henry notes that in attempting to "learn the nature of the universe from Newton" (25) he fell victim to the lust of that great thinker as well. After the conflict between More and Newton over Henry occasioned the discovery that their views on Descartes were not as dissimilar as they once imagined, the two men "fell to tearful embraces," arranged for Henry's dismissal from Cambridge, and decided to "move into the same lodgings, where, so they declared, they would couple the splendours of the physical world to the glories of the ideal, and listen ravished to the music of the spheres" (26). In the process of creating this humorously bizarre and wholly improbable circumstance, Barth displays a rather thorough acquaintance not only with the natural philosophy of the period, but also with the manner in which Descartes reinforced the Pythagorean mathematical conception of truth that was the basis for the speculations of both Galileo and Newton. As Henry puts it, "all these Platonic gentlemen of Christ's and Emmanuel Colleges are wont to sing the praises of Descartes, inasmuch as he makes a great show of pottering about in mathematics and the motions of heavenly bodies, like any Galileo, and yet unlike Tom Hobbes he affirms the real existence of God and the soul, which pleases them to no end" (24). It is not simply that Henry finds the metaphysical dualism which assumes that transcendent and eternal truth is represented in number absurd, all of his mocking refutations of that model are consistent with the metaphysics implied in the new physics.

In explaining to Eben, for example, why he is so fascinated with the notion of twins, Henry provides a description of the relationship between all seeming antinomies that should make good sense in the light of our previous discussion of the implications of quantum theory. "The fact is," says Henry, "I love not part of the world, as you might have guessed, but the entire parti-colored whole, with all her poles and contradictories" (529). After giving Eben an exhausting lecture on the role of twins in myth and legend, Henry asserts that all that appears opposite, even forces as formidable as "God and Satan," are "hatched from one egg" (534). Sensing that every particular is a manifestation of one fundamental unity, Henry declares himself "Suitor of Totality, Embracer of Contradictories, Husband to all Creation, the Cosmic Lover" perpetually overcome with a craving for the "tenor of the mortise, the jointure of the polarities, the seamless universe" (536–37).

As a result of Burlingame's influence Eben eventually learns to regard the old absolutes as "vain constructions" or subjectively based ideas, and yet he also asserts that it is these vain constructions that give rise to "all nobleness allowed to fallen man" (680). Barth is, then, suggesting once again that subjectively based and hence relative values can serve a worthwhile function in human experience as the foundation upon which we realize, through interactions with others, our best conception of human nature. The importance of action as a fundamental ingredient of this morality is underscored when Eben notes before marrying Joan Toast that the crime he stands indicted for is "the crime of innocence, whereof the knowledge must bear the burden. There's the true Original Sin our souls are born in; not that Adam learned, but that he had to learn—in short, that he was innocent" (801). Under the guise of innocence Eben sought to disengage himself from all aspects of experience that did not approximate his conception of ideal forms and values. Since the preservation of this innocence precluded full dependence upon and involvement with others, and, consequently, knowledge of the chaos, confusion, and paradox endemic in the life experience, Eben's crime has been his refusal to come to terms with his humanity. Since Joan Toast is viewed by Eben as "sign and symbol" of the world, his acceptance of her in marriage signifies his commitment to life in a process environment.

In *Giles Goat-Boy*, which will be discussed in greater detail later, Barth examines more closely the manner in which reality for human beings is constructed, and concludes that the reality of everyday experience (our shared as opposed to private conceptions of the real) is a collective fiction generated, maintained, and transformed by members of a given culture. The effort to bracket the fundamental assumptions and attitudes at work in that fiction often leads, he suggests, to an examination of those stories, myths, and legends, broadly defined as *literature*, generated by man throughout his experience in culture. In both *Lost in the Funhouse* and *Chimera*, Barth carries the epistemological quest one step further as he conducts an investigation into the machinations of the human faculty responsible for generating the fiction that is reality. A description of the play of the imagination in the act of creating fiction, which is essentially what both narratives provide, is from Barth's perspective nothing less than an investigation into the manner in which man has made himself.

The key to *Lost in the Funhouse* is in the form of a cryptogram which the reader is asked to construct in the first of the fourteen sections of the novel. In the "Author's Note" Barth comments that the "Frame Tale" is "one-, two-, or three dimensional, whichever one regards a Moebius strip as being."[4] The Moebius strip which sits cut and pasted on my desk suggests not only the multidimensional nature of reality, but the symbol for eternity as well. The phrase that continually repeats itself on this particular Moebius strip is "ONCE UPON A TIME THERE WAS A STORY THAT BEGAN" (1). Since it was Einstein's recognition that space and time are one dimension that led to an acceptance of this model as the shape of the universe, Barth is suggesting, like the physicists before him, that in a world of this character man has perpetually been engaged in the business of creating paradigms that condition if not determine his view of reality. The Moebius strip is a frame for the entire narrative in the sense that all the tales in the collection examine various aspects of that process.

To choose a random example, Barth in "Life-Story" focuses on the dilemmas faced by the modern writer, using himself as a case in point. He begins by discussing the development of his own fiction, notes his displeasure at being labeled an avant-garde writer, lists his favorite contemporary novelists, expresses his fear that the novel as well as American society may be dying, analyzes his own psychological make-up, and even takes us into his study to view some interaction between him and his wife (or "imaginary mistresses" [125]) on the eve of his birthday. In order to impress the reader with the fact that this is not "just" a piece of personal history, Barth comments in the "Author's Note" that the "deuteragonist [actor in Greek drama who takes parts of minor importance] of 'Life-Story,' antecedent of the second-person pronoun, is you" (xi). In addition to stepping out from behind the blind which the narrator in a conventional work of fiction provides and exposing himself instead as author or creator of the fiction being read, Barth makes the point that we in the process of reading that fiction also become actively involved in the creation of it because interrelations or correspondences between the particulars in the tale are established in terms of our own context or situation. Like the physicists, Barth is recognizing here that the x factor in all observational processes which cannot be finally ignored is the world-constructing mind of the individual.

In "Anonymiad" Barth, drawing upon one of several versions of the life of Homer, gives us a playful autobiographical account of the experience of a goatherd turned minstrel who wins favor in the court of Clytemnestra and Agamemnon in Mycenae only to fall victim to a scheme perpetrated by his wife which leaves him stranded on a "Zeus forsaken" (162) island in the Mediterranean Sea. Having little taste for the banalities of court, he discovers that "by pretending that things had happened which in fact had not, and that people existed who didn't, I could achieve a lovely truth which reality obscures— especially when I learned to abandon myth and pattern my fabrications on actual people and events; Menelaus, Helen, the Trojan war. It was *as if* there were this minstrel and this milkmaid, et cetera; one could I believe draw a whole philosophy from that *as if*" (186). He creates the world of *as if* on parchment made from the skin of goats found on the island and invents the term *fiction* to describe this new mode of expression. After realizing that the only "valid point of view" from which to work was "first person anonymous," the name of the fiction became "Anonymiad" (192).

The suggestion is that the writer of fiction, whose archetypal representative is Homer, is inclined to be bored in even the most stimulating circumstances, and seeks to remedy that condition by allowing his imagination to restructure perceptions of environment. The result can be the creation of the world of *as if*, the realm of fiction, which functions as the basis for a new philosophy in the sense of providing an alternate conception of the real. If the fiction seems to contain a "lovely truth which reality obscures," or possibilities for thought and action yet to be realized in human experience, then the alternate conception is assimilated into subjective experience and communicated to subsequent generations as part of its inherited culture in literature. Since the fiction will eventually shape conceptions of the real and govern perceptions of environment, the fiction is the reality. In the "Bellerophoniad" section of *Chimera* all this is expressed more boldly and succinctly by Barth's representative modern artist Jerome B. Bray:

Inasmuch as concepts, including the concepts fiction and necessity, are more or less necessary fictions, fiction is more or less necessary. Butterflies exist in our imaginations, along with existence, imagination and the rest. Archimedeses, we lever reality by conceiving ourselves apart from its other things, them from one another, the whole from unreality. Thus Art is as necessary an artifice as Nature; the truth of fiction is that Fact is fantasy; the made up story is the model of the world.[5]

In each of the three novellas contained in *Chimera*, Barth examines the interplay between the vast storehouse of inherited fiction called mythology and the life of the imagination. The novel suggests that these made-up stories which determine taken-for-granted conceptions of the real are incessantly acted upon and transformed by the imagination as man struggles to overcome his sense of exhausted possibilities, represented in the novel as writer's block. In "Dunyazadiad" an archetypal storyteller (Scheherazade) is visited by a twentieth-century storyteller (Genie) who becomes the source of the stories which quite literally sustain her life. The fact that the stories provided by Genie are taken from the *Arabian Nights* makes the point that literary fictions sustain the myths that continue to function as the basis upon which our conception of the real evolves and transforms. In "Perseid" a mythological hero learns about life from art. Calyxa's murals not only reveal to the failed hero that events in his own past, like killing the Gorgon for King Polydectes, were originally misconceived by him, but they also entice him into an act of creation culminating in a major internal transformation. In the seventh panel of Mural ii, the panel which Calyxa could not complete for him, Perseus portrays himself looking into the eyes of the Medusa he once sought to destroy and perceiving a renewed and more acceptable self. As the story closes Perseus is able to "imagine boundless beauty from my experience of boundless love" (142) which has in the telling become the tale immortalized and "nightly rehearsed as long as men and women read the stars" (142). "Bellerophoniad," which is far too complex to deal with in this summary fashion, is essentially a portrayal of the modern imagination struggling with the innumerable possibilities for choice within the context of 3,000 years of inherited culture. Polyeidus, a metaphor for the act of the imagination, changes shape incessantly. Since "Polyeidus is the story" (246), "Bellerophoniad" is an artifact produced by the imagination portraying the imagination in the process of producing. Once again Barth's intention is to better understand the process through which man has created himself.

In *Giles Goat-Boy* Barth implicitly assumes, along with the quantum theorist, that the either-or as logical paradigm is a dynamic of our mental life that is not ontologically grounded in the life of nature, and proceeds to advertise some very great dangers in our continued and unquestioning reliance upon it. Drawing on the work of modern mythographers and comparative religionists like Otto Rank, James George Frazer, Freud, Jung, Joseph Campbell, and Lord Raglan, Barth creates a mythic hero with all the essential characteristics of the heroic type revealed in myth and literature who undertakes a pilgrimage that closely resembles the pilgrimages of great mythic heroes in the past. The world (University) that the mythic hero will attempt to save is divided into two hostile campuses, East and West, which are completely under the control of their respective computer systems—EASCAC and WESCAC. Both computer systems have been outfitted with a military device called EAT, which sends out brainwaves of the same amplitude and intensity as human brainwaves that will either kill individuals caught within the field of transmission or do irrevocable damage to their brain cells. Barth is obviously using the computers to create an allegorical representation of contemporary society, but what is not so obvious is that they also function as an analogue for the human brain. The clever use that Barth makes of the computers as symbol allows him to examine the major forms of valuation that exist in the Western mind while simultaneously conducting an investigation of the logical processes which inform all of those constructions.

WESCAC as it was originally designed operated on a "yes or no" circuitry and remained at this stage of its development, as IBM spokesmen are now fond of telling the public, a tool of man simply because it could not approximate in its workings those mental processes we include under the broad headings of intuition, imagination, impulse, and desire. After the NOCTIS (Non-conceptual Thinking and Intuitional Synthesis) project is completed, the computer not only begins to think like a human being, but also develops, like HAL in the movie version of *2001*, a sense of identity, and, consequently, a will of its own. Programmed in the Cum Laude Project to do genetic and psychological analyses of all students in West Campus in an effort to determine which young men and women could "breed to some approximation of the ideal, and in how many generations,"[6] WESCAC, apparently overcome with that irrational human desire called *lust*, acts in defiance of its human programmers in an attempt to satisfy its sexual need. Virginia Hector, the daughter of the chancellor of the university, is enticed down into the control room and impregnated with sperm manufactured by WESCAC which presumably carries all the genetic characteristics of the ideal West Campus graduate—thus the GILES (Grand-tutorial Ideal Laboratory Specimen) is conceived.

The goat-boy assumes that it is his mission to deprive WESCAC of its power to EAT by changing the AIM (Automatic Implementation Mechanism) of the computer. He discovers early in his journey that both WESCAC and EASCAC draw the enormous voltage necessary for their operation from a power plant completely under the control of an individual named Maurice Stoker. When he asks Stoker why it is he cannot "singlehandedly remove the danger of a third campus riot" (world war) by either turning off the power or threatening to, Stoker tells him that "You don't understand what power is! The furnace doesn't turn off the thermostat! The heart might *kill* the brain, but it can't *decide* to; only the brain can decide" (218).

In order to help the goat-boy better understand the nature and function of the plant, Stoker takes him by elevator an incredible distance downward to the very source of its power—the Furnace Room. As steam valves blow without warning, winches jam, cables break, and pipes burst, male and female workers rush frantically about the Furnace Room giving vent to their every primal impulse and irrational desire in a futile and obviously half-hearted attempt to establish order. In the midst of fights and sexual assaults, which are obviously a source of delight in spite of the fact that they result in numerous injuries, Stoker grins broadly and proclaims: "Here's where your *power* is" (220).

What Barth is doing here, with a playful realism that Freud himself might well have admired, is constructing an analogue of the human brain. As Stoker intimates, EASCAC and WESCAC represent the two cerebral hemispheres where analytical or rational thought processes take place; the power plant represents the more vestigial portion of the brain, known as the brainstem and mid-brain. These portions of the brain not only function in physiological terms as a kind of psychic energizer, but they are also the areas from which the irrational drives and instincts of man presumably emanate. On another level EASCAC and WESCAC, which have in their storage banks all the knowledge accumulated in their respective hemispheres of the globe as well as complete control over the course of events in those hemispheres, represent the mind sets or world views of East and West which tend to overlap in terms of basic functions and capabilities, but which remain, nevertheless, disparate and distinct. As the goat-boy will later discover, his real mission as Grand Tutor is not merely to reprogram the computer in such a way that it can no longer EAT the student body, but rather to change the AIM of WESCAC (Western mind) in a much more pervasive fashion by altering the manner in which it goes about the business of framing out and understanding experience altogether.

Although in carrying out the Cum Laude Project WESCAC did give in to its own lustful desires, it also did what it was programmed to do. WESCAC produces the Grand Tutorial Ideal and provides him with the key to an understanding of the nature of truth which should allow him to fulfill his role as archetypal savior of mankind. When the goat-boy begins his pilgrimage in earnest by matriculating into the University, he receives a circular assignment sheet from WESCAC with the same phrase found on his PAT (Prenatal Aptitude-Tests) card, printed in the following manner on one side of the sheet,

and the list of assignments, which must be completed "At Once, In No Time" (428), on the other. Not realizing that the form of the assignment sheet has any particular significance, the goat-boy assumes at this stage of his development that there is a clear distinction between *Passage* and *Failure* and that it is his role to enlighten all studentdom of the nature of that distinction.

After attempting to complete his seven assignments in this fashion, the goat-boy makes the first of three visits to the belly, hoping that the computer will affirm that he has passed and is, therefore, the Grand Tutor capable of changing WESCAC's AIM. Harold Bray, who also claims to be the Grand Tutor, explains to the goat-boy prior to his first visit to the belly that WESCAC will ask "one preliminary question and three main questions" (560) and that he is to answer each by pressing *either* a "yes" *or* a "no" button. After responding in either-or fashion to the questions posed by WESCAC and emerging un-EATen from the belly, the goat-boy feels that he has completed his assignment and is perplexed that his passage, or his special role as Grand Tutor, is not universally recognized.

During his imprisonment in "Main Detention" (located, appropriately enough, in the Power Plant) he spends four days and nights contemplating why it is that he should have failed considering that he has, in the traditional sense, passed. He eventually concludes that passage and failure, which he had earlier assumed to be irreconcilable opposites, were somehow related: "I had failed everything, everyone, in every sense . . . had flunked myself as I had flunked them; was flunked at the outset for craving to pass . . . 'Passage is Failure!': I saw now what truth was in that remark, and prepared to suffer until the end of terms" (580). Realizing that the either-or concept of truth, which is perhaps the most pronounced feature of the analytical, rational mind set of the Western world, has caused studentdom to be "hobbled by false distinctions, crippled by categories!" (653), he declares that all such distinctions and categories are invalid and must, therefore, be ignored.

Operating on this model he descends a second time into the belly and is unable once again to make appropriate responses to the questions asked by the computer. When "GILES SON OF WESCAC" flashes on the screen, for example, the goat-boy immediately presses the "no" button because GILES and WESCAC were "distinctions as spurious as son and father, but viewed rightly (if after all through the finally false lenses of student reason), the eugenical specimen whereof I was the issue had been drawn as it were from all studentdom, whose scion therefore I was; WESCAC's role had been merely that of an inseminatory instrument, the tool of the student body" (695–96). Although the effort not to rely on preexistent categories during the examination is successful, the assumption that he must make *either* a "yes" *or* a "no" response leads to the creation of new categories and the continued reliance upon the either-or judgments in the act of distinguishing between them. WESCAC, apparently much displeased by the goat-boy's performance, bounces him off the walls of the control room and unceremoniously throws him out the exit port.

Not long after this second failure to pass the finals, it occurs to the goat-boy that the key to the completion of his assignments "At Once, In No Time"was printed on the assignment sheet itself. His final exegesis of that cryptic message is the most concise statement in the novel of the gospel according to the GILES: "The circular device on my Assignment-sheet—beginningless, endless, infinite equivalence—constricted my reason like a torture-tool from the Age of Faith. Passage *was* Failure, and Failure Passage; yet Passage was Passage, Failure, Failure! Equally true, none was the answer; the two were different, neither were they the same; and *true* and *false, same* and *different*— Unspeakable! Unimaginable!" (708–9).

The goat-boy has discovered like the students of quantum theory that the either-or approach to truth, premised upon the implicit assumption that categorical abstractions are real and irreconcilable, is an inadequate tool in dealing with a cosmos in which every particular (mass) is not only a manifestation of one source (energy) but also functions in dynamic relation to every other particular. The alternate mode of truth-seeking revealed in the form of the assignment sheet is also not unlike Niels Bohr's notion of complementarity. Barth, like Bohr, is also suggesting that seemingly opposite constructs be held in mind as complementary views of one reality, and that opposites have meaning in terms of their participation in one another. That which makes the goat-boy's approach to truth more efficacious in the realm of human experience than the either-or approach is that it provides the individual with some basis for undertaking action by allowing him to distinguish between particulars and yet prevents him from positing irreconcilable, categorical distinctions which preclude compromise and ensure conflict. Since all the tasks on his assignment sheet were predicated upon the either-or approach to truth, an approach which the scientifically minded WESCAC knows to be false, the goat-boy completes his real assignment "At Once, In No Time" in the *instant* that he realizes the approach itself is invalid.

When he enters WESCAC's belly for the third and last time having completed his assignment and prepared to pass the finals, he does so coupled sexually with the wife of Maurice Stoker—an incredibly sensuous female who is styled throughout the narrative as *the* archetypal woman. Rather than respond to the questions in either-or fashion as he did on the previous two occasions, he and Anastasia "rose up joined, found the box, and joyously pushed the buttons, both together, holding them as fast as we held each other" (731). Since WESCAC quietly records the yes-no responses and ejects the couple through the exit port with such gentleness that it takes them some time to discover they are no longer in the belly, the suggestion is that the computer has done that which it was previously programmed to do—it has completed the Cum Laude Project by producing the Grand Tutorial Ideal who now done his assignment and passed his finals.

The obvious objection to this conclusion is that the GILES was supposed to be able to change the AIM of the computer and the goat-boy, by his own admission, fails to do so. The fact that WESCAC's AIM remains unchanged makes sense when we remind ourselves that the NOCTIS project was also successful and the computer, therefore, has a will of its own. WESCAC, which has in its storage banks all the scientific, philosophical, and religious learning of the Western world, seems to realize that the change in AIM which should have been a natural consequence of the completion of the Cum Laude Project would not only alter the manner in which the Western mind (WESCAC) functions, but also dramatically affect the content of that mind. Since all of the absolute systems of valuation which Western man has ever devised are dependent upon the use of either-or, categorical judgments, WESCAC's resistance to the elimination of that feature of its inner workings is nothing less than a fight to preserve its own identity. Fearing that the goat-boy might be able to change its AIM if West Campus were to recognize him as the authentic Grand Tutor, WESCAC simply manufactures a false Grand Tutor capable of fulfilling every societal expectation of what a Grand Tutor should be in the Western world.

There are any number of indications that Harold Bray, initially perceived by the goat-boy as a kind of John the Baptist, is not a human being at all, but rather a terribly sophisticated machine produced by WESCAC. He is seen on several occasions giving off machinelike sounds (buzzes and whirs); he has a seemingly endless supply of faces which peel off like rubber masks; and he sends out bolts of electrical energy which can either stun or kill. Bray does not possess a Pat card, which WESCAC is programmed to provide for every student born into the university, and he even admits at one point that he is "not what people think I am" (559). After performing a number of suprahuman tasks (miracles), Bray begins dispensing certifications, documents indicating that the bearer will probably be passed or saved, to every student in the university that wants one. The interesting aspect of these certifications is that they all take the form of either-or, categorical statements. Since Bray is an extension of WESCAC and functions in precisely the same way that WESCAC, or the Western mind, functions, his certifications are immediately accepted as *valid* by the students on West Campus.

After Max Spielman (who is, incidentally, one of the few individuals with the experience and scientific knowhow needed to change the AIM of WESCAC) has been executed, and after the goat-boy has been totally discredited in the eyes of the student body, Bray enters the shaft of electrical energy used to execute Max. As he rises like something "large and obscure . . . rolling and spreading like the smoke itself" (753), WESCAC's mechanical man is performing the last of those symbolic, ritualistic acts which, the computer knows, are expected of Grand Tutors or saviors in the Western world—crucifixion and ascension into heaven.

Although we may find Barth's fondness for obfuscation a little too exaggerated for our tastes, the novel does convey some formidable insights into our contemporary dilemma. We are asked in *Giles Goat-Boy*, to realize that the tendency of Western man to make either-or judgments, or to frame our experience in terms of irreconcilable categorical abstractions, is a principal source of division and conflict in human society. Since this habit of mind is based upon a conception of truth that is not commensurate with the nature of experience in a relative universe, Barth suggests that we abandon it in favor of a new mode of understanding in which we recognize distinctions between particulars while affirming at the same time that those distinctions are not absolute. The intended result is that we should become as much aware of *sameness* as we are of *differences*, which will not only make for a more realistic assessment of a given situation or problem but also greatly facilitate meaningful compromise.

There is, however, one very major obstacle. In order for Western man to cease making either-or judgments he must abandon all abstract systems of valuation which cannot function without making such judgments. Since major systems of valuation like Christianity, Judaism, classicism, Platonism, mysticism, Freudianism, capitalism, communism, and socialism—all of which the goat-boy encounters in one form or another in the course of his pilgrimage—are predicated upon a belief in efficacy of irreconcilable, categorical abstractions, Western man would soon find himself stripped of his previous identity, confronting an alien environment in which traditional definitions of the nature and function of any given particular in relation to other particulars no longer pertain. Gilesianism, although not necessarily unteachable, will win—as the goat-boy discovers—few converts because the Western mind (WESCAC) will doubtlessly resist a change in its manner of functioning (AIM) which necessitates a complete re-evaluation of self and world. And yet Barth suggests the continued survival of mankind may depend upon its ability to do just that.

5 · john updike

In an interview prepared for his collection of nonfiction prose, *Picked-up Pieces*, John Updike says that all his books are "meant to be moral debates with the reader, and if they seem pointless—I'm speaking hopefully—it's because the reader has not been engaged in the debate. The question is usually, 'What is a good man?' or 'What is goodness?' and in all my books an issue is examined."[1] The suggestion that the moral debate seems "pointless" because the reader is not engaged implies that there is a point which Updike in his private ruminations is aware of but has chosen not to make explicit. If it is actually his intention that the moral dilemmas of characters be experienced by the reader as pointless, perhaps the point, like that of the atheistic existentialists before him, is that there is no ontological ground for moral action. It could be that this fiction, like that of Sartre, Camus, and Beckett, is also designed to demonstrate that the blank wall of absurdity is the event horizon of modern man, and that all our efforts to penetrate the nonexistent core of ultimate being will merely frustrate understanding of our actual condition. As even the most casual student of Updike probably knows very well, this is obviously not the case. Even if we could ignore those numerous occasions on which this novelist has publicly identified himself as a believer in God, there is no escaping the conclusion that the problem of belief in supernatural agency as the foundation for moral behavior is the central focus in virtually all his works. Although the god that so many of Updike's central characters struggle to affirm as an active presence in their lives clearly resembles that of the Judeo-Christian tradition, the correspondence is by no means exact. Intense awareness of the condition of sin and strict obeisance to the dictates of moral law are but dimly present in these struggles, and there is much that is attributed to, or associated with, the agency of God, particularly in the area of sexuality, that most "true believers" would find nothing short of blasphemous.

In spite of this divergence from received Western conceptions of morality, we do not detect in this fiction any concerted effort to parody those conceptions or undermine their validity. Updike, as Victor Strandberg notes, confronts the "problem of belief as directly as did Tolstoy and Tennyson a century earlier, but with the added authority of a mind keenly aware of twentieth-century science and theology."[2] The aspect of modern science that most preoccupies this novelist is clearly the new physics. Although, like the other novelists studied here, Updike is aware that the metaphysics implied in the new physics is not consistent with the conception of being that is the basis for ethical thought and behavior in the Judeo-Christian tradition, he does not conclude, as they do, that the received tradition is no longer grounded in an acceptable ontology. The suggestion from the new physics that either-or categorical thinking is not commensurate with the life of nature on its most basic level of functioning does provide some of the justification necessary to escape this conclusion, but what is most interesting about Updike's resolution of the dilemma is the presumption that the dynamic interplay between seemingly irreconcilable particulars in thought, like that between two cosmologies, parallels the relationship between subatomic particles as it is viewed by quantum physicists. The correspondence between activities on the level of subatomic processes and the neurophysiological processes in the brain may not, as yet, have been proven as exact as Updike suggests it is, but that correspondence is, nevertheless, frequently asserted in his fiction. Although the theological arguments that Updike is most in sympathy with were not made directly in response to the threat modern science posed to the old cosmology, his attraction to them is, I think, best explained in terms of the high degree of symmetry between the structure of those arguments and the understanding of the dynamics of human consciousness derived from physics.

Existence for human beings is, says Updike, "to be in a situation of tension, to be in a dialectical situation. A truly adjusted person is not a person at all—just an animal with clothes on."[3] In Updike criticism duality as a metaphysical dimension is usually interpreted as simply a recapitulation of the Platonic conception of being we identified earlier as the single most pervasive assumption in Western philosophical and theological thought. Most critics assume, as Strandberg does, that duality for Updike means essentially the "division of reality into two spheres: earth and heaven, matter and spirit, flesh and soul, with ultimate reality being spiritual."[4] In Updike's fictional universe, however, we do not detect any strict adherence to the notion that being is divided into two discrete dimensions, or any ultimate reliance upon either-or categorical thinking in the effort to discover the relation between them. In fact, much of the confusion that is usual in criticism of this fiction is, I suspect, a consequence of the attempt to impose this model when it does not finally apply.

Although it was Kierkegaard that Updike recognized in his early twenties as a "giant brother . . . beside whom I could walk safely down . . . the street of my life,"[5] it is the neo-orthodox Christian theologian Karl Barth who appears to have offered him the greatest solace in the struggle to sustain belief in supernatural agency. In a review of one of Barth's works entitled "Faith in Search of Understanding," Updike says the following about the impact of modern science upon Western theism:

The cosmological argument, which survived the shift from the Ptolemaic to the Newtonian cosmos, is hopelessly strained between the unimaginable macrocosm of super-stellar astronomy and the inscrutable microcosm of particle physics. And the theological argument (i.e., many things—e.g., the human eye—are intricately designed for purposive ends; ergo, a directing intelligence exists) was administered a mortal blow when Darwin demonstrated how the organic world, for all its seemingly engineered complexity, might be a self-winnowing chaos.[6]

After inferring that Barth's theology is to be taken seriously in spite of the threat posed to the old cosmology by modern science, Updike characterizes this theology as having two faces, the "No and Yes" (273). The *no* is addressed, he explains, to the conception of God as the "great personal or impersonal, mystical, philosophical, or naive Background and Patron Saint of our human righteousness, morality, state, civilization, or religion." And the *yes* is the affirmation of the existence of God as "totalier aliter—Wholly Other" that we cannot reach, and also of the "virtually antinomian doctrine of all-inclusive Grace" (273–74). Updike then offers the following statements by Barth as examples of conceptions of God that are consistent with these initial assumptions: "Metaphysical absolutes are an abomination unto the Lord and abolished in Christ" (275) and "God shatters every syllogism" (281).

If we can suppose that Updike is, in part at least, using this theology to resolve the crisis of belief occasioned by exposure to discoveries made in modern science, we might conclude that it is acceptance of an antinomian doctrine that obviates the conflict between the metaphysics. If it is "faith and faith alone" that provides the salvation ethos, and nothing can or should be said about the actual nature of deity, then the impact of scientific knowledge upon faith need not have any great consequence. Since Updike has obviously not dismissed the threat, and since his fiction is replete with assertions about the nature of God, he is either not a Barthian in any strict sense, or guilty of a very malicious form of intellectual gamesmanship.

Updike's attraction to Barth is best explained in terms of Barth's willingness to recognize the inadequacy of either-or categorical thinking in the resolution of problems of belief. The fact that debates over metaphysical absolutes in Updike's fiction inevitably end in paradox, or that every syllogism in the course of these debates is somehow shattered, does not bespeak the impossibility of belief—it is his mode of illustrating the dynamics of belief in a cosmos in which the one and the many, or the particular and contingent, are interrelated aspects of a unified process. The concept of duality does not function in this fiction as the metaphysical base for discourse that ideally, or even appropriately, reduces itself to a single, abstract, categorical truth. *Duality* is Updike's term for the poles between oppositions in thought that produce tension which, like that of the interplay between matter and energy (the other aspect of its being), is only resolved through entropy or death.

As Updike knows very well, tension between subatomic particles is a function of their interaction with the force of gravity. Love, says the first-person narrator of *A Month of Sundays*, is "the spiritual twin of gravity—no crude force, exerted by planets in their orbits, but somehow simply, Einsteinly there, a mathematical property of space itself."[7] In Updike's fictional universe love not only offers fleeting respite from the tension between the dualities of self and other, it also has the power to create in the individual a profound sense of union with the entire life of the cosmos. Updike conceives of love, in the manner of the Greeks, as manifesting itself in two complementary but distinct modes—eros and agape. Although both are capable of generating a distinctly religious sense of communion with the source of being, it is agape-love which for Updike is the most infallible source of communion, and which best sustains the individual in healthy and meaningful relationships with others.

In the review of the writings of the theologian Denis de Rougement (who has, by Updike's own admission, been a large influence upon his understanding of the psychology of sex) the novelist says: "Our fundamental anxiety is that we do not exist—or will cease to exist. Only in being loved do we find external corroboration to the supremely high valuation each ego secretly assigns itself."[8] Erotic love in a novel like *Couples* is not, says Updike, "about sex as such: It's about sex as the emergent religion, as the only thing left" (486). But Updike also makes it clear in the review that eros is not sufficient to sustain our metaphysical well-being. Since eros is "allied with Thanatos rather than Agape," it "becomes not a way of accepting and entering the world but a way of defying and escaping it" (285). As de Rougement describes its limitations in behavioral terms, polygamy in Western culture is simply "an indication that men are not yet in a stage to apprehend the presence of an actual person in a woman."[9]

It is agape-love in the fiction of Updike that is the true spiritual twin of gravity, which has the greatest power to momentarily negate the tension between dualities in the movement toward communion with the ontological ground of being. It is this love, according to the novelist's spiritual mentor Karl Barth, that allows a man to "give himself to the other with no expectation of return, in a pure venture, even at the risk of ingratitude," or which provides the basis for the "encounter of I and Thou, the open perception of the other and self-disclosure to him, conversation with him, the offering and receiving of assistance, and with joy."[10] Even this form of love is not, however, a condition in which one dwells; it is, as Buber himself recognized, an activity that inevitably involves movement back into the tension of duality.

The poles in the debate over metaphysical absolutes as the basis for moral action in Updike's first novel, *The Poorhouse Fair*, are made explicit in the extended philosophical discourse between Hook, the ninety-year-old resident of the New England poorhouse, and Connor, the young director of the government-sponsored home for the aged. As a scientifically trained idealist who disdains belief in all forms of transcendence, Connor envisions heaven as the perfect society which in the future man might create as a result of advanced scientific knowledge; he experiences no awe or reverence for natural process. Hook, in contrast, embodies Barth's "virtually antinomian doctrine of all inclusive Grace—he not only exhibits a calm acceptance of God who is "wholly other," but also feels no need to elaborately defend his belief. During a discussion about God and creation on a rainy afternoon at the poorhouse, Connor makes a concerted effort to undermine the old man's religious perspective:

"What makes you think, God exists?" As soon as he pronounced the ominous hollow noun, Connor knew absolutely he could drive the argument down to the core of shame that lay heavily in any believer's heart.

"Why, there are several sorts of evidence," Hook said, as he held up one finger and then added a second, "there is what of Cre-ation I can see, and there are the inner spokesmen."

"Creation. Look at the smoke of your cigar; twisting, expanding, fading. That's the shape of creation. You've seen . . . photographs of nebulae: smears of smoke billions of miles wide. What do you make of their creation?"

"I know little of astronomy. Now a flower's creation—"

"Is also an accident."

"An accident?" Hook smiled softly and he touched the fingertips together, better to give his attention.

"Lightning stirred certain acids present in the raw earth. Eventually the protein molecule occurred, and in another half-billion years the virus, and from then on it's evolution. Imagine a blind giant tossing rocks through eternity. At some point he could have made a cathedral."

"It seems implaus-ible."

"It's mathematics. The amounts of time it takes is the factor that seems implausible. But the universe has endless time."

. . . "I do not quite see how any amount of time can generate something from nothing."

"Presumably there was always something. Though relatively, very little. The chief characteristic of the universe is, I would say, emptiness. There is infinitely more nothing in the universe than anything else."

"Indeed, you propose to extinguish religion by measuring quantities of nothing. Now why should no matter how much nothing be imposing, when my little fingernail, by being something, is of more account?"

"Yes, but there is something. Stars; many of such size that were one placed in the position of the sun we would be engulfed in flame. The issue is, can any sane mind believe that a young carpenter in Syria two thousand years ago made those monstrous balls of gas."[11]

Although Hook *believes* that, "there is no goodness, without belief. There is nothing but busy-ness" (81), young Connor's arguments clearly disturb the old man. At the close of the narrative he finds himself "groping after the fitful advice he must impart to Connor, as a bond between them and a testament to endure his dying in the world" (127). But as the final sentence of the novel implies ("What is it?" [127]), no such argument can be found.

It is the tension between these poles in the metaphysical debate that is the basis for Updike's relentless probing into the morality of action throughout the remainder of his work. On one pole there is the modern, scientific view of the life of the cosmos that carries with it two very disturbing implications: (1) if all particulars in nature are interdependent aspects of one unified process, *self* as an actual existing entity in nature may be a fiction of our minds; and (2) if indeterminacy is a feature of this process, then all teleological arguments, as well as all conceptions of ethics founded upon transcendent and immutable law, are, at best, suspect, and, at worst, mere remnants of an outmoded cosmology. Contending with this conception on the opposite pole is belief in God as wholly *other*, which implies the existence of a separate self, or self as a discrete entity, and also serves as the ontological ground for goodness or moral behavior. If we are to be something more than animals with clothes on, we cannot, suggests Updike, escape the tension that accompanies duality, nor would we finally wish to do so. Although this particular manifestation of duality, i.e., old and new cosmologies, may be a function of our historical situation, duality itself, in Updike's view, is not. The tension between seemingly irreconcilable but fundamentally complementary ideas, thoughts, and feelings is simply the condition of human consciousness in a closed system of relation.[12] His sense that this is a "participatory universe" allows him to affirm that the terms for constructing our reality can be transcended through the operation of human love.

The moral debate with the reader in *Rabbit, Run* and *Rabbit Redux* is occasioned by the moral struggles of a character whose consciousness of opposing conceptions of metaphysical reality creates the tension present everywhere in these struggles. The Harry Angstrom left "running" at the close of the first narrative experiences in the sequel, as Updike indicates in the use of the word *redux*, a "return to health after disease."[13] Rabbit's diseased condition in the first narrative, explored in greater depth in *Couples* and *A Month of Sundays*, is that familiar Western ailment described by Barth and de Rougement—the inability to recognize the primacy of agape-love over eros. Rabbit becomes healthy in the second narrative as a result of discovering, experientially, the profound differences between the two, and learning to fashion his behavior more in terms of the love that is, for Updike, most in accord with the generative essence of Being.

Raised, like Updike, as a Lutheran, Harry in *Rabbit, Run* hopes to discover in established religion the spiritual force and authority that would provide a guide for moral behavior, but cannot finally affirm the existence of an omniscient, all powerful deity who with "all His strength did nothing"[14] to prevent the death of the infant Becky. The inability of Harry to categorically affirm the existence of this God does not, however, result in a categorical denial of his existence. The tension that motivates virtually all his actions is a consequence of the effort necessary to reconcile his intuitive sense of identity in the ground of being with the conception of identity that appears both actual and necessary within the context of the old cosmology. The theological argument that most impresses Harry, which he will use later in theological debates with the Episcopal minister Eccles, is articulated on television by the adult Mouseketeer Jimmy early in the narrative: "Know thyself, a wise old Greek once said. Know thyself. Now what does that mean boys and girls? It means, be what you are. God doesn't want a tree to be a waterfall, or a flower to be a stone. God gives each of us a special talent" (14–15). The self-knowledge advocated by Socrates was not, as Rabbit will interpret it, a direct, intuitive awareness of the sources of being. Socrates, as the big Mouseketeer suggests, was counseling reliance upon the analytical or rational mode of self-awareness which might lead to a larger understanding of self as an atomized entity in a mathematically precise and ordered cosmos.

In the first phase of his spiritual journey Rabbit finds himself driving aimlessly south away from Brewer without consciously deciding to do so. After stopping at a gas station and asking the attendant, a slightly drunk old man, for directions, Rabbit confesses that he does not know where he wants to go. The attendant then says: "The only way to get somewhere, you know, is to figure out where you are going before you get there." Rabbit's immediate and curious response is, "I don't think so" (32). The words of the old man, which Rabbit recalls at several points in the remainder of the narrative, strike at the very core of his dilemma. Affirmation of the existence of the Judeo-Christian God seems to involve acceptance of his identity, or his role definitions, as predetermined functions of a cosmic scheme or plan. He is perplexed that resistance to the acceptance, which Eccles characterizes as a clear violation of the moral law, often results in a kind of exalted happiness, and not the terrible sense of separation from God that this minister advertises as the final consequence of wrong-doing.

Sensing that his own faith in ultimate being is considerably less certain than that of Rabbit's, Eccles realizes that his only viable weapon in convincing Rabbit to return to Janice is the traditional Western conception of the hierarchy of being which legitimates his role as interpreter of the higher moral law. Initially shocked by Harry's simple admission that he believes in God (101), Eccles becomes increasingly dismayed as he begins to discover the special character of that belief. After directing Eccles's attention in a moving car to the "un-grandest landscape in the suburbs of Brewer," Harry asserts that "behind all this . . . there's something that wants me to find it" (120). As the two men begin walking to the clubhouse on the golf course, Eccles sarcastically notes: "It's a strange thing about you mystics, how often your little ecstasies wear a skirt" (121).

The connection in Harry between mysticism and sexuality is a good deal more profound than this stumbling pastoral counselor knows. Shortly before making love to Ruth for the first time, Rabbit perceives the light behind the rose window of the church across the street as a "hole punched in reality to show the abstract brilliance underneath," and feels "gratitude toward the builders of this ornament" (78). He not only asked Ruth earlier that they "be" married and that she perform rituals associated with the rites of the marriage bed, he also attempts to make "love to her as he would his wife" (81).

During intercourse, however, Harry "feels impatience that through all their twists they remain separate flesh; he cannot dare enough, now that she is so much his friend in this search; everywhere they meet a wall" (82). When Harry looks once again out of Ruth's window on the following day (Sunday), he does not feel the same gratitude toward the builders of the church steeple that he felt earlier toward the makers of the window. The steeple, perceived as a shadow thrown by the bright sunlight, is, he muses, a "cool stumpy negative in which a few men with flowers in their lapels stand and gossip while the common sheep of the flock stream in, heads down" (86).

Erotic love as Harry conceives it ought to serve as the ground of communication with the God whose presence lends unity and purpose to all created things, but that same God also demands, as he understands it, obeisance to a moral law that forbids the communication of this love outside marriage. Whenever Harry achieves an intuitive or mystical awareness of communion with ultimate being, however, he is wonderfully oblivious to the dictates of moral law. Shortly before meeting Ruth on the date arranged by his old basketball coach, Tothero, Harry's sense of freedom seems so perfect and "so consistent that all ways seem equally good, all movements will put the same caressing pressure on his skin, and not an atom of his happiness would be altered if Tothero told him they were not going to meet two girls but two goats, and they were going not to Brewer but to Tibet" (51–52). As he adjusts his tie into a Windsor knot, the "lines of juncture" at the "base of his throat were the arms of a star that will, when he finished, extend outward to the rim of the universe. He is the Dalai Lama" (53). The notion of self as one with the organic process of the becoming that is the life of the cosmos also appears in a curious Western translation in conversation with Ruth. After he dumps his clothes on her bed and asks if she has any hangers, Ruth says in anger, "Say. You really have it made." Rabbit then responds, "I made you. I made you and the sun and stars" (103). The intuition that God is one with natural process is also present in Rabbit's attitude toward the planting of seeds in Mrs. Smith's garden: "Getting rid of something by giving it to itself. God himself folded into the tiny adamant structure. Self-destined to a succession of explosions, the great slow gathering out of water and air and silicon" (128).

The tension between the two alternate views of deity, imminent and transcendent, is, however, unresolved in Harry. Climbing Mt.

Judge with Ruth in what is apparently a naive pilgrimage to the higher reaches of being, Rabbit, "bothered by God" and thoughts of death, can only conclude that "if there is a floor there is a ceiling, that the true space in which we live is upward space" (108). Late in the narrative, after the death of Becky, Harry is greatly troubled by Tothero's suggestion that "right and wrong aren't dropped from the sky. We make them" (257) for the simple reason that "he wants to believe in the sky as the source of all things" (258). It is this sense of the sky as the source of all things that motivates Harry to tell the mourners at the child's funeral what is for him simply a statement of fact, but which they regard as an all too graphic illustration of his terrible insensitivity. As he stands in the sunshine, he feels that the "sky greets him. A strange strength sinks down into him. It is as if he has been crawling in a cave and now at last beyond the dark recession of crowding rocks he has seen a patch of light; he turns, and Janice's face, dumb with grief, blocks the light. 'Don't look at me,' he says. 'I didn't kill her' " (271).

In light of this discussion, the most revealing passage in the novel is the description of Rabbit after he runs into the woods adjacent to the cemetery: "He feels more conspicuous and vulnerable than in the little clearings of sunshine; he obscurely feels lit by a great spark, the spark whereby the blind tumble of matter recognized itself, a spark struck in the collision of two opposed realms, an encounter a terrible God willed." (275) The tension between opposing charges that allowed matter to emerge in the interplay with the other aspect of its being, energy, is here likened to the tension that is fundamental to consciousness or self-awareness. The implication is that the price paid for consciousness, to use Updike's term, is duality, or perpetual awareness of the tension between complementary but irreducible oppositions in thought. At the close of the narrative the momentary release Rabbit feels from awareness of sin and guilt associated with the cosmology implicit in the ritual behavior of the mourners may result in its own kind of ecstasy ("he runs. Ah: Runs" [284]), but as we learn in *Rabbit, Redux*, the tension between the poles in Harry's consciousness does not subside.

In the sequel, Rabbit remains uncomfortable with the strictures of role definitions he associates with the old cosmology, but maturity has added new dimensions to his struggle and the prospect of meaningful adjustment. He wants, as Janice explains to her car-salesman lover Stavros, "to live an old-fashioned life, but nobody does that any more, and he feels it. He put his life into rules he feels melting away now" (54). As the signs and symbols of the "old-fashioned life"—fidelity in marriage, the job at Variety Press, the house in Penn Villas—are gradually stripped away, Harry engages in another spiritual journey to discover the sources of his identity. His opponents in the metaphysical debate in this narrative are not establishment figures, like Eccles, but two imaginative and intelligent victims of the Vietnam War era—a black radical and veteran of that war, Skeeter, and a disaffected child of affluent society, Jill.

This older Harry prays to the God of the West while riding buses, and asserts in conversation with his sometime-lover Peggy, that "God is everything that isn't people" (102). His initial refusal to question, or even examine, America's role in Vietnam also owes something to his belief in the old cosmology. When Stavros criticizes the war effort in the restaurant, Harry—who has not yet learned that this man is Janice's lover—first assaults him verbally, and then has the intuition that any description of America's actions as a "power play is to miss the point. America is beyond power, it acts as in a dream, as a face of God. . . . Beneath her patient bombers, paradise is possible" (49). Although Rabbit also senses here, as he did in *Rabbit, Run*, a relation between self and world not consistent with the old cosmology, it is exposure through Skeeter and Jill to a metaphysic consistent with the new physics that eventually allows him to entertain alternate perspectives on the war.

The first of Rabbit's mystical experiences occurs during the evening in which Buchanan, his black fellow worker, invites him to Jimbo's Bar where he is introduced to Skeeter and Jill. Listening to a song performed by Babe, the black blues singer and prostitute who has been caring for Jill, in which the words of Ecclesiastes ("A time to be born and a time to die") are used, Rabbit finds himself suddenly transported: "Her singing opens up, growing enormous, frightens Rabbit with its enormous maw of truth yet makes him overjoyed that he is there; he brims with joy, to be here with these black others, he wants to shout love through the darkness of Babe's noises to the sullen brother in goatee and glasses" (115). The love that Rabbit feels toward Skeeter, who is the opposite of Harry in many respects besides skin color, is agape-love. And it is this love which provides access to the vision of cosmic unity that follows. Feeling unaccustomed to the effects of the marijuana that these "black others" have offered him, Rabbit senses that, "his inside space expands to include beyond Jimbo's the whole world with its arrowing wars and polychrome races, its continents shaped like ceiling stains, its strings of gravitational forces attaching it to every star, its glory in space as a blue marble swirled with clouds." Everything in this ecstatic moment feels "warm, wet, still coming to birth but himself and his home, which remains a strange dry place, dry and cold and emptily spinning in the void of Penn Villas like a cast-off space capsule" (121).

It is agape-love, the spiritual twin of gravity, that bridges the gap between *self* and *other* in Harry's experience throughout the remainder of the novel. And it is this love, in conjunction with the metaphysics consistent with the new physics articulated by Jill and Skeeter, that allows him to begin to perceive the polarities of life and death, order and chaos, creation and destruction, as complementary aspects of one unified process. Jill's version of the new metaphysics emphasizes the fundamental oneness of all events in nature, but she uses that idea primarily as a mode of escaping the painful awareness of *self* as a particular form in the process. Skeeter's emphasis is, in contrast, upon duality as a feature of natural process, but he distorts the meaning of duality in the effort to legitimate his own violently self-destructive behavior. Rabbit, who does not come to an unqualified acceptance of the new metaphysics, manages, nevertheless, to enlarge his capacity for agape-love as a result of exposure to the views of both young people.

During one of the extended metaphysical debates which become usual after Jill and Skeeter take up residence at Rabbit's house, Harry's son Nelson asks Jill what she means in saying that "man is a mechanism for turning things into spirit and turning spirit into things." Jill's explanation is that "the point is ecstasy. . . . Energy. Anything that is good is in ecstasy. The world is what God made and it doesn't stink of money, it's never tired, too much or too little, it's always full." After describing gravity as the force that unifies all material substances as Rabbit did earlier at Jimbo's, Jill tells Nelson that it is our egos that blind us to the perception of the universe as "absolutely clean" and asserts that "matter is the mirror of spirit" (143). What Jill hopes to eliminate, by means of this cosmology, is, as

Rabbit himself realizes, human consciousness, or awareness of self as an actually existing entity in nature. The same notion is present in her effort to explain later in the narrative why she should allow herself to be sexually abused by Skeeter: "I'm not interested in holding anything for myself. It all melts together anyway, you see" (191).

Rabbit's willingness to allow Janice to continue in the relationship with Stavros is not, as she initially interprets it, a sign of his callousness, but one of the first demonstrations in the narrative of agape-love. The difficulty that Rabbit has in acting upon this love is the duality of its effects. In the conversation with Janice in which he indicates that she should remain in contact with Charlie, it comes to Rabbit that "growth is betrayal" (74). Later when his mother urges him not to "say no to life," Harry feels as if "she is asking him to kill Janice, to kill Nelson. Freedom means murder. Rebirth means death" (175). Skeeter, who provides Rabbit with philosophical justification for this view of change, begins with the assertion that "Your God's a pansy. Your white God's queerer than the Queen of Spades," and then offers himself as the "real Jesus" (187). In the interview in *Picked-Up Pieces* Updike expressed his surprise that the critics have not "given serious consideration to the idea that Skeeter, the angry black, might be Jesus. He says he is. I think he probably might be."[15] The comment makes sense in the light of Updike's conception of duality. Skeeter is not the anti-Christ, as some have supposed; he is *the* Christ in the sense that he functions as a conception of this deity that complements, through opposition, received, traditional conceptions.

In his attempt to demonstrate that the Vietnam War is an integral function of the life of nature, and has, therefore, ontological justification, Skeeter draws on two disparate scientific theories on "how the universe was done" (230). While recognizing that the big-bang theory seems correct in terms of the empirical evidence now available to us, he is most intrigued by theorists who view black holes, produced when massive stars collapse into the gravitational field, as pathways into a mirror universe. The war, says Skeeter, is the "local black hole" where the "world is redoing itself. It is the end. It is the tail of the universe we are eating. It is the bottom you have. . . . It is the end. It is the beginning." It is where "God is pushing through" and "Chaos is his holy face" (230). When Rabbit, who remains attached to an either-or categorical approach to the morality of action, asks Skeeter if our being in Vietnam is simply wrong, this Christ of the new dark age responds, "Wrong? Man, how can it be wrong when that's the way it is" (231).

Although Rabbit refuses to accept the notion that deliberately destructive behavior, like Skeeter's, is simply one manifestation of the being that is God, he does come to believe that violence in nature is an integral function of unified process. After being served a casserole by Peggy containing "poor dismembered creatures," Rabbit reflects that there is "no avoiding it: life does want death. To be alive is to kill" (271). At the close of the narrative when Janice shares with Rabbit Charlie's conviction that the war will end when the "big industrial interests" understand that it is "unprofitable," Rabbit tells her about Skeeter's notion that Vietnam "was the doorway into utter confusion" which would eventually lead to a "wonderful stretch of perfect calm, with him ruling, or somebody exactly like him." After Janice asks if he believes this, Rabbit says "Confusion is just a local view of things working out in general" (351). Although Rabbit continues, as he tells Janice in this same conversation, to feel responsibility and "guilt" for all of his actions, he derives some comfort from knowing that the entire cosmos, within which we are contingent but nevertheless particular manifestations, is not in confusion.

The relationship with Skeeter also provides Harry with the best opportunity to experience agape-love as a force capable of obviating momentarily the tension between opposites. His identification with Skeeter through this love is so strong at one point that Rabbit readily admits that he likes "being a nigger," and wants "to be a good one" (262). When Skeeter later in this same discussion asks, "You love me more than you love yourself?", the immediate response is, "Much more" (262). Although he does not finally excuse Skeeter for his complicity in Jill's death in the fire, he also does not categorically condemn him. After he drives Skeeter out of town in Peggy's car to prevent his arrest by the local police, Rabbit wonders if a "Judas kiss" would be proper, and then extends his hand to "shake farewell." Skeeter in his final act of defiance of this representative of the white-power structure spits in his open palm. Rabbit "at first only knows it has happened by seeing: moisture full of bubbles like tiny suns. He chooses to take the gesture as a blessing" (292). Agape-love, the giving of oneself without expectation of reward and with the risk of ingratitude, is here linked to a vision of cosmic unity. Skeeter, who has apparently had little exposure to such love, says in consternation, "Never did figure your angle," and Rabbit answers, "Probably wasn't one" (292). It is agape-love that is at work in the reunion of the Angstroms at the end of the novel. As Rabbit in a motel room that becomes "all interior space," moves his hand along the "familiar dip of her waist, ribs to hip bone, where no bones are, soft as flight, fat's inward curve, slack, his babies from her belly," the novel concludes, "He. She. Sleeps. O.K.?" (352). It is, Updike suggests, the condition of our being that any strong sense of wholeness, unity, and sameness must alternate with a sense of self as individuated, discrete, and different.

Agape-love as the force capable of ameliorating the burden of consciousness of self as a fragile and insignificant activity in nature is the single most pervasive concern in *The Centaur*. In Greek mythology, as Updike notes in the preface, Chiron, the noblest of the half-man and half-horse creatures, is inadvertently struck by a poison arrow. Tormented by the wound that will not heal and longing for death, the immortal Centaur asks the gods to accept his death as atonement for Prometheus. The gods, hearing his prayer and taking away both his pain and immortality, allow Chiron to die "like any wearied man" and he is placed by Zeus as a "shining archer among the stars."[16] Although the choice of Chiron as a mythological representation of George Caldwell does serve to accent his uniqueness, the plight in which he finds himself is, as Updike sees it, familiar to most of us. As Updike suggests in his Paris interview, "The trauma or message I acquired in Olinger had to do with suppressed pain, with the amount of sacrifice that middle-class life demands, and by that I guess I mean civilized life. The father, whatever his name, is sacrificing freedom of motion, and the mother is sacrificing in a way—oh, sexual richness, I guess, they're all stuck. . . . in the irremediable grief in just living, in just going on."[17]

Since Prometheus in one Greek creation myth, in addition to providing the fire that allowed mankind to "learn many crafts," was also responsible for fashioning the shape of man in the likeness of the gods, George's living sacrifice of himself as the teacher of brutish and insensitive youth can be viewed as freeing his son Peter to become a craftsman or "maker" of the shape of human reality through the art of painting. But Chiron, who differed from the other violent and fierce creatures of his kind because of his abundance of goodness and wisdom, was also the teacher of young sons of heroes, and it is George Caldwell's instruction in the "irremediable grief in just living" that provides the impulse for Peter's commitment to the life of the artist. As the mythological Chiron appears under the "Arcadian sun" teaching his pupils about the "Genesis of All Things," he explains that "black-winged Night was courted by the wind, and laid a silver egg in the womb of Darkness" which hatched "Eros." After love "set the universe in motion," he continues, men lived for a time under the rule of Eros in a "world as harmonious as a beehive" with no "cares or labors" and viewed death as "no more terrible than sleep. Then her sceptre passed to Uranus . . ." (78). Since Uranus in Greek mythology is the starry sky and husband to the broad-bosomed earth Gaea, the suggestion is that death became "terrible" in the experience of man as he became conscious of dualities, like that between earth and sky.

The Centaur as science teacher at Olinger High School, wounded by an arrow in the beginning of the narrative as he chalks the probable age of the universe on the board, is obsessed with the extent to which knowledge of the sky makes us more acutely aware of the tenuousness of self as life form on earth. As he stands before his class with his ankle still bleeding from the wound, lecturing on the origins of the universe, the omniscient narrator comments that "astronomy transfixed him; at night sometimes when he lay in bed exhausted he felt his ebbing body was fantastically huge and contained in its darkness a billion stars" (34). After confessing to his class that the enormously large numbers representing the age of the universe and the numbers of stars "remind me of death," he elects to reduce the "five billion years of the universe to our size" and begins describing the evolution of the life of the cosmos within the time frame of one week. As his audience, including the supervising principal Zimmerman, pays curious tribute to eros by engaging in sexual foreplay, Caldwell describes in marvelous detail the manner in which gravitational forces condensed balls of gases to form matter which, he notes, constitutes in the entire universe a "minority of less than one per cent" (35). In describing the appearance of volvox, a genus of tiny single-celled organisms, this formidable teacher notes: "There is no reason intrinsic in the plasmic substance why life should ever end. Amoebas never die; and those male sperm cells which enjoy success become the cornerstone of new life that continues beyond the father. But the volvox, a rolling sphere of flagellating algae organized into somatic and reproductive cells . . . by pioneering this new idea of co-operation, rolled life into the kingdom of the certain—as opposed to accidental—death." By "volunteering for a specialized function within an organized society of cells," Caldwell explains, the "poten-tially immortal [cell] enters a compromised environment" which eventually kills it. The cells that got together and formed the first volvox "were the first altruists, the first do-gooders. If I had a hat on, I'd take it off to 'em" (37).

This is not, as some critics have supposed, a curious scientific justification for Christian charity. In accepting our existence as or-ganisms, or collections of cells, in the evolving, open-ended, holistic life of the cosmos, we are obliged to view death as an integral func-tion of life. Living and dying are not, then, antithetical states, but rather complementary aspects of one process. When Peter asks what Zimmerman meant in his report on his father's classroom perform-ance when he wrote that the "humanistic values implicit in the physi-cal sciences were not elicited" (86), Caldwell responds, "Maybe deep in the atom there's a little man sitting in a rocking chair reading the newspaper" (87). Such values, he implies, are necessarily anthropo-centric, and can be sustained in our dealings with the universe only as articles of faith.

Caldwell's scientifically based awareness that all activities in nature are interrelated aspects of one process is also apparent in a lecture recalled by Peter in which his father wrote the equation "$C_6H_{12} + 6CO_2 + 6H_2O + E$" on a blackboard and then encircled the E. " 'Energy,' " he explains, " 'That's life. We take in sugars and oxygen and burn it, like you burn old newspapers in the trash barrel, and give off carbon dioxide and water and energy. When this process stops'—he Xed through the equation—'this stops'—he double-Xed out the E—'and you become what they call dead' " (142). When Peter asks if the equation can be reversed, his father explains that read backwards it describes "photosynthesis, the life of green plants." The interplay between the two processes, says the Centaur, is the "way the world goes round. . . . Round and round, and where it stops, nobody knows" (143).

The tension between the dualities of scientific and Judeo-Christian cosmologies is a constant in Caldwell's endless pursuit of metaphysical absolutes. Convinced throughout most of the narrative that he is dying of intestinal cancer, he is haunted by the question that his minister father asked shortly before his own death: "Do you think I'll be eternally forgotten?" (73). In conversation at the basketball game with the disinterested Protestant minister March about differences between Presbyterian and orthodox Calvinist views on predestination, Caldwell objects to the notion that that doctrine "must be counterbalanced by the doctrine of God's infinite mercy." The difficulty he has with this idea, explains Caldwell, is that he "can't see how it's infinite if it never changes anything at all. Maybe it's infinite at an infinite distance—that's the only way I can picture it" (189). The duality between belief in God as wholly *other* and *self* as an articulated identity preserved through time, and the belief that life is a unified process in which self eventually dissolves back into the source of being is never finally resolved. The same nature that Caldwell experiences in his own moments of mystical revelation as eternally One is also, as he tells his wife near the close of the narrative, the object of "hate. . . . It reminds me of death" (216).

It is Caldwell's enormous capacity for agape-love that finally precludes the alienating influence which might otherwise have been a consequence of his metaphysical dilemma. In addition to giving of himself to his students with an almost reckless abandon, his encounters with virtually everyone in his experience, no matter how demeaned or demented in appearance and behavior, constitute one of the best illustrations in the modern novel of the dynamics of Buber's *I-Thou* relationship. The physically repulsive hitchhiker, who responds contemptuously to every kind remark and who displays a homosexual attraction to Peter, is described by Caldwell in the "most matter-of-fact tone" as a "gentleman" (72). After discovering that the gloves that were an "expensive and painstakingly deliberate gift" from Peter have been stolen by this man, Caldwell comments simply that "he needs 'em more than I did. That poor devil never knew what hit him" (73). Another similar display of agape-love is the encounter with the youthful but hopelessly dissipated drunk who presumes that Caldwell is sexually involved with Peter and attempts blackmail. Again Caldwell responds with the utmost regard and respect, gives the less-than-grateful derelict money, and then indicates in all sincerity that the young man has "clarified" his own thinking (122).

Although Peter is perpetually annoyed with his father's unwillingness to distance himself from such troublesome people, he is able to find in these displays of agape-love, nevertheless, a source of "hope" (144). But Peter also assimilates his mentor's scientifically based understanding of metaphysical reality. Like his father he is also capable of sensing while lying in bed the fundamental unity of all natural process: "As the sheets warmed, I enlarged to human size, and then, as the dissolution of drowsiness crept toward me, a sensation, both vivid and numb, of enormity entered my cells, and I seemed a giant who included in his fingernail all the galaxies there are" (127). Watching the snow fall after the JV basketball game, Peter is aware of "atoms and atoms and atoms and atoms" suggesting that "out of zero all has come to birth" (179). Later in this same evening as Peter stands in the school parking lot with his father, and looks at the "shadows of snowflakes cast by the light above him," he draws an analogy with the "red shift" phenomenon in astronomy, and muses that the "stars are in fact falling gently through the cone of observation of which our earthly telescopes are but the apex." He then arrives at a kind of metaphorical "edge" in consciousness "where the speed of the shadows is infinite and a small universe both ends and does not end" (191). It is this sense that all manifestations of material substance in the space-time continuum, including the entity called *self*, are interrelated aspects of one unified process that provides the impetus to "go to Nature disarmed of perspective and stretch myself like a large transparent canvass upon her in the hope that, my submission being perfect, the imprint of a beautiful and useful truth would be taken" (218). It is the willingness to assert those "useful truths" that is, as Updike sees it, the mark of our humanity. When Caldwell notices, for example, that the work FUCK on the lavatory wall of the high school has been transformed by some unseen hand to BOOK, his immediate suspicion is that his son may have been responsible (185). It is, suggests Updike, the artist who is capable of reconstituting biological givens into distinctly human realities, and refashioning in the process the shape of those realities.

Although Updike clearly believes that agape-love is the much superior mode of mitigating the tension between opposing cosmologies, the "emergent religion," as he graphically demonstrates in *Couples* and *A Month of Sundays*, is the form of love "allied with

Thanatos rather than Agape." As Freddie Thorne, the dentist and high priest of the new religious order in *Couples*, told his wife, the relationship between the couples, fueled by erotic-love, is a "circle. A magic circle of heads to keep the night out. . . . He thinks we've made a church of each other."[18] Or, as he puts it more explicitly later in the narrative: "People are the only thing people have left since God packed up. By people I mean sex. Fucking" (155). The most avid devotee in the novel to the new religion is not Freddie, whose sexual impotence serves to belie the efficacy of this salvation ethos, but the contractor and builder Piet Hanneman.

Piet, who suffered the early loss of his parents in an automobile accident, is, like most of Updike's central characters, caught up in the tension between scientific and received Judeo-Christian conceptions of cosmology in the effort to relieve intense awareness of the prospect of death. Fearing that there is "no such thing in nature as a point, or perfect circle, or infinitude, or a hereafter" (20), Piet finds "perverse" the assertion made by his sometime mistress and eventual wife, Foxy, that God is not, as he views him, "different" from man but "one and the same" (215). Familiar with the scientific view that matter is "mostly nothing, a titter skinning a vacuum" (271), he is horrified at the thought that "beneath the implacable frozen stars" is revealed "the muffled collapse, the opaque gasp, the unresisted plunge" (273). His anxiety that the matter that composes the self-entity could precipitously dissolve back into the energy field is also evinced as he looks at his daughters sleeping and imagines that they "might fall through into silence. The frail web of atoms spinning" (346). And yet as Angela tells Piet that their marital relationship should perhaps be terminated and that Foxy is a more appropriate spouse for him, it comes to him that "he believed that there was, behind the screen of couples and houses and days, a Calvinist God Who Lifts us up and casts us down in utter freedom, without recourse to our prayers or consultations with our wills" (434).

Erotic love as mode of spiritual communion derives epistemological justification in this narrative directly from concepts in the new physics. While making love to Freddie's wife, Gorgeone, it occurs to Piet that she was "double everywhere but in her mouths. All things double. Without duality, entropy. The universe God's mirror" (58). Piet's conviction that the wedding of the dualities of male and female in intercourse provides respite from death consciousness is apparent in all his sexual activity. Adultery, as he tells Foxy, is a way of "getting out in the world and seeking knowledge" (359), and coitus is a "chamber into universe . . . a blind pleasure tasting of infinity" (456). Oral sex also has special metaphysical import for Piet because mouths "move in the brain's court. . . . When the mouth condescends, mind and body marry. To eat another is sacred" (456). De Rougement's notion that erotic-love is not "a way of accepting the world but a way of defying and escaping it" is clearly at work at the end of the narrative. The dispassionate, almost clinical report on the new circumstances in which Piet and his second wife find themselves is followed by the cryptic statement that "the Hannemans live in Lexington, where, gradually, among people like themselves, they have been accepted, as another couple" (480).

A Month of Sundays consists of a series of wonderfully imaginative and irreverent sermonettes on the metaphysical dimensions of erotic-love with a few concessions paid to character and plot development. The sexual appetites of the Reverend Mr. Thomas Marshfield are matched only by his need to discover religious and philosophical justification for relentlessly seeking to satisfy them. This unconventional Protestant divine also has an extraordinary acquaintance with the new physics which figures large in all his speculations upon the efficacy of the libidinal life. Since the "First Commandment received by human ears" was "Be fruitful, and multiply," Marshfield suggests that there is some theological justification for viewing adultery as "not a choice to be avoided" but a "circumstance to be embraced."[19] Erotic love becomes for this minister, as it does for Piet, a form of worship in that it allows a fleeting sense of communion with the source of being. Viewing this love as the "spiritual twin of gravity" (135), he senses while passing one of his love objects in a corridor a "curious curvature of space-time in which our curt greeting billows and dips" (255). His conviction that sexual coupling involves movement through the tension between dualities in material substances down into the unified energy field even lends excitement to the practice of the ritual acts of his ministry. "There is," he says, "a grandeur, an onslaught of nous and of dizzying altitude, in the act of placing a communion wafer between the parted lips of a mouth that, earlier in the week in which this was the Sabbath day, has received one's throbbingly ejaculated seed" (163). Or, as he puts it more directly later in the narrative, love is "not an e-motion, an assertive putting out, but a *trans*-motion, a compliant moving through" (257).

Quoting from Karl Barth on several occasions, Marshfield also adopts the view of God as wholly *other* who "shatters every syllogism." The God of the West, the "Father of all wonders," works miracles, he says, from which "we can draw no lessons, but that—a splendid lesson—He is not ourselves" (121). Although seeking on occasion to make the understanding of the life of the cosmos derived from the new physics compatible with the received cosmology he is pledged to protect, the discrepancies between the two are once again unresolved. The argument presented to his assistant minister, Ned, that we should "sentimentalize neither the rich nor the poor" for the "material world, viewed spiritually, is a random grid. Wherever we are placed within it, our task is to witness, to offer a way out of the crush of matter and time" (86) does considerable violence to the idea of providential deity. The notion that randomness in the miracles performed by God "is not their defect, but their essence, as injustice (from our point of view, which is that of children) is essential to Creation of differentiated particulars" (125) is more convincing in that it provides scientific justification of a sort for free election, but it also does not rest comfortably with the concept of a divinely ordained cosmos.

The impossibility of discovering metaphysical absolutes is more dramatically accented on other occasions when Marshfield characterizes his ministry as "an act of fraternity amid children descended from, if not one Father, certainly one marriage of molecular accidents" (101), or asserts that "there is no afterlife. Any preacher's son can tell you that, just read your molecules" (151). And yet conversely, in the dance between the polar oppositions of cosmologies, the metaphysics implied in the new physics creates in Marshfield the belief that he is "really fifteen billion light-years in diameter and shaped like a saddle" (221), and lends credence to his argument against the existentialists: "Existence precedes everything; *esse est deus*" (263).

The question of "What is goodness?" in this narrative is perhaps as pointless as Updike could possibly make it. Although there is some practical wisdom in Marshfield's notion that, "Doing right is, to too great an extent, a matter of details, of tinkering" (228) and some truth in the assertion that "ethical passion" is the "hobgoblin of trivial minds" (228), the commitment to erotic-love as salvation ethos is once again shown as a fleetingly satisfying but ultimately debilitating stance. Removed from his parish by an outraged vestry, estranged from his wife and children, the last portion of the narrative consists of a frantic appeal for sexual favors from the only female present at the desert retreat for failed Protestant ministers. As he prepares to leave he confesses to the love object that he is "terrified" by the prospect of re-entering the world, that his life is at "loose ends," that he "cannot cope" (270). The description in the concluding paragraph of the eyes of this woman as they engage in sexual intercourse as "looking up into mine, with an expression without a name, of entry and alarm and salutation," is followed by a curious prayer: "I pray my own face, a stranger to me, saluted in return" (271). Erotic love as the only religion left is not only depicted in this instance as a way of defying and escaping the world, it is also shown as alienating the individual from the sources of his identity in other respects as well.

I do not perceive that Updike has the same preoccupation with concepts from the new physics in *Of the Farm*, *Marry Me*, and *Bech*, but he definitely exhibits this absorption in his most recent novel —*The Coup*. The dictator of the newly created African state of Kush, Colonel Ellelou, is a movable feast of opposing cosmologies and political ideologies. Although the architect of a government in which the "pure and final socialism envisioned by Marx" and the "theocratic populism of Islam's periodic reform movements" serve as "transcendent models,"[20] his exposure to the metaphysics implied in the new physics obviates all belief in transcendent absolutes and provides ontological justification for the concept of duality. After assimilating in his youth a form of nature worship in which spiritual agency is a felt presence in all natural events, he is exposed during the period in which he is a student at an American liberal-arts college to both Marxist socialism and the understanding of the nation of Islam proselytized in the sixties by Malcolm X. His "arid-book-learning" in works ranging from "Plato to Einstein" does not provide access to that which seems incontestably "true," but results in "a steady explosion" in which "the sheltering gods" are "all shattered" (177).

The "death of religions the world over," muses Ellelou, may be followed by the birth of "a new religion . . . in the indistinct hearts of men, a religion without God, without prohibitions and compensatory assurances, a religion whose antipodes are motion and stasis, whose one rite is the exercise of energy, and in which exhausted forms like the quest, the vow, the expiation, and the attainment through suffering of wisdom are, emptied of content, put in the service of a pervasive expenditure whose ultimate purpose is entropy, whose immediate reward is fatigue, a blameless confusion, and sleep" (103). That which keeps mankind from dissolving into a "heap of dust, of individual atoms," however, as he tells Ezana, the principal advisor who will eventually participate in the coup that removes him from power, is duality. "Peace," as Ezana views it in society, is, explains Ellelou, a form of "entropy" in that a "principle of contention is intrinsic to Nature, from the first contentious thrust of bare existence against the subliminal void." The heavens that appear serene as "witnessed by astronomers, shine," he continues, "by grace of explosion and consumption on a scale unthinkable, and the glazed surface of marble or the demure velvet of a maiden's eyelid are by the dissections of particle physics a frenzy of whirling and a titanic tension of incompatible charges" (130–31).

In this narrative Updike not only uses concepts from the new physics as ontological justification for his view of duality, he also incorporates the notion that knowledge is a metaphoric representation that serves to coordinate a greater range of experience and not an absolute transcription of reality. The "dictatorship of the proletariat" is not, for example, in Ellelou's view, subject to "proof," but serves as a "handle on reality that otherwise would overwhelm us" (154). Similarly government, as he understands it, is "mythological in nature," and the business of the societal reformer is simply to "concoct a counter-myth" (174). Recognizing that the realities of his "people are not static, but in the process of transformation," it is his ambition to "help create new realities" (216).

It is this perspective that allows this thorough-going relativist to create the persona of the dictator who could require that any "man caught urinating in a standing position, instead of squatting in the manner of Mohamet and his followers" be "detained and interrogated" (95), or who could unhesitatingly lop off the head of the representative of the old religious and political order, King Edumu IV. As the emblem in the eyes of his people for ideological and cultural purity, Ellelou can readily accept his function in the interplay of dualities as the "curse upon the land" that occasioned the extended drought while at the same time arguing successfully that if he were to reappear after the coup in a public execution the "counter-counter-revolution would be launched" (301). Living in Nice at the close of the narrative on the comfortable pension provided by the new leadership in Kush in recognition of his symbolic function in the on-going revolution, Ellelou concludes his autobiographical account in his characteristic dualistic mode: *"Those who have gone before them also plotted, but Allah is the master of every plot: He knows the deserts of every soul.* The man is happy, hidden. The sea breeze blows, the waiters ignore him. He is writing his memoirs. No, I should put it more precisely: Colonel Ellelou is rumored to be working on his memoirs" (318).

Although this most recent of Updike's fiction definitely signals his ability to deal with concerns other than those of the American middle class, it is the extension of the moral debate with the reader into larger social and political realities that represents the most drastic change in orientation. The imaginary African nation of Kush is also the scene of ideological warfare between the two superpowers whose headlong pursuit of global domination is not tempered by any recognition that the assumptions upon which their symbolics are constructed are not absolute. The decision by the Soviets to electronically wire the severed head of King Edumu to spout propaganda to tourists is perhaps more absurd but certainly no less brutal in its effects than the American humanitarian gesture of vaccinating cattle, which upsets the ecological balance and brings on the drought. Updike, accused by Norman Mailer and others of xenophobia, could well be on the verge of moving into the broader arena, already occupied by figures like Barth and Pynchon, where the greatest obstacle to our continued survival is the manner in which we use our minds. In future novels by Updike we might expect the force of the true spiritual twin of gravity to be exerted in this larger context in which the activity of artist as architect of alternate constructions of reality is desperately needed.

6 · kurt vonnegut, jr.

In his address to the American Physical Society in 1969 Kurt Vonnegut, Jr., felt obliged to warn his audience that "if you want an outside opinion on your profession, you hired the wrong man. I've had the same formal education you people have had, more or less. I was a chemistry major in college."[1] Vonnegut's formal education in chemistry at Cornell prepared him for a good deal of informal education in physics during the three-year period in which he served as a public relations man for the General Electric research laboratory in Schenectady, New York. The job gave him the opportunity to know, as he put it in a recent interview, "hundreds of first class scientists . . . low temperature guys and crystallographers and electron microscopists and all those guys."[2] Another scientist then working at that laboratory, a cloud physicist with whom Vonnegut has consistently maintained a very close relationship, was his brother Bernard Vonnegut. None of this background is necessary, however, to demonstrate this novelist's fascination with the implications of discoveries made in modern science. References to scientific concepts are, in fact, so pervasive in his work that Vonnegut became for a time, as he puts it, "a soreheaded occupant of a file drawer labeled 'science fiction' " which was not at all comfortable because "many serious critics regularly mistake the drawer for a urinal."[3]

Vonnegut resembles science fiction writers in that he does on occasion play fast and loose with scientific insights to make the unusual or bizarre seem more credible. An understanding of wave phenomena appears, for example, to have inspired the notion in *The Sirens of Titan* of the "chrono-synclastic infundibula" that allows Niles Rumfoord and dog to appear as "one node of a wave phenomenon extending all the way from the Sun to Betelgeuse."[4] The "ice-nine" that destroys the world in *Cat's Cradle* obviously grew out of Vonnegut's knowledge of the bonding properties of liquids in response to changes in temperature. Both the time travel of Billy Pilgrim in *Slaughter House-Five* and the suggestion that the force of gravity can be variable in *Slapstick* owe something to relativity and quantum theories. When most science fiction writers use science in this way, however, the focus is generally not upon problems in metaphysics, but rather upon spectacular effects. Vonnegut is very much a metaphysician who has, as Eliot Rosewater tells the writers attending a science fiction convention in *God Bless You, Mr. Rosewater*, "guts enough to really care about the future, who really notices what machines do to us, what cities do to us, what big, simple ideas do to us, what tremendous misunderstandings, mistakes, accidents and catastrophes do to us."[5]

In an address to the graduating class at Bennington College in 1970, Vonnegut made a statement about the effects of modern scientific discovery upon religion which may at first seem quite odd coming from a writer of contemporary fiction: "A great swindle of our time is the assumption that science has made religion obsolete. All science has damaged is the story of Adam and Eve and the story of Jonah and the Whale. Everything else holds up pretty well, particularly the lessons about fairness and gentleness. People who find those lessons irrelevant in the twentieth century are simply using science as an excuse for greed and harshness." Since Vonnegut earlier in the same speech identified the notion that "humanity is at the center of the universe, the fulfiller or the frustrator of the grandest dreams of God Almighty" as the "most ridiculous superstition of them all,"[6] we might presume that all he really intended was to send those young graduates out into the world fully appreciating abuses of poetic license. Add to this the claim made in another public address that "biochemistry is everything,"[7] and we might be inclined to take seriously another of Vonnegut's more memorable public announcements: "You understand, of course, that everything I say is horseshit."[8] Although Vonnegut takes pleasure in advertising himself as a grossly sentimental muddle-headed idealist, there is, as we shall see, much internal consistency in his thought.

The outlines of the metaphysic that can be traced to ideas from physics begin to emerge clearly in his second novel, *The Sirens of Titan*. After Niles Rumfoord, one of Vonnegut's many scions of the American aristocracy of wealth, pilots his spaceship into the chrono-synclastic infundibula, it comes to him "in a flash that everything that ever has been always will be, and everything that ever will be always has been" (25–26). Perhaps the best way to understand Niles's sudden mystical insight is to consider the parallels between Vonnegut's fantasized space phenomenon and ideas from physics. The chrono-synclastic infundibula which, like a black hole, consumes Niles is an immaterial wave scattered through space-time capable of manifesting or "materializing" the shape of Niles and his dog at certain points in the field. That Vonnegut was drawing upon Einstein's theory that matter is simply a point in the space-time continuum in which the gravitational field is extremely intense seems obvious, but not so apparent is the use made here of Einstein's conception of the relationship between matter and energy. The metaphysical sleight-of-hand trick goes something like this: if all the configurations of matter existing in what we term past, present, and future are manifestations of the energy represented in the equation $E = MC^2$, and if all that energy can be said to fully exist in the now, then Niles is in some sense correct in claiming that "everything that has been always will be, and everything that will be always has been" (25–26). Since energy is never lost but merely transferred, the universe is perpetually full and can never be anything but itself.

Niles's recognition that "all things are one" inspires him to establish a new religion called "The Church of God the Utterly Indifferent" which has only two teachings: "Puny man can do nothing at all to help or please God Almighty, and Luck is not the hand of God" (180). Niles chooses as the prime example that luck is not a feature of any cosmic plan, or that it is simply another name for hazard or accident, the fact that "Malachi Constant was born the richest child on earth" (181). The impossibility of reconciling Judeo-Christian cosmology with the modern scientific view of the cosmos is very much in evidence in the invocation of the Reverend C. Horner Redwine of The Church of God the Utterly Indifferent: "O Lord Most High,

Creator of Galaxies, Soul of Electromagnetic Waves, Inhaler and Exhaler of Inconceivable Volumes of Vacuum, Spitter of Fire and Rock, Trifler with Millennia—what could we do for Thee that Thou couldst not do for Thyself one octillion times better? Nothing" (215). Believing that the "brief period of repentance and horror that usually follows bloodshed" (174) provides the most opportune moment to establish a new religion, Niles arranges for the war between earth and his army from Mars. The next event in this unusual religious "pageant" calls for the "miraculous" appearance of a "space wanderer" (Malachi) who will not remember his own name and yet be able to recite the words sacred to all followers: "I WAS A VICTIM OF A SERIES OF ACCIDENTS, AS ARE WE ALL" (229). This fundamental doctrine of the new religion apparently grew out of Niles's perception after absorption into the chrono-synclastic infundibula that events in the cosmos are a "chaos, and no mistake, for the Universe is just being born. It's the great becoming that makes the light and the heat and the motion, and bangs you from hither and yon" (39). The effects of the indeterminacy principle are, Niles suggests, quite detectable on the macro level as well.

All of which would be well and good if it were not for Niles's ability to fulfill the impossible dream of the Newtonians and predict with absolute certainty that which will occur in the future. When he sets himself up as the head of the new religion, for example, he offers a demonstration of his ability to work miracles by predicting "fifty future events in great detail" (180). His most formidable long-range prediction is that Malachi, Beatrice, and their son Chrono will eventually find themselves residing on Titan, one of the moons of Saturn. What Rumfoord eventually discovers, much to his anger and dismay, is that a civilization of robots called Tralfamadorians had been manipulating human history for thousands of years in order to deliver a piece of metal (Chrono's good-luck piece) necessary for the repair of a spaceship piloted by one of their number named Salo. Seemingly great feats of the human will and imagination like Stonehenge and the Great Wall of China were actually, Niles discovers, messages to Salo from the home planet like: "Replacement part being rushed with all possible speed" (271). Although the advanced technology of the Tralfamadorians is obviously capable of exercising great influence over human beings, Vonnegut makes it clear that the system was not "particularly accurate" (273). There were instances in which entire civilizations struggled to build large structures intended as messages to Salo that "would poop out without having finished the message" (273). Add to this the fact that Salo's ship "accidentally" broke down in the first place and Salo's irrational dismantling of himself after being rejected by Niles, and we realize that the clockwork universe of Newton is not what Vonnegut had in mind.

The moral truth contained in this tale—a basic precept in all the major religions and clearly not contradicted by discoveries made in modern science—is that, as Malachi tells Salo, "a purpose of human life, no matter who is controlling it, is to love whoever is around to be loved" (313). Even the harmoniums on Mercury, creatures shaped like spineless kites with "no more thickness than the skin of a toy balloon" (185), have the need to communicate to one another, "Here I am, here I am, here am I" and to respond, "So glad you are, so glad you are, so glad you are" (186). The immensely more intelligent, technologically advanced robots of Tralfamadore use their enormous resources to travel as far out into the cosmos as possible to deliver a similar although somewhat less emotive message—"Greetings" (301). If, as the quantum theorists suggest, every activity in the cosmos involves and in some sense is every other activity, then love, which intensifies our sense of communion with the other, clearly has its place in natural process.

In *Cat's Cradle* the attempt on the part of a free-lance writer to research the life of one of the fathers of the atomic bomb for his book about the day Hiroshima was bombed (August 6, 1945) eventually carries him to a Caribbean island republic called San Lorenzo. There he encounters a number of practitioners of a new religion called Bokononism whose founder, originally a black man named Lionel Boyd Johnson, is still on the island. The novel is not, as most critics have perceived it, simply a baleful commentary upon Western man's self-destructive commitment to the technology of warfare. It also sets forth a metaphysic entirely consistent with concepts from the new physics. The first sentence of the *Books of Bokonon* reads, " 'All of the true things I am about to tell you are shameless lies.' My Bokononist warning is this: Anyone unable to understand how a useful religion can be founded on lies will not understand this book either. So be it."[9] The new religion is premised, then, upon the now-familiar notion that all so-called truths, religious or scientific, are simply metaphors for a life process that will never be fully described or contained by them. The approximate or relative nature of truth, as Barth suggested earlier, is acceptable because such truths are useful and necessary in providing the conceptual ground or framework for human interaction. The inability of the intellect to represent the world to the individual in its actuality is also made more palatable by the fact that, as Bokonon tells his followers, there is "unity in every second of all time" (55–56). If all the activities in the cosmos are in some sense one activity, as the physicists suggest, the metaphors, fiction, or "lies" evolved by man in his effort to make his experience meaningful are part of that activity.

In virtually all Bokonon's pronouncements we find this same very neat correspondence with ideas from physics. "Busy, busy, busy," the phrase whispered by the Bokononists in recognition of "how complicated and unpredictable the machinery of life really is" (51), implies awareness of the indeterminacy principle. The inevitable tension in all atomic events between positive and negative charges parallels Bokonon's "theory of what he called 'Dynamic Tension,' his sense of a priceless equilibrium between good and evil" (74). Good and evil are not considered by Bokonon as categorical opposites, but rather as poles between one activity like that between him and the president of the Republic. All the wonderfully imaginative terms of the new religion like *karass*, *wampeteer*, *durass*, *duffle*, *stuppa*, and *granfalloon* are clearly intended as metaphors for that which tends to occur, generated by a creature that, as Bokonon puts it, "got to tell himself he understands" (124). The God that Bokonon imagines himself thumbing his nose at in the concluding paragraph of the novel is also metaphor, or, as Bokonon would tell it, just another "foma."

Perhaps we should also note that Dr. Felik Hoenikker made the cat's cradle from which the title of the novel derives for his son Newt from a string wrapped around a novel describing the end of the world (16). As the architect of the atomic bomb and inventor of ice-nine bends down to show the cat's cradle to his son, he invites him to "See? See? See. . . . Cat's cradle. See the cat's cradle? See where the nice pussycat sleeps?" (17). Newt, thoroughly frightened by his father's uncharacteristically playful gesture, comments as an adult: "No wonder kids grow up crazy. A cat's cradle is nothing but a bunch of X's between somebody's hands" (114). This revelation is obviously not worth much unless we remember that the little x's or marks normally created by Dr. Hoenikker are contained in scientific formulas that allowed for the creation of some very formidable implements of destruction. Vonnegut's moral lesson here seems to be that the interrelatedness of all things, which the release of ice-nine into the atmosphere at the close of the narrative rather ironically demonstrates, should make us aware that none of our actions or behaviors are finally isolated from others. There is, then, no such thing as pristine innocence. Scientists like Hoenikker who explore the possibilities of physical interactions in nature as if they were simply playing with some giant puzzle are obviously not to be tolerated.

In *Slaughter House-Five* concepts from the new physics not only provide justification, however slight, for the notion of time travel, but also inform the commentary on the nature of human perception in time. Billy Pilgrim, survivor like Vonnegut of the allied bombing of Dresden (February 13, 1945) and prosperous optometrist in Vonnegut's fictional Illium, New York, learned during his captivity on the planet Tralfamadore that "all moments, past, present, and future, always have existed, always will exist."[10] The same argument used earlier in the discussion of Niles Rumfoord's identical realization upon entering the chrono-synclastic infundibula also serves here. If the energy represented in the equation $E=MC^2$ contains within itself all possibilities for the configuration of matter, then it is conceivable, although certainly not likely, that other aspects of its being configured as other moments in time could somehow be known to us. Vonnegut has, incidentally, made a similar but somewhat different claim in a short essay prepared for the collection of his nonfictional work entitled *Wampeters, Foma & Granfalloons*: "Anybody with any sense knows that the whole solar system will go up like a celluloid collar by-and-by. I honestly believe, though, that we are wrong to think that moments go away, never to be seen again. This moment and every moment lasts forever" (184). Eliminate the notion that materializations at other nodes in space-time are possible, like those of Billy in the novel, and we should have little difficulty from the point of view of modern physics in accepting the feasibility of Vonnegut's remarks.

Virtually all Billy's realizations about the character of life in the universe closely resemble those of Vonnegut's other travelers in space-time. When Billy inquires, for example, of the Tralfamadorians what the ultimate cause or reason for his being chosen for the voyage to their planet might be, their reply is, "Why you? Why us for that matter? Why anything? Because this moment simply is" (76–77). A related bit of Tralfamadorian wisdom also offered in response to Billy's need for explanations is, "All time is all time. It does not change. It does not lend itself to warnings or explanations" (86). The correspondences with the new physics are obvious.

We do find, however, in this novel some fresh applications of ideas from physics in Vonnegut's metaphorical description of the manner in which received conceptions of the nature of time condition our view of experience in time. Since the Tralfamadorians could not begin to imagine what time looked like to Billy in his zoolike enclosure on Tralfamadore, the guide asks the crowd to imagine the earthling's head "encased in a steel sphere which he could never take off. There was only one eyehole through which he could look, and welded to that eyehole were six feet of pipe." Further refinements in the metaphor have Billy strapped to a steel lattice which was bolted to a flatcar on rails, and there was no way to turn his head or touch the pipe. Although the flatcar moves at various speeds, angles, directions, Billy can see only "the little dot at the end of the pipe" (114). The metaphor is appropriate in that most of us continue to conceive of time as a linear progression of events moving in causal fashion from the remembered past into an imagined future. Our tendency is, then, to focus upon the future time, directly in front of us, that metaphorical dot at the end of the pipe, and ignore actual time which is the condition of our being in the space-time complex that is the cosmos. If we could somehow perceive that relationship in time, as the Tralfamadorians apparently can, we would sense our involvement in all space-time and hence our activity as every event (past, present, and future) everywhere in the cosmos.

In *Breakfast of Champions*, $E=MC^2$ is boldly scrawled in the middle of a page late in the narrative followed by the authorial comment that, "It was a flawed equation, as far as I was concerned. There should have been an 'A' in there somewhere for *Awareness*— without which the 'E' and the 'M' and the 'C,' which was a mathematical constant, could not exist."[11] If all conceptions of the nature of reality are, as the new physics suggests, subjectively based constructs, then it is, indeed, our awareness of this equation, or any idea for that matter, which makes for its existence. Human awareness, or more accurately the imaginative faculty that creates the ideas that make that awareness possible, is the subject under investigation in *Breakfast of Champions*. It is this awareness, Vonnegut suggests, that spares us from being simply "huge, rubbery test tubes . . . with chemical reactions seething inside." "Bad chemicals and bad ideas . . . the Yin and Yang of madness" (14) can, as we see most graphically in the case of successful businessman Dwayne Hoover, result in behavior over which the individual has no conscious, rational control.

And yet the imaginative act as another condition of awareness is not only capable of creating Dwayne and all other characters in the narrative, it can make a novelist a character in his own fiction. While Dwayne is en route to the cocktail lounge in the Holiday Inn from which he will shortly emerge as a one-man riot, the narrator indicates that the "Black and White and water" that has just been ordered "wasn't for any ordinary person. . . . That drink was for me" (192). When Dwayne is finally subdued after doing considerable damage to both person and property, the narrator notes that he "came out of the riot with a broken watch crystal and what turned out later to be a broken toe" (274). As a final demonstration of the power of the imagination to make and transform the world of experience, Vonnegut appears before a dismayed Kilgore Trout, the science-fiction writer whose own bizarre works of the imagination loom large in many of Vonnegut's earlier narratives, and transports him to the "Taj Mahal and then to Venice and then to Dar es Salaam and then to the surface of the Sun, where the flames did not consume him—and then back to Midland City again" (292). Vonnegut is not simply stepping out from the blind of his fiction and revealing himself as narrator, which is after all a gambit he has used many times before, but also affirming the possibility of freedom in a cosmos in which indeterminacy makes imaginative choice a possibility.

It is clear in *Breakfast of Champions*, as it is in virtually everything Vonnegut has written, that the major problem of Americans is that they lack the communal ethos necessary to sense that they fully belong to and participate in a culture. He elaborates further upon this position in this novel, however, by suggesting that one of the major sources of that dilemma is that Americans attempt to "live like people in story books." It is the storyteller who is responsible for making "people believe that life had leading characters, minor characters, significant details, insignificant details, that it had lessons to be learned, tests to be passed, and a beginning, middle and end" (209). The painful result of exposure to such fiction is that Americans have come to believe that America is a "dangerous, unhappy nation of people who had nothing to do with real life." Vonnegut resolves to "shun storytelling" in this sense and "write about life. Every person would be exactly as important as any other. All facts would also be given equal weightiness. Nothing would be left out. Let others bring order to chaos. I would bring chaos to order, instead, which I think I have done." The effect of this fiction, says Vonnegut, would be to convince his readers that "there is no order in the world around us, that we must adapt to the chaos instead" (210). Underlying the several layers of irony usual in his more serious statements, readers discover here a view of the nature and function of art that closely resembles that perceived earlier in the fiction of Barth and Fowles. In addition to asserting that reality is a product of the human imagination and is perpetually transformed by it, Vonnegut suggests that it is the duty of the artist to break Americans of the habit of attempting to order experience in terms of the old cosmology present in the work of "old-fashioned" storytellers. He pledges himself to write fiction that is *like* his understanding of the character of life in that it is not premised upon a belief in the hierarchy of being and makes no suggestion that a rational scheme or design is at work in experience. The artist, in training Americans to adapt to the requirements of chaos, is not inviting them to despair, but rather to begin to divest themselves of habits of mind which Vonnegut clearly believes distort their relationships to themselves and to the environment.

In *Player Piano* and *Mother Night* a metaphysic derived from the new physics can also be seen at work but without the dramatic, clearly distinguishable effects witnessed in the narratives we have already discussed. The most visible emblem of the overly structured, terribly mechanized society in *Player Piano* is a computer system called EPICAC XIV. The system is described by the one-time actor who is now "acting" as President of the United States as "being dead right about everything,"[12] and the "greatest individual in history" (119). The novel makes the obvious point that the human need for meaning and relatedness is not satisfied simply by meeting the needs of individuals through advanced technology, but it is also significant from our point of view that this system, like all technologies in Vonnegut's novels, is flawed. It is not simply that the computer is unable to deal with the paradox and ambiguity that is a rather large factor in the human equation (e.g., its inability to answer the ancient riddle posed by the Shah of Bratpurh); it also is not terribly efficient in supplying the "transducer" necessary to repair the ultrasonic washer in the home of the statistically average American Edgar R. B. Hagstrohm. The decision by the computer to rescind the doctoral degree of the American diplomat Ewing Halyard because he failed to meet a physical education requirement in undergraduate school, which presumes a linear causal connection between segments of the educational process, also points up the absurdity of relying too greatly on such technologies. Underlying all this is the suggestion that the essentially open-ended or indeterminate character of all natural process, which includes the actual functioning of the computer, will always disallow the prospect that human activity can be entirely subsumed by completely efficient systems of social control.

The title of *Mother Night*, as Vonnegut takes care to explain in the introduction, comes from a speech in Goethe's *Faust* in which Mephistopheles identifies himself with the primal darkness and longs for its return. Howard W. Campbell, the American-born writer who becomes an undercover spy in Germany during World War II, notes in the dedication to his "Confessions" that he was a man "who served evil too openly and good too secretly, the crime of his times."[13] The narrative itself, however, reveals that Campbell's crime is not so easily delineated. Frank Wirtanen, the American intelligence officer who convinces Campbell to become an undercover spy, knows how to make the job attractive to him. Based upon Campbell's plays, Wirtanen has realized "that you [Campbell] admire pure hearts and heroes. . . . That you love good and hate evil . . . and that you believe in romance" (41). On another occasion Campbell tells Wirtanen that, "I admire form . . . I admire things with a beginning, a middle, and end—and, whenever possible, a moral, too" (136). Believing that abstractions like *good* and *evil* have real existence as categorical opposites that compete with and dominate one another, Campbell plays the role of American Nazi propagandist in service of the *good* with an all-too-convincing zeal and dedication. For reasons that he does not begin to comprehend, Campbell is guilty of the crime that the government of Israel has charged him with—"Complicity in the murder of six million Jews"

(110). The morality of our action is not, as Campbell wishes it to be, a feature of some cosmic design with a "beginning, middle, and end," but rather the sum, as Sartre suggested, of our activity or the mode of our being. The Adolf Eichmann with whom Campbell is imprisoned, who is also significantly writing memoirs for publication, is, of course, a prime historical example of debased human nature, and yet the broad outlines of Eichmann's philosophical perspective resemble Campbell's in every detail. Like Bernard O'Hare, whose one act of heroism was capturing Campbell at the end of World War II, both Campbell and Eichmann are capable of believing in "absolutely pure evil" (180) which, as Campbell himself rightly observes, is "that part of every man that wants to hate without limit, that wants to hate with God on its side. . . . It's that part of an imbecile . . . that punishes and vilifies and makes war gladly" (181).

The only critic to my knowledge who has talked specifically at any length about the influence of concepts from the new physics upon Vonnegut's fiction is John Somer. Although I cannot agree with Somer's suggestion that exposure to these concepts convinced Vonnegut that it is "impossible for man to initiate himself, to be reborn, to lose himself in the phenomenological world," I entirely agree with his claim that exposure encouraged Vonnegut to bid us "to synchronize our rational awareness of punctual time with our intuitive loving of (what Henri Bergson calls) pure duration, to create . . . an illusion of reality in which we can immerse and lose our ego."[14] The written communications of the Tralfamadorians in *Slaughter House-Five*—whose relationship to time, as we discussed earlier, is very like that Somer describes—consist of "clumps of symbols" each of which is "a brief, urgent message—describing a situation, a scene." Tralfamadorians "read them all at once, not one after the other. There isn't any particular relationship between all the messages, except that the author has chosen them carefully, so that, when seen all at once, they produce an image of life that is beautiful, surprising and deep." The messages also have "no beginning, no middle, no end, no suspense, no moral, no causes, no effects. What we love in our books are the depths of many marvelous moments seen all at one time" (88). Add to this Vonnegut's comment in an interview that his books are "essentially mosaics made up of a whole bunch of tiny little chips" (15), and we might begin to suspect that novelist and Tralfamadorians are not too many light years distant from one another.

Although Vonnegut's fiction has always tended to read like messages from Tralfamadore, the use of short passages and crude illustrations—both of which serve as clumps of symbols—that are not ordered in the Newtonian sense becomes increasingly more pronounced beginning with the publication of *Slaughter House-Five*. It is, I think, clearly Vonnegut's hope that these scattered clumps will not only eventually cohere in the mind of the reader to produce an "image of life that is beautiful, surprising and deep," but also that the experience will convince us of the possibility of knowing the "depths of many marvelous moments seen all at once" (88). In terms of the metaphysic derived by Vonnegut from the new physics, that moment allows us to sense communion with the alpha and omega of all being which *is* every conceivable moment in time.

7 · THOMAS PYNCHON

At Cornell University, where Thomas Pynchon first won a scholarship to study engineering physics and later took a degree in English, one of his professors "wonderingly remembers his apparently voracious appetite for the complexities of elementary particle theory."[1] Although many critics, some of whom have written articles with titles that would seem to belong in the pages of *Scientific American*, have speculated upon the manner in which concepts from physics function as aspects of Pynchon's bizarre fictional landscape, we have yet to appreciate how pervasive such concepts are in the determination of both design and meaning in all his novels. The implications of discoveries made in the new physics are not merely the source of new ideas which Pynchon incorporates into a traditional novelistic framework; they are rather the basis for a radically new conception of the nature of human identity and societal organization, which Pynchon has chosen to express in a highly appropriate but nevertheless extremely problematic narrative mode.

Known to devour complicated treatises in math and physics at one sitting for "fun," Pynchon's acquaintance with ideas from the new physics is formidable, and he is also, as I shall try to demonstrate, quite sensitive to their implications in human terms. It is now a well-established convention in Pynchon criticism to comment that every particular in his narratives interrelates and interconnects with every other particular, but it is not frequently observed that out of that vast interplay of dynamic particulars we do not arrive at that sense of "meaning" we expect to be a consequence of reading highly structured narratives. The patterns or designs that emerge in a careful study of Pynchon's novels tend toward closure, toward that final point of logical connection that would allow us to fix relationships and draw conclusions, but he almost invariably refuses to make those final connections. The analytically trained critic ferrets out a network of antinomies, polar oppositions, either-or configurations in the hope of discovering deep structure and hidden meaning, but the fictions will simply not be contained by such coordinate systems.

Pynchon's acute awareness that the forms resident in our subjective realities are ill-equipped to describe or contain reality itself is probably best illustrated in the title of this first novel. Critics still continue to catalog the repetitions of v's in V. in what is obviously a very frustrating attempt to uncover a closed system of relation. Pynchon's confidence trick on the literary critic, a species of humanity he clearly has very little use for,[2] was to select from the alphabet—that system of characters we use to represent or configure our written transcriptions of the real—the letter which is nicely illustrative of what Pynchon considers to be one of our more invidious habits of mind. V. (note the period) as figure is a beautiful parody of either-or categorical thinking in that the seeming oppositions in the trajectory of the lines can be traced to and in some sense exist in the point of connection which is their base. It is no accident, of course, that the one character in the novel who most assiduously seeks to impose either-or configurations on the tissue of events, Sidney Stencil (note the play on mimesis in the last name), drowns in a whirlpool in the closing paragraph of the novel.

A more accessible statement on the delimiting effects of the either-or is found in *The Crying of Lot 49*. Oedipa Maas recalls viewing a painting in Mexico City which is described in the following manner:

... in the central painting of a triptych, titled "Bordando el Manto Terrestre" [Embroidering the Cloak of Earth] were a number of frail girls with heart-shaped faces, huge eyes, spun-gold hair, prisoners in the top room of a circular tower, embroidering a kind of tapestry which spilled out the slip windows into a void, seeking hopelessly to fill the void: for all the other buildings and creatures, all the waves, ships and forests of the earth were contained in this tapestry, and the tapestry was the world.[3]

On one level the passage is a nice metaphoric description of

Oedipa's plight in the novel as she traces the seeming connections in Inverarity's vast business empire and struggles to believe that her perceptions of its design are actual and not merely symptomatic of growing paranoia. Pynchon offers, however, an additional comment on the following page which makes his motive for metaphor a good deal more obvious: "Having no apparatus except gut fear and female cunning to examine this formless magic, to understand how it works, how to measure its field strength, count its lines of force, she may fall back on superstition, or take up a useful hobby like embroidery, or go mad, or marry a disk jockey. If the tower is everything, and the knight of deliverance is no proof against its magic, what else?" (11).

To understand all lines of force within a force field is, in the view of contemporary physics, an impossibility because to do that would require a knowledge of all events occurring simultaneously in the cosmos. More important, the tower, or the world-constructing mind of the individual, is not "everything," and an acceptance of its limitations, which Oedipa in part at least acquires, is entirely necessary in order to negotiate the world of experience as Pynchon sees it. Paranoia in Pynchon's fiction is not, as some critics have claimed, a viable mode of self-protection in the face of societal breakdown and the demise of controlling symbolics—it is simply the last tower retreat of the individual whose mental tapestry has displaced all sense of relatedness to the human community.

Any critic who chooses to tackle all *Gravity's Rainbow* in one chapter is either terribly ambitious or very foolish or both. The novel is encyclopedic in scope, not unlike Joyce's *Ulysses*, and will doubtless preoccupy critics of the modern novel for many years to come. What I will do here is suggest that the key to an improved understanding of this massive fiction may well be concepts from the new physics, and to indicate some of the directions in which we might move to explore their applications.

The preface—taken from the writings of one of those architects of the rocket technology which could serve to obliterate us all at any moment—is not to be taken without some sense of irony, but it also provides some useful insights into the design and meaning of *Gravity's Rainbow*: "Nature does not know extinction; all it knows is transformation. Everything science has taught me, and continues to teach me, strengthens my belief in the continuity of spiritual existence after death (Werner von Braun)."[4] If von Braun is reading from

138

the new book on nature, and I presume he is, he is quite right in saying that nature undergoes unceasing transformations, and, if the big-
bang theorists are correct, will continue to evolve out of itself new
modes of being. Further, if mass is a form of energy, and if all particles function in terms of and in some sense are all other particles,
there is a continuity in all natural process which includes us even if a
particular configuration of molecular activity (*self*) ceases to be. If
von Braun's deity is like that of Whitehead, the never-finished becoming of nature's process,[5] there is continuity in our spiritual existence after death as well. Pynchon, whose sense of deity definitely
resembles that of Whitehead, provides in the novel seemingly endless
demonstrations of the fact that Western man has great difficulty accepting this new metaphysic because his tendency to impose either-
or categorical systems on the fluid process of life mitigates against
that acceptance.

The following is a description contained in the novel of the
structure of *Gravity's Rainbow*:

No, this is not a disentanglement from, but a progressive *knotting into*—they
go under archways, secret entrances of rotten concrete that only looked like
loops of underpass . . . certain trestles of blackened wood have moved slowly
by overhead, and the smells of coal from days far to the past, smells of naph-
tha winters, of Sundays when no traffic came through, of the coral-like and
mysteriously vital growth, around the blind curves and out the lonely spurs, a
sour smelling of rolling-stock absence, of maturing rust, developing through
those emptying days brilliant and deep, especially at dawn, with blue shadows to seal its passage, to try to bring events to Absolute Zero. (3–4).

As any anthropologist knows, the human environment in large
part is a creation of the human intellect and reflects the forms resident in man's mind. The world that is not ourselves is the mystery,
the void, which we seek to fill up and contain with mental constructs.
The characters in *Gravity's Rainbow* move through man-made constructions, the archways and underpasses that are extensions of the
forms in their minds, but they inevitably encounter the "mysteriously vital growth," the unknown and unknowable in natural process.
The major characters, with the exception of Slothrop at one crucial
point, weave lines of linear connection between people, events, and
circumstances in an effort to obviate the framing process itself by

encompassing and transcending its most basic principle of organization—the either-or. The knotting process, the novel, becomes a kind of Gordian knot which must be cut through by intuition because it cannot be untied by logical analysis alone. The tangled web of the various narrative lines becomes finally Pynchon's way of demonstrating that all systems of analysis, or all closed symbolics, predicated on absolutes lead ultimately to a state of confusion and chaos within which the alienation of the individual is an inevitability. The frequent references in the novel to Goedel's Theorem, which states that we cannot prove any logical system does not contain contradictions in its basic precepts because to prove the system correct we must get outside of it, are also indicative of Pynchon's bias against the Western mode of valuation and truth seeking.

Events in the novel would arrive at absolute zero in a metaphoric sense if the rocket at the close of the narrative had exploded over the Orpheus movie house in Los Angeles, but the rocket does not explode. It reaches, says the narrator, the "last immeasurable gap about the roof of this old theater, the last ΔT" (887). In order to understand what Pynchon means by absolute zero we must comprehend the use of the Δt in the logistics of rocket technology. The Greek letter Δ represents in calculus infinitesimals, and the Δt is a mathematical notation for units of time used to plot the range and trajectory of a rocket in flight. The following is Joseph Slade's admirable attempt to explain the function of the Δt in lay terms:

Here the parabola is sliced up by integrals from a base line stretched between the rocket's point of firing and its point of impact. Those lines are artificial and arbitrary. Along the parabola itself an infinite number of lines can be drawn, and each two of them—as double integrals—bound a moment in time, relative of course to distance. As the rocket moves along its path, and as it passes these artificial divisions, it has passed through a change in time—designated by the Δt. Theoretically, precisely because the number of divisions can be extended infinitely, the rocket can be said to be poised in the sky ("The Perfect Rocket is still up there, still descending" [426], approaching final zero in an asymptotic—approaching but never reaching infinity—curve, like Zeno's famous arrow).[6]

Another aspect of the parabolic shape of the rocket's flight which serves to explain the notion of absolute zero is that if we bisect a parabola each side perfectly mirrors the other. The rocket becomes a kind of universal icon for several characters and groups in the novel

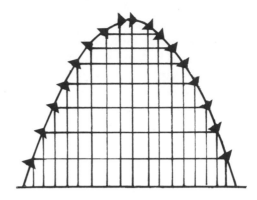

because it appears in flight to reconcile polarities or to unify opposi-tions in approaching absolute zero. Absolute zero is, then, for the rocket worshippers the point of transcendence which takes up into itself all discrepant particulars—it symbolizes the alpha and omega of all being.

What Pynchon has done here with dreadful mastery is to give us a graphic illustration, in terms of our most advanced and lethal tech-nology, of a mode of constructing reality which in his view mitigates against our proper sense of relation to the whole. Since the rocket worshippers frame out experience in closed systems and symbolics, they arbitrarily fragment (put into time frames) their vision of them-selves and others. In the effort to arrive at closure of the system or symbolic, the ultimate $\triangle t$ which is absolute zero, they must deal with all particulars in terms of oppositions, either-or categories, in the hope that all such antinomies will resolve themselves into unity at the final point of transcendence. In physics, as Pynchon knows very well, entropy, a quantity related to the number of accessible quan-tum states available to a system, will tend toward the greatest num-ber of states when the system is isolated. This results in a decrease in the amount of energy available for work as well as more disorder among the atoms in the system. Since characters in a Pynchon novel function, as many critics have noted, in terms of their interrelated-ness or interconnectedness to other characters, we can safely con-clude that he feels that individuals do not in actuality live in isolated systems. The concept of entropy is rather Pynchon's metaphor for our compulsion to construct and maintain closed, isolated systems which induces a sense of dislocation and fragmentation in relation to the whole.

What the rocket worshippers in the novel fail to understand is the nature of the force of gravity. If the resistance of any object to acceleration is a measure of its interaction with the rest of the cosmos, then the rocket at rest in its gravitational field is just as close to absolute zero as the rocket at its highest point of trajectory in flight. What Pynchon implies here in his treatment of the rocket worshippers is that irreconcilable polarities and oppositions are fictions of the mind which have no real existence in nature. Our effort to transcend them to reach the absolute is simply a product of our failure to realize we are at absolute zero without making any effort at all in the sense that our participation in the life of the entire cosmos is a given.

The most pervasive presence in *Gravity's Rainbow* is not a character but an organization or system. The "Firm," controlled by "They," is a vast network of corporations and cartels, like General Electric, Shell, Siemens, I. G. Farben, and Standard Oil. It appears not only to be more powerful than any national government but to manipulate all of them in its own interests. The Firm's authority, as Slade notes, "stems from classical physics, which does rest on cause and effect relationships between forces and objects."[7] The system controlled by They apparently originated after one Kekule von Stradonitz dreamed of an uroborus, saw some uses that could be made of that conceptual form in researching new chemical properties, and gave up his architectural profession to pursue them. In a crucial passage in the novel Pynchon's narrator describes the results in this way:

The Serpent that announces, "The World is a closed thing, cyclical, resonant, eternally returning," is to be delivered into a system whose aim is to violate the cycle. Taking and not giving back, demanding that "productivity" and "earnings" keep on increasing with time, the System removing from the rest of the World those vast quantities of energy to keep its own tiny desperate fraction showing a profit: and not only most of humanity—most of the World, animal, vegetable and mineral, is laid waste in the process. The System may or may not understand that *it's* only buying time. And that time is an artificial resource to begin with, of no value to anyone or anything but the System, which sooner or later must crash to its death, when its addiction to energy has become more than the rest of the World can supply, dragging along with it innocent souls all along the chain of life. (480–81)

The Firm's desire to maintain and extend control over other systems leads to more research into the life of nature in the hope of discovering principles that would allow them to produce more salable technologies and consumer goods—the most important of which are Imipolex G and the rocket. In doing such research, however, the Firm discovers that there are principles in the life of nature which call into question the efficacy of simple causality, hierarchical organization, and closed systems. The inventor of Imipolex G, the mysterious Jamf who did the operant conditioning research on the infant Slothrop, recognizes, for example, that relativity theory has moral implications. In a lecture attended by Pokler, Jamf counsels his students to stay in touch with their lion, his term for their aggressive, territorial instincts: "The lion does not know subtleties and half-solutions. He does not accept sharing as a basis for anything! He takes, he holds! He is not a Bolshevik or a Jew. You will never hear relativity from the lion. He wants the absolute. Life and Death. Win and lose" (673).

As long as individuals continue to see themselves as discrete and separate entities who must dominate or submit to the domination of others in the ruthless struggle for power, the Firm will maintain its control. At the close of another lecture, Jamf encourages his students to " 'move beyond life, toward the inorganic. Here is no frailty, no mortality—here is Strength and the Timeless.' Then his well-known finale, as he whipped the scrawled C-H on his chalkboard and wrote, in enormous letters, Si-N" (676). A commitment to things, to rampant materialism with the concomitant concern with systems of exchange and distribution, is, Jamf gleefully proclaims, an immoral act. Max Weber, whom Pynchon quotes in the narrative, explains why this is the case. The rationalization of our efforts to impose design and pattern on all transactions within the human community easily develops into an irreversible process which depersonalizes and objectifies individuals.[8]

Enzian, who is probably the best spokesman in the novel for Pynchon's views on materialism and technocracy, perceives that the real crises during the war "were crises of allocation and priority, not among firms—it was only staged to look that way—but among the different Technologies, Plastics, Electronics, Aircraft, and their needs which are understood by the ruling elite" (607). If you deify technology, Enzian continues, "it'll make you feel less responsible, but it puts you in the neutered, brother, in with the eunuchs keeping the harem of our stolen Earth for the numb and joyless hardons of human sultans, human elites with no right at all to be where they are" (607). The enemy in *Gravity's Rainbow* is not the ruthless romantic individualism of totalitarian and/or fascist dictators, but rather the ruthless romantic individualism of all leaders, including the Marxists, who dominate through closed systems and symbolics in the name of material well-being. All the other forms of romantic idealism, Pynchon implies, simply serve the interests of such leaders.

The two most ardent devotees to romantic individualism in the novel are Weissman-Blicero and the Hereros Enzian, both of whom are utterly taken with the concept of absolute zero and see the rocket as symbol, or icon, for transcendence of polarities. Virtually all Blicero's thoughts and actions are motivated by his passion to attain the absolute through transcendence of opposites. His imaginatively perverse sexual encounters with Katje, Gottfried (God's peace), and Enzian, his love of Rilke's "Tenth Elegy" (an intensely romantic poem celebrating the impossible union of the actual and ideal) are all manifestations of the desire, as he tells Gottfried, "to leave the cycle of infection and death. I want to be taken in love: so taken that you and I, and death, and life, will be gathered inseparably, into the radiance of what we would become" (844).

Enzian, whose passion to transcend polarities features a curious form of redemption for the Hereros, wants to create a condition in which the "people will find the Center again, the Center without time, the journey without hysteresis, where every departure is a return to the same place, the only place" (370). Since the rocket, says the scientifically minded Enzian, "embraces all deviations in one single act" (271), it symbolizes, like the mandalic form of the Herero village, the union of all seeming oppositions, the ultimate congruence of all either-ors. One might speculate here that Enzian's native mysticism should allow him to accept more readily the implication of the new physics, but, as Pynchon makes clear, Europe came to Africa and "established its order of Analysis and Death" (842). Mandalas in mystical traditions, generally used as meditation devices, are not considered to be transcriptions of nature but rather constructs of the mind. Infected by the Western analytical tradition, Enzian thinks in terms of irreconcilable oppositions that can only be annihilated through a physical event—death. He is, in other words, a thoroughly Western thinker like Blicero.

Pokler is another character manipulated by the Firm in the production of Rocket 00000, but he is more representative of the manner in which the majority of us deal with systems we cannot ultimately affect or understand. Pokler is particularly useful to the Firm because he has technical knowledge of advanced scientific concepts, but continues to construct his subjective reality in essentially Newtonian terms. He is the "cause-and-effect man" (186) who presumes that there is a certain inevitability in a chain of events which precludes radical decision making. As he sits at the very center of the target area during a rocket test, which was the safest place to be because the chances "are astronomically against a perfect hit," Pokler cannot help thinking of "all tolerances of the guidance cooperating toward a perfect shot" (496). In an attempt to convince his wife Leni that astrological predictions have no merit Pokler asserts that no one system can produce a change in any other. To this Leni replies, "Not Produce . . . not cause. It all goes along together. Parallel, not series. Metaphor. Signs and Symptoms. Mapping on to different coordinate systems, I don't know" (186). Since Pokler as a rationalist is incapable of intuiting that all human activity is interconnected and also that much of that activity is irrationally motivated, the designs of the Firm make no sense to him. Even though he has cause to wonder that the Ilse whom Blicero allows him to see two weeks a year in payment for his work on the rocket might not be the same person from one year to the next, Pokler insists, finally, upon a causal connection between the images of a daughter passing before him and assumes they make up a single identity.

One of the more interesting of the Firm's innovations is the White Visitation and its related intelligence-gathering agencies. Aware of the implications of the new physics, and, consequently, of the limits of rationality, the Firm maintains at "a disused hospital for the mad, a few token lunatics, an enormous pack of stolen dogs, cliques of spiritualists, vaudeville entertainers, wireless technicians. Couéists, Ouspenskians, Skinnerites, lobotomy enthusiasts, Dale Carnegie zealots, all exiled by the outbreak of war from pet schemes and manias damned" (89). The Firm studies such people in an incredible variety of ways in an apparent attempt to discover heretofore unknown processes in nature that will allow them to extend their control over individuals.

The Firm's first director of the White Visitation, General Pudding, believed in "a literal Chain of Command, as clergymen of earlier centuries believed in the Chain of Being" (88). The second, who assumes control covertly, is another either-or thinker with a Newtonian world view. The determinist Dr. Pointsman (whose name means switchman on the railroad in British slang) selects as his sacred text Pavlov's *Letters to Pierre Janet*, and his principal object of study is Tyrone Slothrop. Pavlov was, says the narrator, "fascinated with 'ideas of the opposite.' Call it a cluster of cells, somewhere in the cortex of the brain. Helping to distinguish pleasure from pain, light from dark, dominance over submission" (55). When the idea of the opposite is weakened, Pavlov speculated, the individual enters an "ultraparadoxical phase" which is the condition of mental illness in all its manifestations. Since Slothrop's chance sexual encounters in London, the last location of which he "symbolizes" on a map, coincide with the location of the next German rocket strike after a "mean lag" of "about 4½ days" (99), Slothrop appears to be able to effect a reversal of cause and effect. Pointsman's hypothesis is that Slothrop is capable of a "transmarginal leap" in which "ideas of the opposite have come together, and lost their oppositeness" (57).

The irony is that Pointsman is correct in asserting that Slothrop is capable of such transmarginal leaps, but his capacity to do so does not account for his seeming ability to predict target areas nor is it in any sense a sign of mental disturbance. Another character, Roger Mexico, also predicts the location of strikes, but his method is scientific. Roger uses a Poisson distribution equation, a mathematical system dealing in probabilities of occurrence in the "domain of zero to one" (63), which discloses the overall pattern of strikes but not the precise location of any one strike. As Roger explains to the dismayed determinist Pointsman: "Every square is just as likely to get hit again. The mean hits aren't clustering. Mean density is constant" (63).

Although the odds against Slothrop predicting the precise location of even one strike are astronomical, anyone familiar with the new physics should know that Slothrop's chance sexual encounters are no more predictive of precise target locations than Mexico's probability equations. We could assume that the Firm has arranged for the correspondence by following Slothrop's movements and arranging a strike at the location of his last sexual liaison, but that does not seem likely since the chances of engineering a direct hit are, as we saw in our discussion of Pokler, miniscule. What was overlooked by all the researchers who attempt to explain the correspondence is that Slothrop's behavior does not allow prediction of the precise "time" of the rocket strike. If space and time are one dimension, then we must conclude, no matter how incredible the circumstance, that it is only chance or hazard that makes the patterns on the maps of Slothrop and Mexico identical.

Critics in growing numbers have driven themselves to distraction looking for logical connections which would allow for a rational explanation for this "ambiguity" in the novel. (It is probably the most sardonic trick Pynchon has played on his analytically minded readers to date.) The clues are everywhere, but there is again that gap in logical, linear connections which precludes closure. Slothrop has early connections with the Firm through his Uncle Bland, and his education at Harvard was paid for by the Firm in return for allowing the infant Slothrop to be experimented upon by Jamf. The "Conditioned stimulus$=X$" (97) which Jamf used to evoke the hardon response could be, it is suggested at various points, sound, light, German technical language, and the smell of Imipolex G. There is even some suggestion that the penis which Slothrop thought to be his own is made of Imipolex G, a substance which has "erectile" properties. Perhaps telepathic communication exists between Slothrop and Katje who tells him in lowered voice, "you were in London . . . while they were coming down. I was in Gravenhage . . . while they were going up" (243). Or, ignoring the clues and opting for the simplest explanation, we might conclude that Slothrop is capable of precognition.

What Pynchon has done here, with a vengeance some may fail to appreciate, is to provide another of his demonstrations that the Newtonian world view, which features along with the Western mind itself either-or categorical thinking, simple causality, immutable law, determinism, and discrete immutable substance, is not a viable mode of dealing with experience. The Firm in *Gravity's Rainbow* is Pynchon's way of advertising the dangers on the social, political, and economic levels of continuing to frame out experience in this fashion. The consequence on the level of subjective experience are the usual afflictions of Pynchon's characters—alienation and paranoia.

The way in which to counter this seemingly inexorable movement toward the abyss is, Pynchon suggests, a radical change in our sense of relation to the external environment. The key to understanding how such an assertion is made in *Gravity's Rainbow* is much the same as the key to understanding Pynchon's intentions in his first novel—it is a letter, or in the case of his last novel a scientific notation as well, read as figure. The X as it is used in the description of Jamf's experiment on Slothrop is the unknown stimulus, but it is also an intersection of lines. Slothrop is clearly the nexus through which the knotting-into process of narrative lines cross or connect, but there is another sense of connectedness at work in the novel of much greater importance. The effect of gravity on light traveling unimpeded through the cosmos is to bend it into a trajectory, which we now recognize as the symbol of eternity, until it travels back to precisely its point of departure—the X, if you will, as the place of launch and target area become one. When we last see Slothrop in the novel he is looking up at gravity's rainbow: "and now, in the zone, later in the day he became a crossroad, after a heavy rain he doesn't recall, Slothrop sees a very thick rainbow here, a stout rainbow cock driven down out of pubic clouds into Earth, green valleyed Earth, and his chest fills and he stands crying, not a thing in his head, just feeling natural . . . " (729). The sense of communion which is only hinted at here in Slothrop's vision of the lovemaking of earth and sky is made more explicit at the close of the novel. Having placed his reader in a movie theater about to be annihilated by nuclear energy, Pynchon instructs us all to sing a hymn written by Tyrone's ancestor William:

> There is a Hand to turn the time,
> Though thy Glass today be run,
> Till the Light that hath brought the Towers low
> Find the last poor pret'rite one . . .
> Till the Riders sleep by ev'ry road,
> And through our crippl'd Zone,
> With a face on ev'ry mountainside,
> And a Soul in ev'ry stone. . . . (887)

If we take the hymn out of an eighteenth-century context and read it as another of those interconnected fragments of this fiction, we arrive at some fruitful speculations. If *Hand* is a reference to the God of Whitehead, whom I have already identified as the God of Pynchon as well, then time is quite literally turned in the space-time continuum by the Being which is identical with the process of all nature's becoming. The *Light*, or energy, that can in nuclear explosion bring down a world constructed in terms of closed symbolics (*Towers*) is the same light, or energy, which could allow the *preterite*, Pynchon's term for one controlled by the elect or the system's managers, to sense his oneness with the cosmos. If that were the case the *Riders*, the carriers of information which allows the system to perpetuate itself, would sleep, and a zone, like that in the novel, would emerge in which the possibility of free election exists because the controlling symbolics or systems are not in force. It is then that a holistic vision is possible—a sense of relation which breaks down the barriers between self and world ("a face on ev'ry mountainside"), and reveals all that which seemed inanimate (*stone*) as alive with a force and spirit that is also ourselves. "Now everybody—" sing (887).

8 · TOM ROBBINS

Although the fiction of Tom Robbins may not yet appear on the syllabi of many surveys of contemporary literature, his novels seem to have something like the same following among college students as the fiction of Barth or Pynchon did before they became fully legitimated as makers of elitist art. It is interesting from our point of view, however, that concepts from physics, which are for the most part implicit as structuring principles in the art of the more established novelists, are treated in the fiction of this relative newcomer as concerns that must be reckoned with openly. Robbins boldly assumes his reader's familiarity with the fundamental precepts of the new physics and proceeds to explore their metaphysical implications as if that were the inevitable consequence of confrontation with these new ideas. (It is also significant that Pynchon, whose public statements outside his own novels are almost nonexistent, was moved to write a letter describing *Even Cowgirls Get the Blues* as "a piece of working magic, warm, funny and sane" shortly after reading an advance copy.)

Another unique aspect of Robbins's fiction relating to physics is the recognition that the unitary conception of being in the great religious philosophies of the East (Hinduism, Buddhism, Taoism) is far more compatible with discoveries made in the new physics than the dualistic Western model. As Fritjof Capra nicely demonstrates in a book particularly useful to those seriously interested in Robbins's work, the Eastern emphasis upon the unity and interrelatedness of all things in a cosmos that is forever moving, alive, and organic is rather strikingly close to the understanding of the life process implied in the new physics.[1] Although Robbins is aware of the correspondences and frequently takes note of them, he is clearly not advocating that the spiritually impoverished West take the first boat, metaphorically or otherwise, to the spiritually enlightened East. Even if such a dramatic restructuring of Western consciousness were desirable, it is not, as Robbins makes clear in *Cowgirls*, a possibility. The backlog of inherited culture is simply too great, as Barth suggested in *Giles*, to effect such a transformation within any of our lifetimes. Robbins's intent rather is to hammer away relentlessly at those assumptions about self and world in Western cosmology which he feels are injurious to our emotional well-being and a threat to our continued survival as a species.

The narrator of *Another Roadside Attraction*, a whiz kid who once dreamed of "becoming a great theoretical physicist on the order of Werner Heisenberg or Einstein,"[2] describes in an admittedly "indeterminate" fashion the wonderfully bizarre happenings in the life of Amanda and John Paul Ziller and their zany partner in the greatest heist in any century—Plucky Purcell. Marx Marvelous, as the narrator elects to call himself for a variety of interesting reasons, notes that it was exposure to Heisenberg's Uncertainty Principle that caused him to realize that "every system that science proposed was a product of human imagination," and also that "much scientific truth proved to be as hypothetical as religious allegory" (215). Recognizing that his investigations into pure science, abstract mathematics, and theoretical physics "frequently led him into areas of thought he could only describe as . . . metaphysical," and perceiving some basic similarities between the "mental processes of religion and pure science" he concludes that it is not inconceivable that science "could make a man feel whole" or "produce a kind of exalted happiness" (215). Since Amanda and John Paul Ziller practice "a poetics that anticipates tomorrow's science" (141), Marvelous scrutinizes their thoughts and behavior with the utmost interest.

The metaphysics endorsed by this wonderfully unique couple owes much to Eastern religious thought, but what is most striking is their continued reliance upon concepts from the new physics to illustrate the efficacy of this vision of the nature of being. Knowing that matter is a form of energy and apparently familiar with Einstein's principle of the conservation of energy, Amanda says about the death of any life form that "their forms may become obsolete but their essential energies are eternal. The only thing that ever disappears is the shape of energy" (84). Marvelous, well schooled in these matters, is forced to concur: "As the German biologist Ernst Haeckel established, no particle of living energy is ever extinguished, no particle is ever created anew" (84). The notion from the new physics that all life processes are unified appears quite frequently in Amanda's mystic pronouncements. After concluding in a discussion with Marx Marvelous that it is just as spiritually proper to eat animals as plants, Amanda offers the following explanation for this change in her philosophical position: "At the higher levels of consciousness all things are one anyway. There is no difference between animal, vegetable and mineral. Everything just blends together in energy and light" (189).

Light as emblem for the energy out of which all material form is manifested figures large in John Paul's metaphysical quest. Energy for John Paul was, explains Marvelous, "the only permanent 'thing' in the universe, it was the most (if not only) significant 'thing.' And although he had great respect for sound, he believed that the highest form of energy is light" (239). John Paul speaks of light as if it were "living tissue" (239) and theorizes that "man is nothing but slowed down light" (334). All of which culminates in what must be the strangest attempt to return to the source of being ever recorded in fiction. At the point at which John Paul's corporeal substance, or mass, is presumed to be utterly destroyed by the intense light of the sun outside the protective cover of the atmosphere in Icarus XC, Marvelous notes that "he returned—literally—to energy, dissolving in the pure essence that spawned all life" (326).

The poetics that anticipates tomorrow's science includes a conception of moral law wonderfully consistent with the view of the nature and limitations of natural law in contemporary physics. In analyzing the behavior of the F.B.I. agents guarding the roadside zoo after John Paul and Plucky abscond with the corpse, Amanda notes that such men are "symbol junkies" who find it "much easier to cope with the abstract than the concrete" because this habit of mind disallows "direct, personal involvement" (253). The abstract idea serves to preclude, she says, full engagement in a life process in which "things are usually in a state of flux and always changing" (253). The symbol junkies who claim to have an uncompromising respect for the law fail to realize that laws "have no moral content, they merely symbolize conduct which does" (253). In short, the moral law can no more contain, define, and control human activities than the natural law can contain, define, and control activities in nature.

Marvelous—simultaneously fascinated and appalled by Amanda's higher wisdom—toward the close of the narrative speculates like so many characters in the other fiction discussed here that if abstractions do not in the final analysis represent that which is actual or true in external reality, then the universe is ultimately meaningless. When Amanda concedes that life has no meaning but stipulates that it is not without value, Marvelous suggests that this is a cop-out. She then responds:

"Maybe. But it seems to me that the real cop-out is to say that the universe has meaning but that we 'mere mortals' are incapable of knowing that meaning. Mystery is part of nature's style, that's all. It's the Infinite Goof. It's meaning that is of no meaning. That paradox is the key to the meaning of meaning. To look for meaning—or the lack of it—in things is a game played by beings of limited consciousness. Behind everything in life is a process that is beyond meaning. Not beyond understanding, mind you, but beyond meaning." (335)

For the quantum theorists the indeterminacy principle, Amanda's Infinite Goof, implies that no static, abstract law or formula can predict to the nth degree the results of interactions on the micro level. There is, then, a mystery in natural process that is quite literally "behind *everything* in life" which will inevitably frustrate our desire to know or discover meaning in the absolute sense. Amanda has no difficulty with this realization because she recognizes that "not knowing" in the sense of being unable to predict the direction and force of physical change is the condition of our freedom. If we are simply one of the expressions of the energy that is all life, then that element of hazard in nature which makes all the happenings in the cosmos ultimately open-ended and hence free is also present in our own experience.

Culturally derived and hence arbitrary conceptions of the real, which Amanda refers to as "content," are useful she says, because it is "content, or rather consciousness of content, that fills the void"

(12) or that allows us to sustain the awareness that we exist in actuality in relation to everything else in existence. But she claims that that which ultimately matters is not the forms in our minds but the quality of our activity as one dynamic aspect of the creative energy of life: "The most important thing in life is style. That is, the style of one's existence—the characteristic mode of one's actions—is basically, ultimately, what matters" (12). The problem with our received notions of the real is that they are too often premised upon obeisance to an authority which limits all too severely the scope or freedom of our activity. The way out of this dilemma is, as Amanda sees it, to use style creatively and thereby alter content: "If our style is masterful, if it is fluid and at the same time complete, then we can re-create ourselves, or rather, *we can re-create* the Infinite Goof within us. We can live on top of content, float above the predictable responses, social programming and hereditary circuitry, letting the bits of color and electricity and light filter up to us, where we can incorporate them at will into our actions" (208).

The strident criticism of the Roman Catholic Church occasioned by Plucky's theft of Christ's corpse from the lower-level catacombs at the Vatican should not be read simply as an ill-mannered attack on one of the greatest civilizing influences in the Western world. The Roman Catholic church is simply a convenient vehicle used by Robbins to point up those features of Western cosmology that delimit our freedom and engagement in a life process whose internal workings now appear to suggest that several major assumptions upon which that cosmology is based are false. Marvelous's field research for the think tank known as the East River Institute of Brain Power Unlimited was premised on the belief that political, economic, and cultural degeneration in America was due to the bankruptcy of traditional Christian values. Although his colleagues at the Institute "linked the floundering and chaos in the church with what they believed to be a corresponding deterioration in general ethics," his own perception is that "America's so-called moral breakdown was largely myth" (157). It is clearly Robbins's hope, and perhaps even belief, that the new cosmology and the new ethics advertised in the novel are already at work in this culture and displacing the old world order. As Marvelous puts it, we stand at the beginning of a "Golden Age" (159).

The Western belief in the real existence of a transcendent realm of being in which immutable truths reside provided the rationale in Robbins's eyes for the view of authority—or all societal organization for that matter—as hierarchical. Catholicism, as Plucky notes in a letter to the Zillers, is "a duality of good and evil" and hence "a microcosm of secular society." What he hates about the Church is the same thing he hates about society: "Namely, authoritarians. Power freaks. Rigid dogmatists. Those greedy, underloved, under-sexed twits who want to run everything" (186). In the imaginary dialogue between Tarzan, a pagan who is unaccountably outfitted with a contemporary knowledge of religious history, process philosophy and physics, and Jesus Christ, Tarzan claims that prior to the ascendancy of the ancient Hebrews "folks were more concrete. I mean they didn't have much truck with abstractions and spiritualism" (302). Living close to the world of vegetation it was then easy to perceive, he says, that "energy is never destroyed" and that "death came from life" (303). It was only when the "original tribes of Judah—quit tilling the soil and became alienated from vegetation cycles that they lost faith in the material resurrection of the body," developed a "new and unnatural fear of death," and, consequently, the "concept of spiritual rebirth" and "Supreme Spiritual Being" (303).

After Christ explains that it is his special mission to assist man in rising above the carnal nature of such "phallic and vegetarian cults," Tarzan retorts, "Rise to what, Jesus? To Abstractions? And Alienation?" In the beginning, he continues, was not the "Word," for life "is reproduced from life, while resurrection—the regeneration of seeds, the return in the spring of leaves that fell in the autumn—is of matter, not of spirit." In response to Christ's objection that the pagan belief in the organic unity of natural process is "unsophisticated," Tarzan reminds Christ that science in a couple of thousand years will "determine that life originated when a cupful of seawater containing molecules of ammonia trapped in a pocket in a shore rock where it was abnormally heated by ultraviolet light from the sun" (304). If we could resuscitate, Tarzan suggests, that early sense of the essential unity of life that our science has now proven to be demonstrably true, then we might develop enough reverence and respect for our natural environment "not to sell it out or foul it up" (304).

Other basic features of Judeo-Christian cosmology are parodied after Christ announces that he intends to "change the world" and eradicate "evil." Tarzan gleefully proclaims that change has always been "perpetual" in the cosmos and will continue with "no help whatsoever," and that good and evil "have to coexist in order for the world to survive" (305). Unlike Tarzan, Christ, as an either-or thinker not yet familiar with quantum physics, is incapable of seeing apparent opposites as complementary aspects of one process. In the dialogue with Tarzan Jesus becomes so confused that he has "difficulty articulating the activity in his brain," and finally blurts out: "If you think carnally then you are carnal, but if you think spiritually then you are spirit." Apparently angered by Tarzan's suggestion that it is possible to think both ways, Jesus concludes the exchange by yelling: "You're either with me or against me" (306).

The importance of either-or categorical thinking and a belief in the existence of transcendent absolutes, perhaps the most basic features of Judeo-Christian cosmology, as mechanisms of control is further underscored by both the ardent efforts on the part of the authorities to recover the corpse and their willingness to allow it destroyed in Icarus XC. The decision by Ziller to expose that mass which is himself and the corpse to the solar radiation produced by the sun, that "yellow dwarf star" that converts "four million tons of matter into energy every second in accordance with Einstein's basic formula, $e = mc$ squared" (266), is itself a curious parody of the old cosmology. The name of the experimental aircraft has, of course, both mythical and iconographical referents. Icarus, son of Daedalus, failed in his efforts to fly to the sun, and the XC, frequently found on sarcophagi and early medieval and classical religious art, represents Jesus Christ. The implication is that Christ the man, originally known as Joshua ben Miriam, could not, as Icarus could not, transcend the limitations of his humanity and elevate his corporeal substance to some nonexistent higher mode of being or functioning. Since ascension into heaven is an impossibility in a universe consisting only of that vast cosmic interplay of the two aspects of its being, matter and energy, Ziller, the great lover of light, pays tribute to that highly imaginative religious thinker called "the light of the world" (307) by arranging for a situation in which his body can undergo, as quickly as possible, the only transmutation of being that can ever occur in nature. The fact that the shape of the experimental aircraft resembles that of Ziller's whopper hot dog, that "pillar of democracy, the pride of the Yankees, the boneless eagle of free enterprise" (238), provides additional, ironic commentary on the unfortunate uses made in the West of the teachings of a man whose "one real insight during his life" was that the "kingdom of heaven is within" (297).

Robbins's second novel, *Even Cowgirls Get the Blues*, is also replete with references to concepts from the new physics, but the emphasis here appears to be on the potential impact of these concepts upon our understanding of the nature and function of time. We have assumed in the Judeo-Christian tradition not only, as Newton formalized it, that time is a separate dimension, but also that our experience in time is a linear, rational progression with beginning, middle, and end. Einstein's relativity theory in addition to proving that time cannot exist separately from space also demonstrated that perception of events in time is relative because it is dependent upon the position of the observer in relation to the observed event. Quantum theory invalidates the notion of linear, rational progression of events in time because of the quantum interconnectedness of all subatomic events and also because of the indeterminate nature of these processes. Outfitted by one of nature's chance mutations with incredibly oversized thumbs, Sissy's commitment to hitchhiking is justified as a mode of being-in-time by appealing to concepts from physics: "Einstein had observed motion and learned that space and time are relative; Sissy had committed herself to motion and learned that one could alter reality by one's perception of it."[3] When her thoroughly bourgeois analytically minded husband-to-be criticizes Sissy for traveling her whole life without "destination," she alludes to the indeterminacy principle in her response: "What is the 'direction' of the earth in its 'journey' where are the atoms 'going' when they spin?" (92).

The "clocks" constructed by the Clock People and the clock in the Chink's cave on Siwash Ridge overlooking the Rubber Rose Ranch, occasion an extended, rather formal philosophical discourse upon experience-in-time in light of what is now known in physics. Robbins's parody of the accepted view of time as a series of discontinuous units which divide up, contain, and measure experience, takes the form of the huge seven-foot-wide and thirteen-foot-tall hourglass in the clockworks. Approximately thirteen hours are required for the acorns to funnel through the waist of the device representing the twenty-six-hour day of the Clock People. Our own twenty-four-hour day may be a bit more commensurate with the

diurnal revolutions of this planet moving about its sun, but the measure is, finally, simply an arbitrary convention like that of the Clock
People. The presence of the second clock in the clockworks, the pool
fed by the underground stream that "flows directly into the San
Andreas Fault" (221) containing catfish who have the uncanny ability to "register earthquakes as far away as Los Angeles . . . four weeks
in advance" (222), suggests that the Clock People do on some level
apprehend time as flow or process, but their apocalyptic vision of the
end of time which will issue in "a continuum they call the Eternity of
Joy" (218) is, as the Chink points out, a vestige of the old cosmology
not commensurate with present, scientific knowledge. Although the
Clock People do, Robbins suggests, rightly perceive that the "universe is simultaneously many and One" (219), a perception that allows for a high degree of individual freedom while simultaneously
encouraging the sense of being one with the whole, their notion of
beginnings and ends is simply not appropriate in a universe in which
change that is fundamentally indeterminate in character is constant.
The problem with the Clock People's perception of time, says the
Chink, is that their "waiting for the Eternity of Joy was virtually
identical to the Christians waiting for the Second Coming. Or the
Communists waiting for the worldwide revolution" (230). They are,
as he puts it more succinctly, "just more victims of the disease of
time" (231).

As the Chink observes in a statement that Werner Heisenberg
could well have admired, life is "a dynamic network of interchanges
and exchanges, spreading in all directions at once. And it's all held
together by the tension between opposites." Order in nature is always accompanied by disorder and "it is the balance of tensions between the order and disorder, the natural laws and natural randomness, that keeps it from completely collapsing" (235). The problem,
as the Chink sees it, is that "man has a pronounced bias for order. He
not only refuses to respect or even accept the disorder in Nature, in
life; he shuns it, attacks it with orderly programs. And in so doing, he
perpetuates instability" (236). The Chink's clockworks, a collection
of "garbage can lids and old saucepans and lard tins and car fenders"
(240), is designed to help him sustain an awareness of the randomness or indeterminacy of natural process that makes freedom a
human possibility. Laws, as the ostensible narrator Dr. Robbins
notes, "that pretend that reality is fixed and nature is definable are

antilife" (314). It is our belief in the existence of such laws, nicely fostered by classical physics, which, the novel suggests, causes us to live within the narrow confines of received conceptions of the real and precludes an active, imaginative realization of life's enormous possibilities.

The Chink's acceptance of the notion, supported by his study of "the science of the particular" or the "laws governing exceptions," that reality is subjective leads to the recognition that "freedom—for humans—is largely an internal condition" (210). That which seems actual depends, says Sissy, on "how you look at it, that everything, always, depends on how it is perceived, and that the perceiver has the ability to adjust his perceptions" (303). Our world-constructing mind, which becomes something of a character in its own right in this narrative, makes use, Robbins suggests, of an arbitrary mode of constructing reality that delimits all too severely our perceptions of self and world. It is rational thought, defined by the narrator as a "brain game that is widely, if poorly, played" (133), that Robbins fingers as the culprit. Although "recent neurological research indicates," notes the medically trained Dr. Robbins, "that the brain is governed by principles it cannot understand" (161), we continue to presume that rational analysis, predicated upon a belief in abstractions and either-or categorical thinking, can answer the "Ultimate Questions." In the dialogue between thumb and brain, the brain even suggests that something like the indeterminacy principle is a feature of its own internal life: "Because the truth is, my neurons occasionally fire spontaneously in the absence of a stimulating signal. I'm subjected to a fair amount of randomly generating currents. It isn't as orderly in here as you might imagine" (360). The brain confesses that it is capable of "a different kind of thinking" that "might be more useful in the Universe," but only a handful of "poets, madmen, artists, monks, hermits, composers, yogis, shamans, eccentrics, magicians, anarchists, witches and rare bizarre subcultures such as the Gnostics and the Sierra Clock People—have used my thinking in unusual and unpredictable ways, with interesting results" (362). It is sleeping and dreaming, a state of consciousness in which, says Freud, analytical thought processes are but minimally present, which the brain claims to do best: "it may be my true vocation" (362).

The tendency in the West to frame out experience in terms of a hierarchical system of abstractions has led to the development of a civilization that the Clock People view as "an insanely complex set of symbols that obscures natural process and encumbers free movement" (222). This belief in a rigorous distinction between the higher and the lower was not, Robbins suggests, originally a pronounced feature of Christianity and was also conspicuously absent from Western religious cosmologies that predate the Judeo-Christian. Christianity, says the Chink, was an "Eastern Religion" containing truths that bore strong resemblance to those found in religious cosmologies premised upon a unitary conception of being like Buddhism and Hinduism. The supreme deity in the West, he continues, "prior to the Eastern alien Jehovah" venerated from Neolithic days by the "peoples of Britain and Europe" was a "bawdy goat-man who provided rich harvests and bouncy babies; a hairy, merry deity who loved music and dancing and good food; a god of fields and woodlands and flesh" (265). The Christianity that transformed that ancient pagan deity who celebrated life in the here and now into the image of Lucifer was a Christianity transformed and debased by Greek, dualistic thinkers like Saint Paul who caused the light of Jesus to grow "dimmer and dimmer until, around the fourth century, it went out altogether" (268).

The present state of Western civilization is obviously, as Robbins sees it, a product of the belief in a cosmology that assumes that man, existing on some higher plane of being, has a rightful dominion over all nature. There are, says the Chink, "countless ways to live upon this tumultuous sphere in mirth and good health, and probably only one way—the industrialized, urbanized, herding way—to live here stupidly, and man has hit upon that one wrong way" (220). According to the cultural anthropologists, the ability of our prehistoric ancestors to manipulate the thumb in a manner that allowed for the facile use of tools, which resulted in a rapid increase in the size of the brain, eventually making it possible to use symbolic language systems, has culminated in the development of a technology that in the long term could make the planet unlivable and in the short term transform it beyond all recognition in a nuclear holocaust. Robbins highlights what he considers to be our profound stupidity at the close of the novel by suggesting that Sissy and Dr. Robbins will be protected from the effects of the nuclear disaster in their cave dwelling on Siwash Ridge and will become, like Adam and Eve, the "first parents" of generations of men outfitted with thumbs that make any elaborate use of tools an impossibility. In this garden there will be no God-parent and forbidden fruit, for the cosmology derived in part from the Chink and firmly implanted in the minds of these enlightened scientifically minded primitives, counsels full participation in a unified, holistic life process that is essentially indeterminate in character and hence not governed by any fixed, immutable laws.

We need not conclude, of course, that concepts from physics will occasion a commitment to the bizarre and essentially adolescent lifestyle of Robbins's major characters, but it is difficult not to take seriously his philosophical speculations upon their metaphysical import. When writers of popular fiction like Robbins borrow concepts that not so very long ago were merely the esoteric concerns of a small community of scientists and make them accessible to something like a mass audience, I suggest that it is time to begin contemplating the appearance in our culture of a revolution in thought of the first order. Academic humanists who have grown accustomed to thinking of physics, or of all science for that matter, as a dull, predictable and, in their own terms, essentially unimaginative pursuit that has very little to do with the "real" business of life, may very well be in for a shock.

9 · doN dEliLlo

Although Don DeLillo's six published novels are considerably more limited in scope of reference and range of implications than the three novels of Thomas Pynchon, there is remarkable similarity between these novelists' individual conceptions of the contemporary human dilemma. Both assume that the tendency of Western man to construct reality in terms of closed systems and symbolics is not only without epistemological foundation, but also functions as program and guide for the fragmentation of individual identity and the possible extinction of the entire race of man. They also share the conviction that the continued survival of human civilization is dependent upon a fundamental restructuring of the dynamics of our world-conceiving minds, and each favors a return to a more primal sense of being that allows for an enlarged awareness of self as manifestation of one unified process. Although DeLillo, like Pynchon, is preoccupied with exposing the principle of the either-or as the most invidious dynamic in the construction of closed systems and symbolics, the purging from consciousness of abstract systems definitions of reality is normally accompanied in his fiction by a renewed awareness of the denotative aspect of language. DeLillo apparently feels, more strongly than Pynchon, that by detaching ourselves from the word as *Logos*, and placing greater emphasis upon the function of the word as concrete referent, we would be better able to construct an alternate reality more consistent with the metaphysics implied in the new physics.

The system under investigation in *Americana* is the electronic communications network, and the aspect of that system that receives the most careful scrutiny is the filmic image. David Bell, the youthful and thoroughly American protagonist, discovers in his work as a network producer that "words and meaning were at odds. Words did not say what was being said or even the reverse."[1] This "child of Godard and Coca-Cola" (256) whose father and grandfather were both legends in the advertising industry, conceives of himself and others as little more than a compilation of images derived from a lifetime of exposure to movies and television programming. There is a tendency in this culture, speculates David early in the narrative, to regard the lens of the motion picture camera as "history. What the machine accepts is verifiably existent; all else is unborn or worse" (4). His belief that conceptions of self are increasingly the projections of identity marketed by commercial films and television leads to the conclusion that the authentic or unique self is being trivialized out of existence. David comes to perceive everyone as a "living schizogram" (50), and feels that his "only problem" is that his "whole life was a lesson in the effect of echoes, that I was living in the third person" (58).

The metaphysical dimension of this transformation of our sense of self by the moving filmic image into the "third-person singular" is explored by thirty-seven-year-old sculptor Sullivan who makes the westward journey with David and his other zany friends. "We become," she explains, "documentary. We become newsreels telling what we think is the truth. Our listener is really no more than a fragment of the dark. The true audience is the darkness itself" (114). Since the architects of this truth are the media managers who fashion images of the idealized self for the purpose of marketing products, the American dream, previously thought to be a function of received political and religious ideologies configuring in the lived experience of our cultural forebears, becomes increasingly the province of advertising. As David sees it, this new American "dream made no allowance for the truth beneath the symbols, for the interlinear notes, the presence of something black (and somehow very funny) at the mirror of one's awareness." Bombarded all of his life with the "institutional messages, the psalms and placards, the pictures, the words" of the advertising industry, he senses that "all the impulses of the media were fed into the circuitry of my dreams," and that he has become, finally, "an image made in the image and likeness of images" (125).

Exposure to media entices Americans, suggests DeLillo, to view gratification of impulse in terms of the likeness or image of self that appears in advertising to have the most access to scarce commodities. As David puts it in lines written for a character in his home movie on American identity, "It moves him [the viewer] from first person consciousness to third person, the man we all want to be. . . . To consume in America is not to buy; it is to dream. Advertising is the suggestion that the dream of entering the third-person singular might possibly be fulfilled" (257). What is finally "merchandised," he explains further, is the prospect of altering the image of the self for purposes of consumption, as opposed to refashioning, or reconstructing, the environment to create larger possibilities for growth and satisfaction. This segment of David's film also includes the comment: "Advertising discovered the value of the third person but the consumer invented him. The country itself invented him" (258). What this invention cannot represent, in that it reduces self to a set of single, composite, unidimensional images, is the richness and variety of experience in a diversified culture replete with contrasting lifestyles and traditions. In the absence of extensive associations with the deep structure of received traditions and communal ethos that communicates the "truth beneath the symbols," the individual ceases to be highly individuated and also suffers the loss of any profound sense of relation to that which is *other*.

David's film, which in its final version runs nearly a week (327), serves as a transcript of what he describes as his "great seeking leap into the depths of America, wilderness dream of all poets and scoutmasters, westward to manifest destiny . . . westward to match the shadows of my image and my self" (325). The reasons that this ambitious enterprise is not likely to be successful are best understood by Sullivan. Like so many of DeLillo's characters, David is fascinated with numbers, assumes that "numbers have power," and also that the "whole country runs on numbers" (119). The attempt to recover an authentic self in the film is wrong-headed in Sullivan's view because it mirrors self through numeration, or through a vast accumulation of static frames of film. This obsession with numbers is, she tells David, "somewhat less than Euclidean in its sweep and purity; that one of my main faults was a tendency to get blinded by the neon of an idea, never reaching truly inside it; that to follow a number to infinity was not necessarily to arrive at God" (120). As David watches Sullivan gracefully cut up some bacon immediately after she makes this judgment, he wonders that the bacon might "represent the insignificance of numbers; the futile quest for infinity; the indivisible nature of God as opposed to the fractional promiscuity of numbers? Was it all a lesson in prime matter and substantial form?" (120). The suggestion that the ontological ground for all individual existences is energy in the space-time continuum that is identical with the ultimate being of God is reinforced later in the narrative when Sullivan notes that "all energy runs down, all life expires, all except the force of all in all, or light lighting light" (315). David's only previous exposure to this conception of metaphysical reality was a course in college on Zen philosophy in which he was drawn into the perception that "emptiness is fullness. Become the book. Become the bamboo. The darkness ran shallow green.Then it was black, welcoming as deep space, and I sighed audibly and advanced into a fresh galaxy" (170).

Having spent all of his twenty-eight years, as he sees it, "in the movies" (269), David has received far too much conditioning in the business of fragmenting experience into static images to easily embrace a holistic vision of the cosmos. He is bemused by but cannot finally comprehend the message of the terminally ill executive at the network who writes in one of his enigmatic underground memos: "To square the circle is child's play. It is the reverse which leads to beatific vision" (213). Since a movie is a series of still photographs in square frames, David's attempt to encircle or define his cultural identity by making a movie is child's play in a literal sense. Although it is clearly his intent that the film, like the radio transmissions picked up while traveling in the van, should create the impression that "all was in harmony" and that there is "logic beyond delirium" (195), the finished product has quite the opposite effect. The fragments of Americana (events, people, places) that David hopes to weave into a composite image of his identity not only fail to cohere, the movie viewed in the sequence in which it was filmed "becomes darker and more silent as it progresses" (327). In its entirety the film "functions best," David concludes, "as a sort of ultimate schizogram, an exercise in diametrics which attempts to unmake meaning" (328). The collage of images that records the activities that represent, in David's perception, the life of the culture deconstructs not into essences of identity, but rather into an ultimate cleavage between oppositions void of all signification.

And yet the film as testament to his willingness to become an artist dealing in the "complexities of truth" has been, as he eventually realizes, "successful" (328). It is not simply that he learns from the experience that he was engaged in "merely a literary venture, an attempt to find pattern and motive, to make of something wild a squeamish thesis on the nation's soul. To formulate. To seek links" (330). The movie actually succeeds in the sense that it demonstrates, like the novel itself, the impossibility of imposing closed systems or symbolics, constructed in terms of the either-or, upon the essentially fluid and indeterminate life process. This is not, however, as DeLillo suggests in the conclusion of the narrative, a widely accepted truth in American culture. Ten minutes after David Bell, image and product of the "third-person singular," boards an aircraft to return to the mecca of the advertising industry in New York, "a woman asks for his autograph" (358).

In *End Zone* DeLillo is not, as some of the earlier reviewers presumed, drawing a simple-minded comparison between American football and modern warfare. What he has done in this narrative, with admirable ingenuity, is draw extensive parallels between the game as exemplar of all closed systems used in the construction of human reality, and the nuclear defense system. He then deconstructs the former in order to expose the latter as our most terrifying manifestation of the same habits of mind. Like Barth and Pynchon, who also dare to think the unthinkable in confronting the very real prospect of nuclear holocaust, the culprit for DeLillo is not the irremediable organization of our instinctual life, but the structure of our arbitrarily developed and potentially malleable symbolic universe.

Gary Harkness, the star running-back whose two major intellectual interests are the special character and appeal of football and the technology of nuclear war, attends four major universities before being recruited to play football for Logos College. The college, founded by a deaf mute, has undertaken an ambitious new football program under the direction of head coach Emmett Creed whose own illustrious career had been virtually destroyed when he broke the jaw of a second-string quarterback two years earlier at another university. The suggestion in the choice of names for coach and college that the game functions as emblem for systems definitions of reality is reinforced throughout the remainder of the narrative. Creed, "famous for bringing order out of chaos,"[2] conceives of football as a "complex of systems" which ideally "interlock" in some final "harmony" (163). He is described as the "name giver" (110), the "man upstairs" (76), and as a combination of "Satan" and "Saint Francis" (195).

Although Gary enjoys playing football because the "thoughts" of the football player "are wholesomely commonplace, his actions uncomplicated by history, enigma, holocaust or dream" (3), his deconstruction of the game reveals increasing resemblances between this system and the dramatically more lethal system of nuclear technology. He begins with the realizations that "language moves masses of people or a few momentous objects into significant juxtaposition" that is "almost mathematical," and that "history is the angle at which realities meet" (35). Our attraction to sport may, he conjectures, be a consequence of a "benign illusion, the illusion that order is possible" (89), and football is particularly attractive in this regard because it is the "one sport guided by language, by the word symbol, the snap number, the color code, the play name." We may derive pleasure from the "game's unique organic nature," but it is also "not just order but civilization" (90). When the essential structure of football is bracketed out in the pick-up game in the snow through the elimination of huddles, customary gestures and postures, and even plays and opposing lines of players, what remains is the fundamental opposition between "man with ball" battling others "to keep possession of ball." The either-or as fundamental feature in the construction of systems is inescapable in football just as it is in all other systems and "double consciousness" (105), as Gary's metaphysically minded fellow-player Bing points out, is just as inescapable here as it is elsewhere. Another player on this remarkable team, Ted Joost, even dreams about closure of the entire system of football with the use of a computer broadcasting "signals" to receivers in the helmets of every player in every game then being played (108).

Gary's intense fascination with the "possibilities of nuclear war" begins with his exposure to a book assigned in a course on "disaster technology" at the University of Miami (17). Even in the face of serious depression over his seemingly perverse interest in the subject, Gary is irresistibly drawn to this display of the "rationality of irrationality," in which "tens of millions die" and entire cities are destroyed (17). After receiving permission at Logos College to audit an AFROTC course devoted, in part, to a study of "aspects of modern war" (40), Gary arranges for a private meeting with the instructor, a Major Staley, to exchange views on the problem. As Gary explains to Staley, there is a "kind of theology at work" in the manufacture of weaponry with such over-kill capability. We have made a god, he says, of the "force of nature itself, the fusion of tritium and deuterium" and the "big danger is that we'll surrender to a sense of inevitability and start flinging mud all over the planet" (62). Following a graphic description of the effects of nuclear blasts on cities and people, the major comments that "war is a test of opposing technologies" configuring on such a high level of abstraction that "nobody has to feel any guilt. Responsibility is distributed too thinly for that" (66–67). It is, as Gary comes to view it, the underlying systems organization of the arsenal that sustains its growth, mitigates responsibility for its existence, and which may, as the mind that creates it hungers for closure, eventually lead us to the apocalypse. This last prospect begins to seem even more likely to Gary when the major, in another private conversation later in the narrative, tells him that the "big problem with war games, whether they were being played at the Pentagon, at Norad or Fort Belvoir, at a university or think tank, was the obvious awareness on the part of the participants that this wasn't the real thing" (180). The nuclear defense system becomes real, or ceases to function as simply an abstract schema of the possible, when, the major suggests, it is put into use. Closure in this system requires, in other words, the wedding of the ethereal war game, or war as unrealized possibility, with the war itself. "It could," as the major wryly puts it, "happen" (181).

"Detachment" in the examination of "timeless questions" is, Gary muses during a conversation with his roommate, "needed only for the likes of astrophysics, quantum mechanics, all painstaking matters so delicate in their refracted light that intellects such as ours would sooner yield to the prudish machine" (38). And yet the machine, the pattern-forming, logocentric world-constructing mind, operates in terms of principles, like discreteness of individual substances and the either-or, that are inconsistent with the behavior of the massless photon. The basic unit of the language system, words, can, as Gary discovers at an early age, "escape meaning" (14). Attracted by the notion of "oneness with God or the universe or some equally redoubtable super-phenomenon" (15), Gary, in a curious effort to return to the source of being not unlike that of Ziller in *Another Roadside Attraction*, elects to reduce the mass of his body by not eating. As his fast continues he takes long walks in the desert adjacent to campus where he becomes increasingly enchanted by the starkness and silence of a landscape in which words—"The sun. The desert. The sky" (69)—begin to seem detached from the connotations and associations of the language systems and appear tied to their denotative function. It is, Gary speculates, in "silence [or] some form of void, freed from consciousness, [that] the mind remakes itself. What we must know must be learned from blanked-out pages. To begin to reword the overflowing world" (70).

Frustrated by his inability to finally apprehend the silence where language deconstructs itself to this first, basic function as referent to the concrete, Gary is driven at one point to writing a "long hysterical letter on the subject of space-time" which, although he knows little about the subject, "practically wrote itself" (170). After becoming finally disenchanted with football as a mode of relating to organic nature, and learning that Taft, the black running-back in the "Taft and Gary, Touch and Go. Thunder and Gore" (124) backfield, is similarly preoccupied with mass destruction of the innocent, Gary eliminates liquids from his diet as well. At the close of the narrative, this quester after an alternate metaphysic describes himself being carried to the infirmary and fed through plastic tubes (200).

Great Jones Street, which is, I think, DeLillo's least impressive, most transparent narrative, details the adventures of Bucky Wunderlick, self-described "hero of rock 'n roll,"[3] as he attempts to remove himself as salable commodity from a system, in this instance the musical recording and distributing industry. Apotheosized by a group of societal drop-outs, called the Happy Valley Commune, because he seems committed, as they are, to a return to the idea of privacy in American life (17), he receives a package containing a new street drug developed by this group that is clearly considered a more valuable commodity than he is. While being pursued by a host of bizarre characters who wish to secure the package to make profits through the illegal underground drug distribution system, Bucky, like David and Gary, also seeks to withdraw into the silence of awareness without symbolic content. In this narrative, however, the retreat into silence, or into the apprehension of reality void of systems constructs, does, in fact, occur.

Early in the narrative Bucky declares that he is "interested in endings, in how to survive a dead idea" (3–4). The dead idea is not simply the concept or image of self fashioned by the music industry as a salable commodity, but *idea* as function in the symbolic organization of human reality. In a transcript of an interview inserted into the text, a member of the "Issues Committee of the Permanent Symposium for the Restoration of Democratic Options" implies that Bucky's music, which has such enormous appeal in American popular culture, is merely "noise." At this point Bucky purportedly responds: "Noise, right. It's a natural force. We're processing a natural force. Electricity in nature every bit as much as sex in nature" (102–3). When asked later in the interview if it is only "loud noises" that "explain the Wunderlick formulation or ethos," the superstar confesses that his "whole life is tinged with melancholy" and that the "more I make people move, the closer I get to personal inertness" (105). Since the lyrics of Bucky's songs, which either celebrate sex or seek to sanction inertia, are virtually unintelligible on the actual recordings, the suggestion is that his success is to be explained in terms of the widespread appeal of an ethos consisting only of a compulsion to escape consciousness of self through motion. Although this motion is in response to systematic manipulation by the recording industry, motion that mitigates awareness is, DeLillo suggests, simply motion. As Bucky discovers first hand in his relationship with his girlfriend Opal, this ethos provides a sense of "connection" only in the shared commitment to "go harder, take more, die first" (12).

The need on the part of young people in this culture to experience language in more direct relation to the source of being is reflected in the almost instantaneous appeal of what appears to be a nonsense phrase, "Pee-pee-maw maw," on the most recent of Bucky's albums. The phrase, as he explains in the same interview, was first used by him as a "childhood incantation," but probably originated in "twelfth century England or the Vikings or the Moors." The chant appeals, he explains, because it "can be traced to the dawn of civilization" (106–7), or to that first phase of linguistic development during which the word had presumably not yet lost its power to signify fusion between man and his environment.

The mastermind behind much of the elaborate scheming to take possession of the product developed by the Happy Valley Commune is a mysterious denizen of the underground drug distribution system named Chess. Expert, as his name implies, in the business of elaborately orchestrating movement within preestablished guidelines or patterns, Chess theorizes that Americans are "seeking the wrong kind of privacy, the old privacy, never again to be found." The need to withdraw, he suggests, is occasioned by "sensory overload. . . . Technology. Whenever there's too much technology, people return to primitive feats. But we both know that privacy is an inner state" (252). His solution is not, however, to abandon systems definitions of reality that tend toward closure, but rather to simplify systems. Closure in the effort to recover the drug means, as Chess puts it, that "we're compelled to use it. We have the drug so we're forced to administer it." Since the drug "damages the cells in one or more areas of the left sector of the human brain" resulting in "speech loss" (255) and has no market value, it is administered to Bucky.

When asked by Chess if he has any "last words" before the drug is introduced into his organism, Bucky quickly responds, "Pee-pee-maw-maw" (256). During the period in which he suffers complete loss of verbal skills, or a quite literal return to silence, Bucky finds himself "unreasonably happy, subsisting in blessed circumstance, thinking of myself as a kind of living chant. I made interesting and original sounds." The drug, as it turns out, is "less than lasting in its effect," and the first word that Bucky is capable of uttering is "mouth" (264). As the rumors about the whereabouts and activities of the missing cult hero continue to proliferate, Bucky decides that when the "season is right I'll return to whatever is out there. It's just a question of what sound to make or fake" (165).

Although DeLillo in *Ratner's Star* is definitely exercising poetic license in suggesting that human civilization originated at a much earlier date than can be supported by scientific evidence, we discover in this narrative not only an impressive acquaintance with concepts from the new physics but also the manner in which these concepts inform his artistic vision. Billy Twillig, fourteen-year-old Nobel laureate in mathematics, did not, like Einstein, "learn to talk until he

was past the age of three," at which point he "spoke with his mind
and to his mind."[4] After discovering at an early age an extraordinary
ability to conduct this internal dialogue in mathematical codes, Billy
learns to take pleasure in inhabiting that "lonely place in his mind"
where he is "free from subjection to reality, free to impose his ideas
and designs on his own test environment. The only valid standard for
his work, its critical point (zero or infinity), was the beauty it possessed, the deft strength of his mathematical reasoning" (117). This
ardent disciple of the Pythagorean mathematical idea leaves his research post at "The Center for the Refinement of Ideational Structures" (26) to journey to a vast, internationally funded scientific
laboratory and think tank called "Field Experiment Number One."
It is the hope of the highly unorthodox directors of this project that
Billy will succeed where others have failed in decoding radio messages emanating in space from the vicinity of the body known in astronomy as Ratner's star.

Billy, who reasons so thoroughly in the realm of the mathematical that he conceives of himself as "having two existences, right and
left in terms of an equation," and who also fears that the mathematical side "might overwhelm the other, leaving him behind, a name
and shape" (129), functions in the narrative primarily as a vehicle
through which DeLillo discourses upon the inability of closed scientific paradigms to fully contain or define natural process. Mathematical reasoning, with "its claim to necessary conclusions; its pursuit of
connective patterns and significant form" (13), is premised upon assumptions, as Billy's mentor Softly points out in a "work in progress," that are a product of an outmoded cosmology. "The unat-
tested cadence of the heavens," writes Softly, "had been based on the
circles of Ptolemaic calculations, a format supported by the Polish
monk Copernicus. . . . Motive soul drove the planets and it was held
that every orbit described a musical scale. The problem of course and
solution as well were distinctly mathematical" (45).

The influence of the old cosmology also causes us to continue to
assume, like one of the directors of Field Experiment Number One,
that "there is no reality more independent of our perception and
more true to itself than mathematical reality" (48). Billy's decision to
become a mathematician was a consequence of a series of dreams in a
single night. The first two "concerned the terror of nature not understood," but in the third the world suddenly appeared "comprehen-

sible, a plane of equations, all knowledge able to be wielded, all nature controllable. These were dreams generated by the motion of a straight line, a penciled breath of linear tension between day and night, the limit that separates numbers, positive from negative, real from imaginary, the dream edge of discrete and continuous, history and prehistory, matter and its mirror image" (64). This is, of course, the conception of the ontology of number envisioned by Galileo and formalized by Descartes which, as DeLillo knows very well, does not mirror reality in the manner we once thought it did.

Although Schwarz, one of the physicists working with Billy, is committed, like most members of the actual community of physicists today, to developing a "totally harmonious picture of the world system" (49), he also realizes that there is, in quantum physics, the "lack of cause and effect in the behavior of elementary particles" and that "certain basic components of our physical system defy precise measurement and definition" (49). A historical overview of this dilemma is offered by LoQuadro, another philosophically minded physicist at Field Experiment Number One. The dream that grew out of the first scientific revolution in the "seventeenth century" that it would just be a "matter of time before all knowledge was integrated and made available, all the secrets pried open" has not, he notes, been realized. The problem is not merely that scientific knowledge "refuses to be contained," but also that the "world itself keeps pushing out" and "breaking through" (65–66).

Late in the novel DeLillo, as omniscient narrator, deals directly and at some length with the metaphysical implications of the new physics and draws some fairly definite conclusions. Addressing the reader as a hypothetical physicist, DeLillo says: "having dismantled the handiwork of your own perceptions, in order to solve reality, you know it now as a micron flash of light scattering matter in a structure otherwise composed of purely mathematical coordinates" (431). The prospect that the mathematical coordinates can provide a direct transcription of self is doubtful, he notes, because "in the wave-guide manipulation of light and our nosings into the choreography of protons, we implicate ourselves in endless uncertainty." DeLillo then asserts that this is "the ethic you've rejected. Inside our desolation, however, you come upon the reinforcing grid of works and minds that extend themselves against whatever lonely spaces account for our hollow moods, the woe incoming. Why are you here? To unsnarl us from our delimiting senses?" (432) This compulsion to define the essence of our being as mathematical or scientific entity will eventually, he concludes, "make us hypothetical, a creature of our own pretending, as are you. Geometric space of any number of dimensions. Awareness of not being self-aware" (433).

DeLillo, like Pynchon, is definitely not advocating an end to scientific investigation, nor does he mean to belittle the enterprise in the least. He is using present scientific knowledge to make the case that closed systems of abstractions that tend toward closure are not only invalidated by this knowledge, but provide a virtual guarantee that the entire human experiment will come to an abrupt halt in nuclear war. Although this is precisely what takes place at the conclusion of *Ratner's Star*, DeLillo is far more explicit here than in his other narratives in delineating those features of language, or those terms in the construction of the symbolic universe, that have driven us, in his view, to this absurd predicament.

The closure of economic and political systems that brings on the holocaust appears, first of all, to be the consequence of the effort by a bizarre business tycoon named Troxl to establish complete control over the international money market. "We admit," says Troxl, "to a lust for abstraction. The cartel has an undrinkable greed for the abstract. The concept-idée of money is more powerful than money itself. We would commit theoretical mass rapine to regulate the money curve of the world" (146). The most effective way to accomplish this aim, explains Troxl, is to "acquire air space. We make motion studies in and out. We lease and sublease multi kinds of time— makeshift, standby, conceptual et all forth. Then we either buy, sell, retain or incite revolution, all totally nonprofitless, done merely to flux the curve our way" (147). As the cartel, renamed significantly "ACRONYM" (412), begins to establish a monopoly over all "model building organizations" (413), including Field Experiment Number One, it becomes increasingly more effective in moving the international monetary exchange system toward closure. As this movement occurs, global tensions increase proportionally. "We can measure," explains Softly, "the gravity of events by tracing the increasingly abstract nature of the technology. One more level of vagueness and that could be it" (281).

The same compulsion to transform human reality into an idée fixe by containing it within abstract systems definitions is also at work in the effort to develop in the Logicon project a "universal" language that would facilitate communication with extraterrestrial beings like those initially thought to be transmitting the radio message. As Lester Bolin, who is most involved in the project, explains, this metalanguage cannot be spoken by a computer until they "figure out how to separate the language as system of meaningless signs from the language about language" (339). The problem, as the anthropologist Wu realizes, is that such a metalanguage cannot "mirror the world" because it involves the "impossible attempt to free reality from the structures it must possess as long as there are humans to breed it" (392). Like any closed scientific paradigm that seeks to contain the open-ended, essentially indeterminate processes of nature, that which is finally mirrored is not the world but subjectively based human constructs. Since this mode of defining or explaining does not take into account the role of the observer in the participatory universe of the new physics, it communicates only itself.

The spokesman for the alternate metaphysics consistent with the new physics in this narrative is Shazar Lazarus Ratner, the impossibly aged and decrepit physicist after whom the star was named, who remains alive, ironically to be sure, only by virtue of an elaborate artificial life-support system. Ratner, like Whitehead, conceives of God, whom he refers to in the manner of orthodox Jews as "G-dash-d," as identical with the endless process of becoming that is the life of the universe (230). Underlying the perceived world is, he says, the "hidden. The that-which-is-not-there. The neither-cause-nor-effect. The G-dash-d beyond G-dash-d. The limitless. The not-only-unutterable-but-by-definition-inconceivable" (217). The inability to perceive, in normal states of consciousness, our proper relation to the ontological ground of Being is, suggests Ratner, largely due to the fact that "everything in the universe works on the theory of opposites" (219), including language. The lesson learned in quantum physics that "all things are present in all things. Each in its opposite" (219), has meaning, implies Ratner, only when we allow ourselves to "go into mystical states" and "pass beyond the opposites of the world and experience only the union of opposites in a radiant burst of energy" (218–19). Although transcendence of oppositions in language systems is a precondition for apprehending our actual condition in metaphysical terms, this does not, as Ratner sees it, diminish the power or importance of language. "If you know the right combination of letters," he says, "you can make anything. This is the secret power of the alphabet. . . . The alphabet is itself both male and female. Creation depends on an anagram" (222–23). The point of Ratner's somewhat rambling discourse is that although oppositions are both useful and necessary in the construction of our knowledge of the cosmos, and have real existence in the life of the cosmos itself, we must balance this understanding against the recognition that they are manifestations of one fundamental unity, and are, therefore, not absolute.

Although there is certainly no archeological evidence to support the assertion made at the conclusion of this narrative that a technologically advanced race of men managed to destroy their own civilization over a billion years ago, DeLillo does draw on some recent discoveries in astrophysics in fashioning his own fanciful explanation for the source of the radio signal. Ratner's star, which is eventually found to be a "binary dwarf" consisting of red and white stars (179), resembles Pulsar 1913+ 16 which was first discovered by radio astronomers in Puerto Rico in 1974. This pulsar, now called a "binary pulsar" because it orbits closely around another collapsed star forming a binary or two-star system, also flashes radio energy seventeen times a second. At this point, however, DeLillo departs from the scientifically verifiable in suggesting that the star exists in a "mohole totality" within which the "laws of physics vary from one observer to another" (185). It is this new conception of relativity that explains why the star is capable of absorbing radio energy and emitting it at irregular intervals, and which also leads to the conclusion that the radio signal picked up at Field Experiment Number One was beamed into space by some earlier civilization of men.

When the scientists working on the Logicon project begin to sense that nuclear war is inevitable, they summon a "woman from the slums" who supposedly has "unexplained insight into the future" (423). After struggling through a series of violent contortions, Skia Mantikos, whose name means "shadow prophet" (423), manages to utter a single, and from our perspective, very significant word: "Pythagoras" (429). It is important, of course, that the scientists, including Billy, who are privileged to hear this prophetic word do not have the first clue as to what it might mean. All of which serves to communicate DeLillo's fear that because language systems, particularly the mathematical, are assumed capable of revealing the immalleable essence of the real in an ordered, predictable, and closed totality the Western intellectual tradition might well be incapable of even questioning the validity of that assumption.

Both of DeLillo's most recent novels, *Players* and *Running Dog*, can, and, I think, should, be read as attempts to expose the inefficacy of that assumption. The central characters in these narratives move through a complex maze of overlapping systems that appear initially to be manifestations of economic and political realities, but which are finally revealed to be self-perpetuating entities whose only rationale for existence is the prospect of closure. In *Players*, Lyle and Pammy Wynatt, middle-class residents of Manhattan, move, both figuratively and literally, through space divided up into boxlike configurations and categories whose proper function, or relation in some larger context, is never finally known.

The towers of the World Trade Center, the work place for both characters, do not, as Pammy perceives them, "seem permanent. They remained concepts, no less transient for all their bulk than some routine distortion of light."[5] Similarly the elevators and lobbies in this emblem of interlocking systems of social control are regarded by Pammy as "spaces," but the entire structure remains enigmatic as "a condition, an occurrence, a physical event, an existing circumstance, a presence, a state, a set of variables?" (41). On a more prosaic level Queens is described by Lyle as having an "endless something about it. It's like a maze without the interconnection. A blind maze" (43).

Lyle's preferred escape from the constraints of his environment early in the narrative is through television watching, but he is not the typical American viewer. Turning the "channel selector every half minute or so, sometimes more frequently," he enjoys "jerking the dial into fresh image-burns." This activity, described as a "discipline like mathematics or Zen" is pleasurable because he hopes to discover in the "electrostatic glow" of the television screen "a privilege state between wave and visual image, a secret of celestial energy" (14). This deconstruction of the filmic image, patterned by photons bombarding the screen, by rapidly turning the dial is an exercise in which he seeks to apprehend more directly the source or ground of being that is identical in his view with the unified energy field of the new physics. The same motivation also explains his willingness, in the absence of any ideological perspective whatsoever, to assist the anarchists in their plot to disrupt the international monetary system by blowing up its headquarters in the World Trade Center.

When Lyle, chosen to participate in the plot simply because he works for the Exchange, asks one of the anarchists, Marina, why it has been targeted, she explains that the intent is "to disrupt their system, the idea of worldwide money. It's the system that we believe is their secret power. It all goes floating across that floor. Currents of invisible life. . . . The electronic system. The waves and the charges" (93). The anarchists, who view theory as "an effete diversion" and who are committed only to destruction (94), feel compelled to act immediately for fear that the system will "go underground. Or totally electric. Nothing but waves and currents talking to each other" (95). Lyle has no difficulty accepting the motivation of the anarchists because he has "seen the encoding rooms, the microfilming of checks, money moving, shrinking as it moved, beginning to elude visualization, to pass from a paper existence to electronic sequences, its meaning increasingly complex, harder to name" (95). Later, walking down Nassau Street in New York City, he senses that the financial "district grew repeatedly inward, more secret, an occult theology of money," and that at its "inmost crypt might be heard the amplitude pulse of history, a system and rite to overshadow men's senses" (115). The financiers, or systems managers, who are invisible in the actual operations of the system, are not motivated, it seems, by lust for money, power, or even love of control, but rather by a quasimystical contemplation of the movement of the system toward closure. "Financiers," as the anarchist Rafael is reported to have described them, "are more spiritually advanced than monks on an island" (93).

In his most recent fiction DeLillo seems quite intent upon demonstrating that systems are not isolated phenomena that compete with one another in separate regions of thought or experience, but overlapping and interpenetrating modes of constructing reality which may finally become one indistinguishable force. Although this point is made more insistently in *Running Dog*, there is considerable overlap of systems definitions of reality in *Players* as well. As Kinnear, yet another anarchist, puts it: "It's this uncertainty over sources and ultimate goals. . . . It's everywhere, isn't it? Mazes, you're correct. Our big problem in the past, as a nation, was that we didn't give our government credit for being the totally entangling force that it was. . . . All these convolutions and relationships" (91). The effect of this uncertainty on the individual is, as Pynchon also noted, extreme paranoia in which nothing can ever finally be known as itself. "Behind every stark fact," says Kinnear, "we encounter layers of ambiguity" (91). The overlapping of terrorist and police networks and apparatus (102) creates, for example, considerable ambiguity as to the actual identity or allegiance of virtually everyone, including Lyle, who move inside these networks.

The motel, as an emblem of space most amenable to reduction through systems definitions to categories and discrete functions, a notion that was first introduced in *Americana*, is the device that frames *Players*. The novel opens with the statement "SOMEONE says: Motels. I like motels. . . . I'd like to go from one to another to another. There's something self-realizing about that" (1), and closes with a chapter entitled "The Motel." The concept in its "concrete form," muses Lyle in this chapter, is conducive to "Inwardness spiraling ever deeper. Rationality, analysis, self-realization" (182). As the concluding sentence of the narrative suggests, however, the rational or analytical mode of self-examination operating in a subjective universe replete with systems definitions of reality does not reveal the unique structure of the self, but quite the opposite: "The propped figure Lyle, for instance, is barely recognizable as male. Shedding capabilities and traits by the second, he can be described (but quickly) as well formed, sentient and fair. We know nothing else about him" (184–85).

Running Dog is remarkably similar to *Players* in both theme and structure, and contains few surprises for those who have carefully followed the development of DeLillo's art. The protagonist of this narrative, like that of *Players*, is caught up in the mesh of activity associated with overlapping systems, and, although he comes to a considerably more violent end, suffers the same identity confusion and loss of any sense of meaningful relation to the external world. Here, as in *Great Jones Street*, the representatives of interlocking systems are intent on taking possession of a product. The product in this narrative is a film believed to have been shot in Hitler's bunker in Berlin in April 1945. Predictably DeLillo uses this device as an excuse to discourse further on the symbolic content and cultural significance of the filmic image.

Interested in acquiring the film are a dealer in erotic art, a twenty-two-year-old "master of distribution and marketing" of erotica, a U.S. Senator who owns "over a million dollars of sexually explicit art," and the director of "Radial Matrix"—a one-time covert government agency transformed into a private business enterprise.[6] Although Senator Percival, who gives an account of the history of Radial Matrix, perceives no significance in the name of the organization, the implications of this choice of name are difficult to ignore. The words *radial* (branching out in all directions from a common center) and *matrix* (used in mathematics to refer to a set of numbers or terms arranged in rows or columns between parentheses of double lines) conjoined to form one phrase, describe rather neatly the tendence of systems to impose—in their outward circular growth—binary, categorical definitions or functions upon that which is subsumed under their control. Since Radial Matrix in the narrative pretends to be "a systems planning outfit," but actually serves as "a centralized funding mechanism for covert operations directed against foreign governments, against elements within foreign governments, and against political parties trying to gain power contrary to the interests of U.S. corporations abroad" (74), it is a particularly lethal manifestation of systems consciousness. The organization also reflects in a broader context the bipartite, divisive aspect of this mode of constructing reality in that the activities of such organizations, claims the Senator, "satisfy the historical counter-function. They fill those small dark places. And they're illegal. Run counter to the Spirit and letter of every law, every intelligence directive, that pertains to such matters" (74–75). The fact that the government "has lost control of its own operation" (75) is consistent with DeLillo's conviction that systems are self-perpetuating entities that will eventually defy the attempt by systems managers to delimit or even define their movement.

The film shot during the final days of World War II in the bunker of Hitler, who was not at all reticent to admit or act upon his own impassioned commitment to closed systems and symbolics, becomes such a sought after commodity not only because it is presumed to be the "century's ultimate piece of decadence," but also because it "moves" (20). As Moll, reporter for *Running Dog* magazine and sometime lover of Selby, notes: "The modern sensibility had been instructed by a different kind of code. Movement. The image had to move" (80). Movement of the static film image projected on the screen is, of course, illusory, and the representation of self in those images carries the same implications here as it did in *Americana*. Concomitant with the outward expansion of systems definitions of reality is, as Lightborne, the dealer in erotic art, explains, the apparent effort to put the "whole world on film." "We are filmed," he says, "as we shop, work, drive cars, and get medical checkups." "What," he asks, "circles the earth constantly? Spy satellites, weather balloons, U-2 aircraft. What are they doing? Taking pictures" (149–50).

The pictures taken by organizations for purposes of definition and control are, as it turns out, different in kind from those shot in Hitler's bunker. This home movie, believed to be made by Eva Braun, consists of perfectly ordinary footage of Magna Goebbels and her children and what appears to be Hitler doing a pantomime of Charlie Chaplin. That Hitler, who used the moving filmic image for purposes of propaganda more extensively and successfully than any leader of his time, should style himself in the image of an image (Chaplin) is simply a restatement of DeLillo's thesis that film has the power to reduce the individual to the third-person singular. That Chaplin in the *Great Dictator* played Hitler also nicely reinforces the thesis. What most impresses the viewers of the film, Moll and Lightborne, in addition to the fact that it "seems so real" (229), is that the "whole bunch" must be "movie-mad" to be making a home movie when artillery shells are probably "raining down" all around them (237). The suggestion is that Hitler, as product of the filmed documentary and newsreel, or as "an image made in the image and likeness of images," could also not finally distinguish between self as media product and self as an actually existing entity.

The character most directly affected by the machinations of competing but overlapping systems is Glen Selby. As an operative of Radial Matrix, he initially appears on the staff of Senator Percival posing as an expert in erotic art while actually seeking to gather information about the Senator's investigation of the operations of Mudger's organization. As he tells Moll during their first encounter, "I believe in codes" (33), and as the omniscient narrator notes later, virtually all of his activities are "carried on beneath the level of ordinary life" (54). After Mudger elects to sever his connection with Radial Matrix in order to make "movies" (138), he decides that

Selby, aware of that previous connection, must be eliminated. Pursued throughout much of the narrative by an assassination team recruited by Mudger from the South Vietnamese army during his involvement in that conflict, Selby returns to the "Marathon Mines" where he had previously received "extensive weapons training," participated in "small scale military operations," and studied "coding and electronic monitoring," "foreign currencies," and "international banking procedures" (153), courtesy of Radial Matrix. In the retreat to the now-abandoned training center Selby hopes to escape consciousness of systems reality, or, as he puts it, the "incoherence. Selection, election, option, alternative. Codes and formats" that make "choice a subtle form of disease" (192). The severance of a connection with the operation of systems is, in DeLillo's fictional universe, impossible once the individual allows himself to be defined in terms of them. The subject is not merely eliminated, his head is cut off by the surviving member of Mudger's assassination team in order to provide "evidence that the adjustment had been made" (240).

Perhaps the best summary statement on the relationship between DeLillo's somewhat arcane subject matter and his motivations and intentions as artist comes from the novelist himself. The list of names and accomplishments of the most recent recipients of the Nobel Prize in *Ratner's Star* contains the following entry:

LITERATURE—Chester Greylag Dent. . . . the award as "recognition of a near century of epic, piquant disquisitions on the philosophy of logic, the logic of games, the gamesmanship of fiction and prehistory, these early efforts preparing the way for speculative meditations on the unsolvable knot of science and mysticism, which in turn led to his famous afterthoughts on the ethereally select realms of abstract mathematics and the more palpable subheights of history and biography, every published work of this humanist and polymath reflective of an incessant concern for man's standing in the biosphere and hand-blocked in a style best characterized as undiscourageably diffuse."(306–7).

DeLillo has not, of course, been working for a century, but the remainder of the description has some approximate validity. In spite of the bleakness of his vision of the future of man, the concern about the future is earnest and extremely thoughtful.

10 · physics, metaphysics and the form of the novel

Assuming, as I have claimed, that ideas from the new physics are putting the lie to features of consciousness that have been consistently reinforced in Western culture for some 2,500 years, our acceptance of the death of the old notions of substance and relation, which is necessarily a kind of death of ourselves, will not come about simply as a result of rearranging intellectual constructs. If the contemporary novelist is to illumine the pathways into a new era of consciousness, and induce us to travel them with the full conviction of our emotions as well as our intellect, clearly something more must be expected of him than mere thematic treatment of concepts from physics within a traditional novelistic framework. We must be made to inhabit a fictive landscape in which the metaphysics commensurate with the new physics is pervasive and implicit throughout, a landscape in which idea and mode of realization have achieved some final union in both narrative form and technique.

The brave novelist who attempts to construct such a landscape confronts, however, a major and seemingly insurmountable difficulty—the metaphysical assumptions implicit in Newtonian physics are equally implicit in the art form that was also a product of the eighteenth century. Novelists of the period operated upon the same received conceptions of substance and identity, space and time, movement and change, that served as the metaphysical foundations of classical physics, and also made use of the same logical paradigm as the glue to hold these discrete aspects of physical reality together —the principle of the either-or. Since the literary conventions that make a novel a "novel" are themselves grounded in the outmoded metaphysic, the imaginative artist who invents a new set of conventions in accord with an alternate metaphysic would not appear to be writing novels at all.

Although some of the tenets of realist fiction have clearly been abandoned in the novels discussed here, even those narratives that are most innovative technically, like those of Barth and Pynchon, pass as novels, nevertheless, precisely because received narrative conventions have not been altogether abandoned. The first phase of assimilation of the new metaphysic into the art of the novel is, then, both obvious and inevitable—it is a self-conscious rebellion against the conventions. The rebellion, particularly in the more experimental fiction, takes the form of parody, and provides a number of fascinating indications about the direction in which the novel of the future may evolve. If the novelists have failed to move in that direction themselves, it is not due to any reprehensible lack of imagination or artistic integrity. It is simply that the conventions of the novel that would make that movement possible have not yet been established.

The reliance of the early novelists upon common-sense conceptions of space and time, reified by Newton, was, as John Vernon has suggested recently, an enormously important influence upon the evolution of both narrative form and technique.[1] We begin only now to study that influence because our acquaintance with the alternate conception of space-time in the new physics allows us to perceive it as something other than a taken-for-granted aspect of physical reality. From this new vantage point the traditional bases for narrative (time, motion, change) not only take on the appearance of strangeness, they also lose their ontological authority. In an effort to arrive at this perspective we will delineate some extensive, but not necessarily exact, correspondences between Newtonian physics and the novel as subjectively based paradigms for the organization of physical reality. The assumption, or bias, at work here is that each paradigm reflects upon and is grounded in Western metaphysics, and that the set of narrative conventions that grew out of that tradition, which distinguishes the novel from other forms of literary expression, can be brought into sharper focus by playing off the correspondences in the two metaphors.

This examination of "tendencies to occur" in narrative conventions should demonstrate not only the extent to which received conventions in narrative frustrate the efforts of contemporary novelists to create a fictional landscape in which the alternate metaphysic is a feature of both design and function, but should also help us better appreciate why, again for metaphysical reasons, the possibilities of the novel-as-form seem, at least to a select number of novelists and critics, "exhaustible." There are any number of narratives (*Tristram Shandy, Heart of Darkness, Wuthering Heights, Ulysses* and *Finnegans Wake, Nightwood,* and virtually any Faulkner) for which these generalizations about received narrative conventions prove absurdly reductive and terribly inadequate. It is, however, necessary to indulge in conscious exaggeration of the impact of metaphysical assumptions upon these conventions in order to develop, in one chapter, a somewhat distorted, but not finally unrealistic, picture of the form of the novel which, in rough outline at least, remains in force.

The early novelists assumed, as Newton did, that space is that which is void of substance; it is an empty container that exists logically prior to that which it contains. When substance, composed of discrete, immutable atoms, enters that space in classical physics, it *displaces*, and is, therefore, *separate* from, the space itself. Since time in this scheme is the other dimension of being, distinct from the existence of objects that move and change, movement, and the time in which it occurs, are, as Capek notes in his discussion of atomism, eliminated as internal dynamics of the life of substance.[2] Operating upon the same metaphysically based assumptions, the eighteenth-century novelist created characters that move through the space of the novel experiencing change primarily as a function of interaction with other external substances (characters and their attendant things), and time as existing "somewhere" outside of consciousness. Since time placed outside of consciousness must be spatialized, as lines, clocks, and calendars, in order to be represented at all, the architects of the novel fashioned a fictional universe in which real time, or time as an actual condition of being, ceases to exist. Although characters in these novels do, of course, sense subjectively that time is passing, real time makes an appearance as that which it is clearly not by anyone's reckoning—points located in space.

One obvious objection here is that the socialization process in all cultures, regardless of metaphysical orientations, involves, at least within the context of our own psychological paradigms, internalization at some early stage of development of a sense of *self* as disparate from the realm of the *other*. Since the maintenance of the idea of self, fundamental to psychological well-being, is largely a function of reflecting upon the differences in interpretation made by ourselves and others of the results of interactions with external substances, the fact that the eighteenth-century novelist represented change primarily as a function of that interaction does not seem particularly earth shaking. That which is distinctive about the treatment of change in these novels, however, is the extent to which it does not result in any radical transformations in the subjective experience of characters. Characters may change their definition of self in terms of social, political, or economic status as a result of movement to some new location in relation to other, moving substances, but consciousness tends to remain a discrete, atomized entity, sealed-off from the world of full being, and immune to any fundamental alterations in internal structure.

The organization of the movement of the character-substance through space is *plot*, a word that as a verb also refers to the action of locating points on a plane by means of coordinates between two points. Since the early novelist mapped his own locations in terms of coordinates marking relative positions of substances in space, and the relations of moving substances to spatialized points in time, plot became, quite literally, the map of the novel's space. Eidetically reduced, the essence of plot was, and remains, a system or network of lines delineating interrelationships between moving substances. Motion in the map space of the novel, given the correspondence in conceptions of space and time, also resembles motion as it was conceptualized in classical physics in two important respects: the movement of the character-substance is linear and causally connected, and tends to culminate, like the classical experiment, in arrival at some fixed, preordained location where results of interactions are fully known.

Defoe's Crusoe remains, for example, unswervingly industrious, pious, practical, and shrewd, the very epitome of middle-class virtue, throughout his twenty-eight-year residence on the island right up to the inevitable, preordained rescue by the English vessel. As the one-time mariner charts and maps the space of his domain for his own use and comfort, change is represented almost entirely in terms of his triumphant manipulation of external things. Pamela in Richardson's novel moves from lower-middle-class family to wife-of-country-gentleman with her own essence similarly intact. The sweet, tolerant, forgiving Pamela, equipped, of course, with enough middle-class shrewdness to bargain her virginity at the top price, moves linearly, although in this case vertically as well, up the social ladder to her own preordained location simply by remaining that which she was in the very beginning. Similarly, the linear movement of Fielding's Tom Jones establishes threads of connection that form a maplike configuration in which Tom's true identity in relation to a class structure is known—he is now and has always been the illegitimate child of the sister of Squire Allworthy. Marriage with the essence of high-spirited, intelligent, independent, and beautiful female nature, Sophie, and the expansion of economic status and power that will accrue by joining the neighboring estates, is now an inevitability.

The logical principle fundamental to the organization of all particulars in the map space of the novel is the either-or. It is this aspect of the formal logic of the West, everywhere present in the polar oppositions that structure the objective space of narrative, that makes logical coherence possible. And logical coherence continues to be the most explicit criterion for aesthetic unity in all our literature. The most encompassing of these oppositions is that between mind and world, between the agency that maps the landscape and the landscape itself. If the dualism between mind and matter, fostered by classical physics, is of any consequence whatsoever in Western thought, how in epistemological terms could novelists begin to presume that they could provide in fictive space the semblance of correspondence with the form of objective space itself?

The explanation lies, I think, in another metaphysically based assumption which we traced earlier to the wild imaginings of Pythagoras—the notion that mind through reason and contemplation could know the essence of physical reality. The novelist was confident in his ability to depict the objectively real in fiction because he implicitly assumed, as Newton did, that its essential structures were known to him. Since the conceptual forms inherent in the construction of the fictive landscape were presumed to have actual existence in the life of nature, the objective space of the novel, to use the eighteenth-century metaphor, was regarded as the mirror held up to objective space itself. The distinction between map (subjectively based paradigm) and landscape (forms and substances external to consciousness) that has become both obvious and problematic from the modern scientific view was, for this reason, easily blurred for novelists, just as it was for classical physicists.

The primary opposition within the novel itself, between the character-substance and all other external presences in the map space, clearly implies that the world is a thing apart from the people who occupy it. When movement, change, and time are made external to the life of the character-substance, it follows that, as Capek puts it, "Qualitative variety as well as qualitative transformation are psychic additions to the perceiving mind; they do not belong to the nature of things."[3] This split in the novel between consciousness and the objects of perception extends and reinforces, along with Newtonian science, the split between mind and world that was an early consequence of ontological dualism in Western metaphysics. Reader identification with characters inhabiting a fictive landscape irrevocably distinct from their own being, a landscape replete with fragmented, discontinuous particulars which in their consciousness at least are not finally synthesized, might well be another, heretofore hidden, source of alienation in the experience of modern man.

The alienating influence of metaphysically based assumptions about the character of physical reality has an indirect impact, albeit a more dramatic one, in realist and naturalist fiction with the reliance upon deterministic models for the organization of human experience. Balzac's view of character in *La Comédie Humaine* as zoological specimens modified by natural and social conditions, or Tolstoy's conception of character as sums of historical tendencies that inexorably determine place and function in the larger scheme, obviously owe something to the scientific determinism legitimated by Newtonian science. The conviction of the naturalists that awesome and unseen *forces* in "Life, Nature, History" wholly determine the location and direction of change for the character-substance shows a rather obvious dependence upon the Newtonian conception of natural law. The idea of fixed, transcendent and immutable natural law is, for example, very much in evidence in Zola's efforts to apply to the treatment of character the experimental method of the natural sciences, and in Dreiser's seemingly endless demonstrations that characters are merely functions of nature, manipulated without consideration by hidden, immaterial agencies.

The distinction in point of view between novelist and classical physicist virtually dissolves in naturalist fiction. The eye of both novelist and scientist is the objective recorder of causally connected events; it is the godlike, immaterial, knowing essence positioned at such a remove from the materials under investigation as not to interfere with the outcome in the least. Since the lens through which the objective eye of the narrator views substance is the forces, or laws, which move them, characters in naturalist fiction become even more atomized than they were in earlier fiction. Their subjective realities, compressed to the limit, become airtight, stultifying, boxlike containers in which unwilling products and victims of the natural engage in inchoate and fruitless speculation upon their proper relation to a world in which individual thought and feeling are inevitably disjunctive and incongruent with external reality.

The analogy between character in this fiction and the atom of classical physics is made even more complete when we consider that both are unconscious of the reified essences that determine the results of their interactions. True human freedom can be incorporated into the novel, says Sartre, only when the future does not preexist for any of the characters.[4] The burden of the preexistent future—ameliorated for the early novelists, as it was for Newton, by acceptance of the possibility of divine intervention—takes on the oppressive weight of terrible certainty in the godless universe of naturalism that has remained to some degree in the experience of the novel ever since.

Although in more recent fiction the growing recognition that chance, hazard, or indeterminacy as a feature of natural process has greatly diminished the emphasis upon neat, mathematical correspondences between forces and the movement of character-substances, the map space in which the movement occurs, and the conventions of narrative congruent with that structure, have not undergone any major transformations. The fear on the part of contemporary novelists, popularized by Barth, that the possibilities of the novel as form have been exhausted, that an entropic heat death of the entire genre may already be in progress, is due in no small part to the inability of the contemporary novelist to circumvent received conventions and make the conception of space-time legitimated by the new physics operational in narrative.

That sense of exhausted possibilities is perhaps best represented in the fictive landscape of a novelist who is the self-proclaimed architect of a *new novel*, but who, in fact, has simply pushed the metaphysically based assumptions about space and time in the old novel to their logical, and absurd, conclusion. Borrowing from Sartre the notion that the *en soi* is irreparably distinct from the *pour soi*, and that the individual, consequently, is locked away in the abyss of his subjectivity, Robbe-Grillet asserts in *For a New Novel* that "things are there and they are nothing but things, each limited to itself."[5] In divesting all objects in fiction of any subjective significance and reducing the world to a purely visual presence, Robbe-Grillet has created a fiction whose structure is, in many fundamental respects, more Newtonian than that of the eighteenth-century novel.

Most obviously, the philosophical premise upon which this art is constructed infers that the classical division between primary and secondary qualities is precisely that which Newton and Descartes presumed it must be without appeal to transcendence in some form —absolute. The absence of any synthesizing intelligence in this fiction, other than that of the character-reader, makes it difficult, if not impossible, to configure distances between locations at any remove from objects themselves, to look down upon relative positions of substances and gain a sense of overview. The lack of the synthesizing intelligence also explains why time, spatialized with a peculiar vengeance by Robbe-Grillet, is experienced by the reader as such a tedious and mind-numbing affair. Any suggestion of passage or flow of time, other than the still pictures of locations in space recorded by the watchful and insistent, but certainly less than human, narrative eye, would suggest that human signification has been surreptitiously at work.

The so-called new novel is, then, not new because it relies wholly upon metaphysically based conceptions of the nature of space and time that have structured the novel from the very beginning; it can be called *new* only in the sense that it makes explicit in narrative form and technique the logical consequences of the full implementation of that structure. The result is map space pure and simple. In Robbe-Grillet objects in the fictive landscape have finally become that which metaphysically based assumptions about space and time in narrative have always implied that they must be in the absence of an ontological principle that would bridge the gap between perceiver and perceived—discrete and discontinuous substances devoid of all human signification. If Robbe-Grillet's novels exude the sense of exhausted possibilities, which they appear to do in a very studied manner, it is because the conventions of his narratives, grounded in a metaphysical tradition that presumes ontological dualism, are indeed, exhaustible when transcendence in any form, and hence the duality of being, is denied. What is clearly needed to enliven the sense of the possible in narrative is something that Robbe-Grillet's so-called new novel does not begin to provide—an entirely new set of conventions grounded in an alternate metaphysic.

In the new physics *things* or substances, including our own bodies, are processes in the space-time continuum that involve and in some sense are all other processes, and the matter that composes substance is simply one manifestation of a unified field of energy at the point at which gravity is extremely intense. Operating upon this understanding of the nature of things, the architects of the new fictional landscape are not likely to find the traditional conception of character as discrete, discontinuous, sealed-off substance very useful. All of the novelists studied here make concessions thematically to the notion that life is a unified process, within which character is an evolving and unified function, but none has yet to discover a way within the texture of narrative itself to suggest that an actual fusion between subjective and objective realities, as interrelated activities of that process, has occurred. Each parodies the notion of character as fixed, unchanging substance, with particular emphasis upon the power of static constructs (roles, masks, reified essences) to fragment the experience of self and to obviate any full, Heideggerean, sense of being-in-the-world, but characters remain, nevertheless, sealed-off subjectivities.

Nicholas Urfe in *The Magus*, Amanda and John Paul Ziller in *Another Roadside Attraction*, and Harry in *Rabbit, Run* and *Rabbit Redux* achieve, for example, a drug-induced awareness of cosmic unity, but the result is mere description of an alternate state of consciousness that cannot, by definition, be fully incorporated into the reality of everyday experience. Similarly, Barth's Burlingame and Polyeides represent character as evolving process, but the process is an internal dynamic projected upon external reality as masks of identity that become barriers to full participation and intelligibility in the realm of the *other*. Pynchon's treatment of Slothrop as a strung-out series of patterns of self, or repetitions of forms, that come together, but do not logically cohere, as a nexus of lines involving the activities of both self and world, is a far more imaginative approach to the problem. The use of lines to configure the connection is, however, nicely illustrative of the difficulties involved in the effort, as Pynchon might put it, to "interface" received conventions of characterization with the metaphysics implied in the new physics. Although the lines as metaphor parody the conventional conception of the movement of character-substance as neat, linear progression in the map space, they also imply a relation between disparate points, and hence an irreconcilable division between subjective and objective realities.

The novelists have apparently been more successful in drawing upon ideas from physics to modify conventions in narrative governing the role of the narrator himself. The observer in the new physics is not only the carrier of paradigm-induced expectations that make the experiment and govern the outcome of the process of observation, he is also part of the activity of the experiment itself. This notion is more easily incorporated into narrative because it legitimates experiments in narrative technique without completely undermining the observer's, or narrator's, role as commentator upon and interpreter of events. Barth's frequent reminders in his later work that the truth of fiction is that fact is fantasy, or the appearance of narrator as character in fiction (Barth, Fowles in *The French Lieutenant's Woman*, Vonnegut) might well have been derived, in part at least, from the acquaintance of these novelists with the role of the observer in physics. The appearance in Robbins's novels of Tarzan, Christ, or the human brain and thumb, as characters like any other, also bespeaks a new freedom in the use of narrative that is rather easily legitimated by this aspect of the new science.

It is, however, in the treatment of plot that the novelists have discovered their greatest opportunity to parody received conventions in narrative that are incommensurate with the metaphysical implications of contemporary physics. On the most obvious level there is an open-endedness in the movement of the character-substance that denies the prospect of arrival, and the resolution of conflict, in a fixed location. Even Fowles, who is, along with Updike, comfortable with the constraints of plot as it has been traditionally conceived, takes care in *The Magus* to suggest that the scene that appears climactic, the trial, is actually a metaphor for closed, rationally constructed paradigms that cannot contain or define fluid process. The variable conclusions to another of his conventionally plotted narratives, *The French Lieutenant's Woman*, serve the same function. Among this group of novelists the most subtle and radical parodies of plot as the system of lines marking actual relationships between moving character-substances in the map space are those of Barth and Pynchon.

Ebenezer in *The Sot-Weed Factor* is a representative eighteenth-century man traveling as he conceives it through a space that is clearly Newtonian. His efforts to disclose within the fabric of events the location of atomized substances as functions of some rational design leads him into one comically absurd predicament after another, and, finally, to the recognition that, as Burlingame tells him, "the pointed order of the world" lives only in his fancy. Plot in this narrative, as Barth states explicitly on several occasions in *Lost in the Funhouse*, is a subjectively based construct accepted by both reader and narrator as just another of those necessary illusions that are the price of admission into the world of *as if*. In *Giles* Barth externalizes within the space of the narrative the forms of the mind and the principle of their organization, the either-or, that are the essential ingredients of plot in realist fiction. As we follow the indeterminate and irrationally motivated movements of character through the University (world) structured by WESCAC (Western mind), the impulse to plot, or to organize experience in life or literature in the manner of the realists, is revealed as not only absurdly destructive for the individual, but potentially disastrous for all human civilization.

Pynchon's refusal to allow the lines of linear connection to arrive at closure in both *V.* and *Gravity's Rainbow* can also be read as parody of plot in realist fiction. In *Gravity's Rainbow*, as in *Giles*, the closure of narrative lines, or the final imposition of plot, becomes a metaphor for all subjectively based paradigms that demand closure upon the structure of human life. Since the closure of narrative lines in *Gravity's Rainbow* would have required that the rocket over Ravenhage reach and explode at ground zero, Pynchon, like Barth, is obviously convinced that our continued reliance upon this mode of organizing experience is not to be taken lightly.

A more accessible parody of received conceptions of plot is Oedipa's attempt in *Crying of Lot 49* to draw the lines of connection between points in space which will, she hopes, disclose the hidden structure, or plot, of the Tristero. Although her own movements are clearly random and arbitrary, she happens upon what appear to be the signatures of the system in every conceivable circumstance: in a Jacobean revenge drama, on a lavatory wall, in a bar or a munitions factory, and, most pervasively, in the seeming machinations of the hopelessly complex postal delivery service called WASTE. Oedipa's expectation, like that of the reader, is that mind-rending puzzle will be transformed into meaningful, rational pattern with the addition of the last, hidden point of connection in the yet undisclosed scheme. The conspicuous absence of this last point of connection in the narrative is Pynchon's way of suggesting that the network of causally linked lines in the systems, or plots, which we use in life or literature to reduce a fundamentally indeterminate process to static, logical configuration, are fictions of our mental landscape arbitrarily imposed upon an actual landscape that cannot be contained or defined by them. Our compulsion to do so is, as Pynchon sees it, not only the source of alienation, but also the stuff from which paranoid delusion—Oedipa's struggle in the novel—is made. DeLillo, as we saw in some detail earlier, is similarly preoccupied with the dehumanizing, alienating influence of closed systems definitions of reality in virtually all of his fiction.

Although Vonnegut's fiction from a technical standpoint is not as highly textured or configured as that of Barth or Pynchon, he alone among the novelists studied here has arrived at a conception of plot which, as a thought experiment at least, is commensurate with the metaphysics implied in the new physics. The model is the written communications of the Trafalmadorians. Their messages consist, as we noted earlier, of "clumps of symbols" free of any Newtonian emphasis upon beginning, middle, end, cause or effect, but arranged so that the "depths of many marvelous moments" can be instantaneously known when read "all at once" by the recipient. There is, of course, good reason to suspect that plot for the Trafalmadorians is not likely to be very useful to the plot makers on this particular planet. The novels of earthlings will doubtless continue, for a while at least, to consist of linear progressions of words on a page which, in spite of the assurances of the apostles of speed-reading techniques, will not be apprehended "all at once" by any of us. There is, however, one aspect of this bizarre formula which is much more suggestive of new possibilities in narrative than we might initially expect—

the notion that a novel could be written as cleverly arranged "clumps of symbols."

Symbols in literature, as Charles Feidelson has demonstrated, are capable of uniting part and whole, and, therefore, of configuring discrete aspects of reality as a single unity.[6] Assuming that consciousness, including all modes of perception, is, like any other event in nature, simply another manifestation of energy in the space-time continuum, the symbol, with its capacity to integrate in consciousness external and internal realities, could well become the vehicle through which traditional oppositions in the space of the novel can be blended. Symbolic language, which once served to reveal, as figures like Eliade have claimed, the "basic oneness of several zones of the real" to man in primitive cultures,[7] could conceivably function in the same way for modern scientific man now that his science has demonstrated that the primitive is not so primitive after all. Since the sustained use of symbolic language to wed antinomies like character and setting, motion and stasis, space and time, would undermine received conventions in the narrative so completely as to make them nonexistent, we should not anticipate any rapid developments in this direction very soon. We might well expect, however, some greater reliance upon the integrative function of symbols by those novelists of the future who undertake to incorporate within their fiction the metaphysic implied in the new physics simply because it is the only established literary device abundantly suited to that purpose. DeLillo's efforts to rediscover the denotative aspect of language, or the word as concrete referent, as a precondition for constructing alternate symbolics is indicative, I think, of a renewed emphasis upon this function of symbolic language.

In the absence of yet-to-be-imagined conventions in the novel congruent with the new metaphysic, all speculations at this juncture upon the possible form or structure of the new fictional landscape are, I suspect, idle. During this period of waiting, however, we can look forward to these developments with no small degree of excitement, and not for the fairly mundane reasons that they will provide grist for the omnivorous critical mill, or prove that the possibilities of the novel have not been exhausted after all. The headier prospect is that the novel, as the art form best equipped to extensively articulate the relationship between objective and subjective realities, could serve as the artistic medium through which Western man might rediscover in lived experience a sense of being-in-the-world as something other than a sealed-off subjectivity cruelly victimized by external forces. The essential problem of the hero, or anti-hero, in contemporary fiction is one of identity, and the source of that problem is Cartesian dualism made absolute in the absence of transcendence. For the contemporary hero in fiction, says Hassan, the "essence of the self and the essence of the world are not one and the same, and the broken pattern of all his actions recalls the futile courage of a Sisyphus toiling to unite one pole of experience to the other."[8] Immersion in the realm of the *other* is such a terrifying prospect in the contemporary novel because its existence is perceived as a function of that which is wholly separate from it in ontological terms —human consciousness. If the novelist of the future can free himself of the confines of the old metaphysics, well represented in received narrative conventions, and fashion a fictional universe in which polar oppositions between mind and world become, as the quantum theorists insist they must be, interrelated dynamics of one unified process, perhaps we could put the story of Sisyphus back into the context of Greek mythology where it now clearly belongs.

The awareness of our hypothetical future novelist that life is an open-ended, essentially indeterminate process could also make for a renewed emphasis upon what novelist as Newtonian scientist could not really entertain in the realist and naturalist movements—the ineffable and mysterious. In the absence, says Jaspers, of any "sense of the infinite vastness of what is beyond our grasp, all we succeed in conveying is misery—not tragedy."[9] The misery that is so prevalent in contemporary fiction is due in no small part to the inability of Western man to celebrate that sense of the infinite. Without it, as Blake intuited in the age of Newton, the "bounded is loathed by the possessor," and that which passes as art is merely the patterned repetitions of the already known and dully familiar.

The vastness of what is beyond our grasp in the new physics is as near as the dance of particles that make up the substance we call our bodies, and as far as matter in regions of the cosmos that will probably remain forever undetectable to us. And yet the energy that is matter is as near as it is far, manifesting itself everywhere in the space-time continuum as the perpetually new, inexhaustible essence unfolding and folding upon itself in the never finished becoming of its own being. And more wonderful still, all indications are that every effort we make to arrive at a definitive understanding of its nature will probably, given the quantum interconnectedness of all events and the indeterminacy principle, dissolve before the discerning intellect like the smile on Lewis Carroll's Cheshire cat. If this is not the stuff out of which great art is made, I suggest we stop looking for it altogether.

Preface

1. Gerald Holton, *Thematic Origins of Scientific Thought* (Cambridge, Mass.: Harvard University Press, 1974), pp. 48–49.

2. Quoted in Harry Hoijer, "The Sapir-Whorf Hypothesis," *Language and Culture*, American Anthropological Association, Memoir no. 79 (1954), pp. 95–96.

3. Ibid., p. 102. See Joseph H. Greenberg, *Essays in Linguistics* (New York, 1957), pp. 56–65, and Leslie A. White, "The Origin and Nature of Speech," *Twentieth-Century English* (New York, 1940), pp. 99–103 for a more detailed discussion of these matters.

4. Holton, *Thematic Origins*, p. 31.

5. Karl H. Popper, *The Logic of Scientific Discovery* (New York: Basic Books, 1959), p. 317.

6. Martin Deutsch, *Evidence and Inference in Nuclear Research*, ed. Daniel Lerner (Glencoe, Ill.: The Free Press, 1959), p. 98.

7. Henry Pierce Stapp, "The Copenhagen Interpretation," *American Journal of Physics*, 40 (1972): 1112.

8. Holton, *Thematic Origins*, p. 448.

9. See Tony Tanner, *City of Words* (London: Cape, 1971). The preoccupation with the self-limiting, restraining, and distancing function of linguistic reality is, for example, perceived by Tanner as something of an obsession among writers of the American contemporary novel. That obsession is, suggests Tanner, principally a consequence of the "tenacious feeling in America that while older countries are ridden by conventions, rules, all sorts of arbitrary formalities which trap and mould the individual, in America one may enjoy a genuine freedom from all cultural patterning so that life is a series of unmitigated spontaneities" (p. 15). Although I do perceive some validity in this assumption, it also strikes me that the examination of the epistemological limits and the ontological foundations of language by the present generation of novelists is not being conducted only by

Americans, and also that it is different in kind, even in the American tradition, from that conducted by Melville, Hawthorne, Poe, or James. There are, of course, gross similarities, but the intellectual concerns that promote the examination are quite different in the modern period from those at work in the creative efforts of the first great generation of American novelists. And one of those concerns, which is definitely a palpable presence in the work of novelists studied by both Tanner and me, is the new paradigm for the organization of material reality.

Common Sense and the Nature of Things

1. John Dewey, *The Quest for Certainty: A Study of Knowledge and Action* (New York: Putnam, 1929), p. 115.
2. Werner Heisenberg, *Physics and Philosophy* (New York: Harper and Row, 1958), p. 72.
3. Ibid., p. 71.
4. Copernicus, *De Revolutionibus*, quoted in Gerald Holton, *Thematic Origins of Scientific Thought* (Cambridge, Mass.: Harvard University Press, 1974), p. 82.
5. Holton, *Thematic Origins*, pp. 69, 70–71.
6. Kepler to Herwart von Hohenburg, February 10, 1605, published in Holton, *Thematic Origins*, p. 72.
7. Kepler to Johann Brengger, October 4, 1607, published in Holton, *Thematic Origins*, p. 76.
8. Holton, *Thematic Origins*, p. 86.
9. Kepler to von Hohenburg, February 10, 1605.
10. *Dialogo sopra i due Massimi Sistemi del Mondo*, in *Le Opere di Galileo Galilei* (Firenze: Edizione Nazionale, 1898), 7:35.
11. Alexandre Koyré, *Metaphysics and Measurement* (Cambridge, Mass.: Harvard University Press, 1968), pp. 42–43.
12. See Aristotle *Physics* 7. 5. 249b, a50 250a; *De Caelo* 3. 2. 301e.
13. Galileo, *Dialogo*, pp. 229, 423.
14. Koyré, *Metaphysics and Measurement*, p. 95.
15. Galileo Galilei, *Dialogues Concerning the Two Great Systems of the World*, in *Mathematical Collections and Translations*, trans. Thomas Salusbury (London, 1961), 1:99.
16. Galileo Galilei to Grand Duchess Christini, 1615, in *Mathematical Collections*, 1:80.
17. See account and comments on sources in G. Milhaud, *Descartes savant* (Paris, 1922), p. 47.
18. René Descartes, *Principles of Philosophy*, Part 1, principle 76, in *Philosophical Works*, trans. Haldene and Ross (Cambridge, Mass.: Harvard University Press, 1911).
19. *Principles of Philosophy*, Part 1, principle 1, in *Philosophical Works*.
20. Isaac Newton, *Opticks*, 3d edition, corrected (London, 1721), p. 376.
21. Ibid., pp. 345, 328.
22. Frank E. Manuel, *Isaac Newton Historian* (Cambridge, Mass.: Harvard University Press, 1963), p. 1.

23. Frank E. Manuel, *Portrait of Isaac Newton* (Cambridge, Mass.: Harvard University Press, 1968), pp. 12, 22.
24. Isaac Newton, "System of the World" in *Mathematical Principles of Natural Philosophy*, vol. 3 (London, 1803), p. 10.
25. Newton, *Opticks*, pp. 351, 377.
26. Newton, *Mathematical Principles*, Part 1, principle 9.
27. Ibid., Part 2, p. 311.

Metaphysics and the New Physics

1. Thomas S. Kuhn, *The Structure of Scientific Revolutions* (Chicago: University of Chicago Press, 1970), pp. 5, 52–53.
2. Albert Einstein, "Autobiographical Notes," in *Albert Einstein: Philosopher-Scientist*, ed. P. A. Schilpp (LaSalle, Ill.: Open Court, 1969), p. 45.
3. Ibid., pp. 3, 5.
4. Albert Einstein, "On the Method of Theoretical Physics," in *Ideas and Opinions* (New York: Dell Publishing Company, 1973), pp. 246–49.
5. Ilse Rosenthal-Schneider, "Reminiscences of Conversations with Einstein," July 23, 1959, quoted in Holton, *Thematic Origins*, p. 236.
6. Gerald Holton, *Thematic Origins of Scientific Thought*, p. 307.
7. Albert Einstein, "Aether und Relativitätstheorie," trans. W. Perret and G. B. Jeffrey, in *Physical Thought from the Pre-Socratics to the Quantum Physicists*, ed. Shmuel Sambursky (New York: Pica Press, 1975), p. 479.
8. Herman Minkowski, "Space and Time" (An address to the Eightieth Assembly of German National Scientists and Physicians, Cologne, Germany, September 21, 1908). Reprinted in A. Loen, A. Einstein, H. Minkowski, and H. Weyle, *The Principles of Relativity* (New York: Dover Press, 1952), p. 75.
9. Albert Einstein and Leopold Infield, *The Evolution of Physics* (New York: Simon and Schuster, 1961), p. 197.
10. James B. Conant, cited in *The Limits of Language*, ed. Walker Gibson (New York: Hill and Wang, 1962), p. 17.
11. Albert Einstein, cited in Melic Capek, *The Philosophical Impact of Contemporary Physics* (Princeton, N.J.: Princeton University Press, 1961), p. 53.
12. Werner Heisenberg, *Physics and Beyond* (New York: Harper and Row, 1958), p. 76.
13. Max Jammer, *The Conceptual Development of Quantum Mechanics* (New York: McGraw-Hill, 1966), p. 271.
14. Max Born, *Atomic Physics* (New York: Hafner, 1957), p. 102.
15. Werner Heisenberg, cited in James B. Conant, *Modern Science and Modern Man* (New York: Columbia University Press, 1953), p. 40.
16. J. Robert Oppenheimer, *Science and the Common Understanding* (New York, 1956), pp. 42–43.
17. Léon Rosenfeld, "Niels Bohr in the Thirties: Consolidation and Extension of the Conception of Complementarity," in *Niels Bohr: His Life and Work as Seen by His Friends and Colleagues*, ed. Stefan Rozental (New York: John Wiley and Sons), p. 121.

18. Oscar Klein, "Glimpses of Niels Bohr," in *Niels Bohr*, p. 74.

19. Holton, *Thematic Origins*, p. 146.

20. Henry Pierce Stapp, "The Copenhagen Interpretation," *American Journal of Physics* 40 (1972): 1104.

21. D. Bohm and B. Hiley, "On the Intuitive Understanding of Nonlocality as Implied by Quantum Theory," in *Foundations in Physics* (Princeton, N.J.: Princeton University Press, 1961), p. 319.

22. Henry Pierce Stapp, "S Matrix Interpretation of Quantum Theory," *Physical Review* 3 (1971): 1303 ff.

23. See Hugh Everett, III, " 'Relative State' Formations of Quantum Mechanics," *Review of Modern Physics* 29, no. 3 (1957): 454–62.

24. See J. A. Wheeler, "Genesis and Observership" in *Proceedings of the Fifth International Congress of Logic, Methodology, and Philosophy of Science*, ed. R. E. Butts and J. Hintikki, part 2 (Boston: Reidel, 1977), pp. 3–33.

25. Stephen Brush, "The Chimerical Cat: Philosophy of Quantum Mechanics in Historical Perspective," *Social Studies in Science* 10 (1980): 393–447.

26. Henry Margenau, in *Albert Einstein: Philosopher-Scientist*, p. 250.

27. Mandel Sachs, "Space Time and Elementary Interactions in Relativity," *Physics Today* 22 (February 1969): 53.

28. Evelyn Fox Keller, "Cognitive Repression in Contemporary Physics," *American Journal of Physics* 47, no. 8 (August 1979): 717.

29. Ibid., p. 721.

30. Ibid.

John Fowles

1. William J. Palmer, *The Fiction of John Fowles* (Columbia: University of Missouri Press, 1975), p. 7.

2. John Fowles, *The Aristos: A Self-Portrait in Ideas* (Boston, 1970), p. 20.

3. Jean-Paul Sartre, *Existentialism*, trans. Bernard Frechtman (New York: Philosophical Library, 1948), p. 46.

4. See *The Aristos*, p. 28.

5. John Fowles, *The Magus*, rev. ed. (New York: Dell, 1979), p. 17. The differences between the revised edition of *The Magus*, used as the basis for this discussion, and the earlier edition are not as substantial as some reviewers initially led us to believe. The most pervasive change is that the character Nicholas is made more circumspect and less naive as he progresses through the godgame. The result is that some of the magical, fabulous quality of the first version is sacrificed, but the obvious benefit is that the more bizarre events in the narrative become much more credible. Other changes, like the rewrite of the scene in which Lily-Julie seduces Nicholas before the trial and the much anticipated new ending, simply make explicit what was implicit in the first version.

6. See Jean-Paul Sartre, *Being and Nothingness*, trans. Hazel Barnes (New York: Philosophical Library, 1956), pp. 565–66.

John Barth

1. John Barth, *The Floating Opera* (New York: Viking Press, 1972), p. 15.
2. John Barth, *The End of the Road* (New York: Viking Press, 1969), p. 128.
3. John Barth, *The Sot-Weed Factor* (New York: Viking Press, 1969), p. 132.
4. John Barth, *Lost in the Funhouse* (New York: Viking Press, 1969), p. ix.
5. John Barth, *Chimera* (New York: Random House, 1972), p. 256.
6. John Barth, *Giles Goat-Boy* (New York: Viking Press, 1967), p. 100.

John Updike

1. John Updike, *Picked-up Pieces* (Greenwich, Conn.: Fawcett Publications, 1975), p. 483.
2. Victor Strandberg, "John Updike and the Changing of the Gods," *Mosaic*, 12 (Autumn 1978): 159.
3. *Picked-up Pieces*, p. 485.
4. Strandberg, p. 169.
5. John Updike, *Horizon*, Autumn 1972, p. 105.
6. John Updike, *Assorted Prose* (New York: Alfred Knopf, 1979), p. 105.
7. John Updike, *A Month of Sundays* (Greenwich, Conn.: Fawcett Publications, 1975), p. 135.
8. *Assorted Prose*, p. 299.
9. Denis de Rougement, *Love in the Western World*, trans. Montgomery Belgion (London, 1956), p. 315.
10. Karl Barth, *Church Dogmatics: A Selection*, trans. G. W. Bromiley (New York, 1962), p. 188.
11. John Updike, *The Poorhouse Fair* (New York: Fawcett Publications, 1959), pp. 78–79.
12. Although structuralism in the criticism of figures like Geoffrey Hartman, Harold Bloom, and J. Hillis Miller ("the Yale School") has been enormously influential of late, it is, I think, likely that this somewhat mechanical model, premised on the efficacy of binary opposition and closed systems of relation, will be viewed as inexact, or at least less appropriate, when the metaphysics implied in the new physics is more generally known in the academic community.
13. John Updike, *Rabbit Redux* (Greenwich, Conn.: Fawcett Publications, 1972).
14. John Updike, *Rabbit, Run* (New York: Fawcett Publications, 1960), p. 255.
15. John Updike, *Picked up Pieces*, p. 191.
16. John Updike, *The Centaur* (Greenwich, Conn.: Fawcett Publications, 1963).
17. John Updike, "The Art of Fiction," *The Paris Review*, Spring 1969, p. 69.
18. John Updike, *Couples* (Greenwich, Conn.: Fawcett Publications, 1969), p. 12.
19. *A Month of Sundays*, p. 56.
20. John Updike, *The Coup* (New York: Fawcett Publications, 1978), p. 17.

204

Kurt Vonnegut, Jr.

1. Kurt Vonnegut, Jr., "Address to the American Physical Society," in *Wampeters, Foma & Granfalloons* (New York: Dell, 1976), p. 93.
2. Vonnegut, "Playboy Interview," in *Wampeters*, p. 266.
3. Vonnegut, Preface to *Wampeters*, p. 1.
4. Kurt Vonnegut, Jr., *The Sirens of Titan* (New York: Dell, 1976), p. 21.
5. Kurt Vonnegut, Jr., *God Bless You, Mr. Rosewater* (New York: Dell, 1965), p. 18.
6. Vonnegut, "Address to Graduating Class at Bennington College, 1970," in *Wampeters*, pp. 166, 163.
7. Vonnegut, "Address to the National Institute of Arts and Letters, 1971," in *Wampeters*, p. 176.
8. Vonnegut, "Playboy Interview," in *Wampeters*, p. 239.
9. Kurt Vonnegut, Jr., *Cat's Cradle* (New York: Dell, 1970), p. 14.
10. Kurt Vonnegut, Jr., *Slaughter House-Five* (New York: Dell, 1971), p. 27.
11. Kurt Vonnegut, Jr., *Breakfast of Champions* (New York: Dell, 1975), p. 241.
12. Kurt Vonnegut, Jr., *Player Piano* (New York: Dell, 1974), p. 116.
13. Kurt Vonnegut, Jr., *Mother Night* (New York: Dell, 1974), p. xii.
14. John Somer, "Geodesic Vonnegut; or If Buckminster Fuller Wrote Novels," in *The Vonnegut Statement*, ed. Jerome Klinkowitz and John Somer (New York: Delacorte Press, 1973), p. 238.
15. Vonnegut, "Playboy Interview," in *Wampeters*, p. 258.

Thomas Pynchon

1. Frank D. McConnell, "Thomas Pynchon," in *Contemporary Novelists*, ed. James Vinson (New York: St. Martin's Press, 1972), p. 1034.
2. Pynchon has an agreement with his publisher that stipulates that no critical studies of his own work can be published by them if they wish to maintain their contract with him.
3. Thomas Pynchon, *Crying of Lot 49* (New York: Viking Press, 1967), p. 10.
4. Thomas Pynchon, *Gravity's Rainbow* (New York: Viking Press, 1974), p. 1.
5. Alfred North Whitehead, *Process and Reality* (New York: Free Press, 1960), p. 254.
6. Joseph W. Slade, *Thomas Pynchon* (New York: Warner Paperback Library, 1974), p. 219. Also see Lance W. Ozier, "The Calculus of Transformation: More Mathematical Imagery in *Gravity's Rainbow*," *Twentieth Century Literature* 21, no. 2 (May 1975): 193–210.
7. Slade, p. 215.
8. See Max Weber, *The Protestant Ethic and the Spirit of Capitalism*, trans. Talcott Parsons (New York: Scribner's, 1958).

Tom Robbins

1. Fritjof Capra, *The Tao of Physics* (Berkeley: Shambhala, 1975).
2. Tom Robbins, *Another Roadside Attraction* (New York: Doubleday, 1971), p. 142.
3. Tom Robbins, *Even Cowgirls Get the Blues* (New York: Bantam, 1977), p. 82.

Don DeLillo

1. Don DeLillo, *Americana* (New York: Simon and Schuster, 1973), p. 34.
2. Don DeLillo, *End Zone* (New York: Simon and Schuster, 1973), p. 8.
3. Don DeLillo, *Great Jones Street* (New York: Simon and Schuster, 1974), p. 1.
4. Don DeLillo, *Ratner's Star* (New York: Alfred Knopf, 1976), p. 69.
5. Don DeLillo, *Players* (New York: Random House, 1977), p. 16.
6. Don DeLillo, *Running Dog* (New York: Random House, 1978), p. 49.

Physics, Metaphysics, and the Form of the Novel

1. See John Vernon, *The Garden and the Map* (Urbana: University of Illinois Press, 1973). Vernon's understanding of the metaphysical foundations of the form of the novel is, I think, formidable, and I have drawn heavily upon his efforts here.
2. Melic Capek, *The Philosophical Impact of Contemporary Physics* (Princeton, N.J.: Princeton University Press, 1961), pp. 123 ff.
3. Ibid., p. 79.
4. Jean-Paul Sartre, *Literary and Philosophical Essays*, trans. Annette Michelson (New York: Collier Books, 1962), p. 7.
5. Alain Robbe-Grillet, *For a New Novel*, trans. Richard Howard (New York, 1966), p. 138.
6. Charles Feidelson, Jr., *Symbolism and American Literature* (Chicago: University of Chicago Press, 1953), pp. 57, 60.
7. Mircea Eliade, *Patterns in Comparative Religion*, trans. Rosemary Sheed (Cleveland: World, 1963), p. 452.
8. Ihab Hassan, *Radical Innocence* (Princeton, N.J.: Princeton University Press, 1971), p. 114.
9. Karl Jaspers, *Tragedy Is Not Enough*, trans. Harald A. T. Reiche, Harry T. Moore, and Karl W. Deutsch (Boston: Anchor Books, 1952), p. 48.

selected bibliography

The following short bibliography is intended as a research tool for humanists who wish to acquire background in the history and philosophy of science. Although the authors of these works do occasionally rely upon mathematical language to represent scientific ideas, the origins and implications of those ideas are, for the most part, expressed in ordinary language. In the instances in which additional commentary on the content of the work seemed useful or necessary, I have provided it.

Primary Sources

The manner in which the architects of major scientific theories express their views in ordinary language is the source of great insight into the metaphysical assumptions prevalent in their time. These well-known but seldom read texts are particularly useful in that regard.

Aristotle. *Physics.*
Copernicus, Nicolaus. *On the Revolution of the Heavenly Orbs.*
Laplace, Marquis de. *System of the World.*
Galilei, Galileo. *Dialogues Concerning the Two Great Systems of the World.*
Newton, Isaac. *Opticks.*
————. *Principia.*

Secondary Sources

This list provides a selection of books that will give general background, surveys of scientific developments, and bibliographies, as well as a number of items that will be useful to those readers concerned with the metaphysical assumptions and cultural implications of ideas from physics.

Boyer, Carl. *A History of Mathematics*. New York: Wiley, 1968.

Brush, Stephen G. "Irreversibility and Indeterminism: Fourier to Heisenberg." *Journal of the History of Ideas* 37 (1976): 603–30. A solid short history of an important aspect of modern science.

——. *The Kind of Motion We Call Heat, A History of the Kinetic Theory of Gases*. New York: North-Holland, 1976.

——. "Should the History of Science Be Rated X?" *Science*, no. 183 (1974), pp. 1164–72. Reviews the conflict between conceptions of "proper" scientific methods and conclusions drawn by recent historians of science.

Burtt, E. A. *The Metaphysical Foundations of Modern Science*. New York: Doubleday and Company, 1952. A seminal work on the relationship between metaphysics and physics, but concerned principally with classical physics.

Butterfield, Herbert. *The Origins of Modern Science*. London: G. Bell, 1957. Covers the period 1300–1800 and attempts to integrate scientific thought into broader cultural trends.

Capek, Melic. *The Philosophical Impact of Contemporary Physics*. Princeton, N.J.: Princeton University Press, 1961. Important for all concerned with the impact of science upon modern thought, but does not deal with many recent controversies.

Crombie, A. C. *Medieval and Early Modern Science*. Cambridge, Mass.: Harvard University Press, 1959.

Derry, T. K., and Williams, T. I. *A Short History of Technology*. London: Oxford University Press, 1961.

Einstein, Albert. *Ideas and Opinions*. New York: Dell, 1973. Provides many fascinating glimpses of Einstein the man.

Einstein, Albert, and Infield, Leopold. *The Evolution of Physics*. New York: Simon and Schuster, 1961.

Elkana, J., ed. *The Interaction Between Science and Philosophy*. New York: Humanities Press, 1975. Includes an important essay by Stephen Toulmin making the case that modern science has abandoned the Parmenidean axiom that unchanging essences lie beneath changing appearances.

Forman, Paul. "Weimar Culture, Causality, and Quantum Theory, 1918–1927." *Historical Studies in the Physical Sciences* 3 (1971): 1. Recognized by many sociologists as a model for discussing external influences upon the development of scientific concepts.

Greaves, R. L. "Puritanism and Science: The Anatomy of a Controversy." *Journal of the History of Ideas* 30 (1969): 345. Contains useful bibliography on the history of this relationship.

Hall, A. Rupert. *From Galileo to Newton*. New York: Harper and Row, 1963.

Hallam, A. *A Revolution in the Earth Sciences*. London: Oxford University Press, 1973.

Heisenberg, Werner. *Physics and Beyond*. New York: Harper and Row, 1971.

——. *Physics and Philosophy*. New York: Harper and Row, 1958.

Holton, Gerald. *Introduction to Concepts and Theories in Physical Sciences*. 2d ed. Edited by Stephen G. Brush. New York: Addison-Wesley, 1973. A textbook that is particularly useful for humanists without extensive background in science, which provides easy access to scientific concepts while nicely illustrating the relationship of those concepts to the broader cultural context.

———. *The Scientific Imagination*. New York: Cambridge University Press, 1978. This and the following title contain a wealth of insight into the interrelatedness of scientific thought and cultural change.

———. *Thematic Origins of Scientific Thought*. Cambridge, Mass.: Harvard University Press, 1974.

Ihde, Aaron J. *The Development of Modern Chemistry*. New York: Harper and Row, 1964.

Jammer, Max. *The Conceptual Development of Quantum Mechanics*. New York: McGraw-Hill, 1966.

———. *The Philosophy of Quantum Mechanics*. New York: Wiley, 1974. A difficult but important book by the generally recognized authority in the area.

Jeans, James. *Physics and Philosophy*. Ann Arbor, Mich.: University of Michigan Press, 1958. A somewhat dated but nevertheless important account.

Keller, Evelyn Fox. "Cognitive Repression in Contemporary Physics." *American Journal of Physics* 47 (1979): 717–21. Keller makes use of Piaget's studies of cognitive development to explain the resistance of many contemporary physicists to the implications of wave-particle dualism and indeterminacy.

Knight, David. *Sources for the History of Science: 1660–1914*. Ithaca, N.Y.: Cornell University Press, 1974.

Koyré, Alexandre. *Galileo Studies*. New York: Humanities Press, 1978.

———. *Metaphysics and Measurement*. Cambridge, Mass.: Harvard University Press, 1968.

———. *Newtonian Studies*. Chicago: University of Chicago Press, 1965. Excluding Holton, Koyré is perhaps the most formidable and readable of the modern historians of science.

Kuhn, Thomas S. *The Copernican Revolution*. Cambridge, Mass.: Harvard University Press, 1957.

———. *The Structure of Scientific Revolutions*. Chicago: University of Chicago Press, 1970. Although criticized by many historians of science, this book is probably the best-known work in the history of science for the layperson. Kuhn's notions of *paradigm* and *paradigm shift* are now widely used in a number of humanistic disciplines.

Losee, John. *A Historical Introduction to the Philosophy of Science*. London: Oxford University Press, 1972.

Manuel, Frank E. *Isaac Newton, Historian*. Cambridge, Mass.: Harvard University Press, 1963.

———. *Portrait of Isaac Newton*. Cambridge, Mass.: Harvard University Press, 1968. Informed studies by a well-known historian on Newton the man which make extensive use of nonscientific documents, written by Newton, that have only recently been available to historians.

Multhauf, Robert. *The Origins of Chemistry*. London: Oldbourne, 1966.

Neu, John. "History of Science." *Library Trends* 15 (1967): 676–92.

Nicolson, Marjorie. *Science and Imagination*. Ithaca, N.Y.: Cornell University Press, 1956. Contains six articles written from 1935–1940 on the influence of classical physics on English literature.

210

North, J. D. *The Measure of the Universe: A History of Modern Cosmology*. London: Oxford University Press, 1972.

Oppenheimer, J. Robert. *Science and the Common Understanding*. New York, 1956.

"The Relations of Literature to Science: A Selected Bibliography." *Symposium* (1968).

Sarton, George. *History of Science*. Cambridge, Mass.: Harvard University Press, 1959.

Schilpp, P. A. *Albert Einstein: Philosopher-Scientist*. New York: Harper and Row, 1949.

Shapere, Dudley. *Galileo, A Philosophical Study*. Chicago: University of Chicago Press, 1974. Attempts to analyze the writings of Galileo within the context of the Western philosophical tradition.

Stapp, Henry Pierce. "The Copenhagen Interpretation." *American Journal of Physics* 40 (1972): 1112–21. Probably the most concise and readable account to date of the metaphysical and epistemological implications of the Copenhagen interpretation of quantum theory.

Struve, Otto, and Zebergs, Velta. *Astronomy in the Twentieth Century*. New York: Macmillan, 1962.

Whittaker, E. J. *A History of the Theories of Aether and Electricity*. London: Nelson, 1951.

Wolf, A. *A History of Science, Technology and Philosophy in the Sixteenth, Seventeenth and Eighteenth Centuries*. New York: Macmillan, 1952.

index